MW00929469

GOD Still Loves the French

BY

Marc J. Mailloux

xulon PRESS

Copyright © 2006 by Marc Mailloux

God Still Loves The French
by Marc Mailloux

Printed in the United States of America

ISBN 1-60034-284-1

All rights reserved solely by the author. The author guarantees all contents are original and do not infringe upon the legal rights of any other person or work. No part of this book may be reproduced in any form without the permission of the author. The views expressed in this book are not necessarily those of the publisher.

Unless otherwise indicated, Bible quotations are taken from the "New International Version". Copyright © 1978 by New York International Bible Society.

www.xulonpress.com

To my wife, daughter, sisters, and mother;
Five of the best reasons I know for God's creation
of XX chromosomes.

GOD STILL LOVES THE FRENCH

PREFACE

In my first book,* I wrote about the circumstances which led to my conversion on the banks of the Ganges River in India, the subsequent travels to Japan and the Far East, and my return to the West (both literally and figuratively). Like many others, the Lord dragged me into the Kingdom kicking and screaming. Now I was returning to a country to which I once swore I would never return.

France was one of the first countries in the Western world to be evangelized. In the second century, there was already a growing church in Lugdunum (Lyon) of which Irenaeus was the most illustrious overseer. In 177, under the Roman philosopher emperor Marcus Aurelus, the church at Lyon suffered persecution for refusing to partake in pagan Roman emperor worship. A few centuries later, the conversion of Clovis (in 496), the first king of the Merovingian dynasty, marked a significant step in diffusing the gospel throughout Gaul. With only limited access to the written Word, the Church in France as elsewhere fell into major errors in the middle-ages. Then came the Reformation.

By the 16th and 17th centuries, France acquired the dubious distinction of becoming the only country with a significant protestant minority (as much as 40% of the population by 1562, according to some estimates) to reject the Reformation. Had the Lord judged this country for its terrible persecution of so many of His people, "punishing the children for the sins of the fathers up to the third and fourth generation of those who hated Him" (Deuteronomy

5:9)? Coupled with the anti-Christian heritage of the 18th century "Enlightenment" thinkers, this might explain the modern dearth (less than 1% by most estimates) of Bible-believing Christians in the land of Calvin.

Americans have long had a love-hate relationship with the French. Many appreciate the beauties of the French language, culture, and culinary art. Others find the French ungrateful for repeated American sacrifices on their behalf, and dislike their obstinate bent to act independently of our other allies.

Some wonder why the French don't seem to like Americans, not realizing that these negative feelings aren't reserved exclusively for Americans: The French don't seem to like anyone. Other U.S. visitors to Paris come to understand the opinion of the French poet-film director Jean Cocteau who, describing his own compatriots, said that a Frenchman is "an Italian in a bad mood." The Frenchman's general grumpiness may be understandable in a land where not many have the joy of salvation.

It's one thing to visit France as a tourist. It's quite another to live there as we did between roughly 1974 and 1996. The following pages contain anecdotes relating the experiences of an American living in France--first as a language and theology student, later as a missionary.

The intent of this account is to help Americans better understand the French, who can be just as endearing as any other people—especially when one gets away from Paris. Still, I wouldn't particularly mind if the reader has a good laugh or two along the way at the expense of the French. May it please the Lord to use these stories for the edification of those who read them.

---

*Discovery on the Katmandu Trail (1983)

CHAPTER 1

AN UNLIKELY CANDIDATE FOR MISSIONARY SERVICE IN FRANCE

My wife Aline hates the cold. Or, it is more accurate to say she has a pathological fear of winter. The woman has poor circulation, so her hands and feet are, even in summer months, cool as a healthy pup's nose. So obsessive is her aversion to cold that, though we live in S. Florida, she keeps an eiderdown quilt on our bed year-round, save for a two-week period in July. As soon as there's a "cool" night (below 85F), it comes out of the closet and goes back on the bed. I fold it over to her side where it forms a double layer on her. She's never too warm.

I believe that my wife's phobia has altered our entire life course. While finishing seminary, we were invited by a pastor in Quebec to participate in a church-planting effort. I was excited at the possibility of working in ministry in the birthplace of my grandparents, and tried to reassure her that everything north of the border was "cold proof." She wasn't convinced. For her, there are only two seasons in Canada: winter and July.

I managed to persuade her to visit "La Belle Province" with me for an exploratory mission in January of 1981. It probably wasn't the best time of year for me to make my case, but it was the only time we could go.

Arriving at the Vermont-Canada border in northern Vermont, we stepped out of our toasty vehicle for a quick trip to the rest room. It was sunny and the temperature around 20°F, but with a chill factor near zero. Walking back the fifty yards from the facilities through the parking lot, we were overcome by a gust that stole our breath away. As she got into the car, my Provence born wife glared at me and said with the utmost seriousness; "Je ne pourrais jamais vivre ici! L'air est si froid que ça fait mal même de respirer!" (I could never live here. The air is so cold that it hurts one's lungs to breathe !). That was it. Despite the warm hospitality of the Canadian pastor, Aline had already decided to leave Quebec to those whose vocation was to live in artic climate. "Dieu ne m'a pas donné la constitution physique pour supporter le froid" (God did not make me for the cold), she insisted.

I reminded her of the 18th century Danish missionary who went to evangelize the Eskimos in Greenland and whose wife feared the cold. "Tant pis pour elle" (too bad for her) was Aline's response. I even tried the philosophical approach, reminding her that cold, like evil, does not exist ontologically; as evil is the absence of good, cold is just the absence of heat. That didn't work either. Her mind was made up in 1981. The Lord would have to find us a warm climate to serve in.

Seven years earlier I had arrived back in the States from my journey to Katmandu where I'd found the Truth, or rather, the Truth had found me. I was beginning to think I might have a vocation for sharing the gospel in France, the only country where my name might be pronounced correctly. That's no small advantage for it grieves French ears to have to hear their language mispronounced.

There's a true story of an American pastor who was much appreciated by his parishioners despite his butchery of French pronunciation. Our beloved linguistic barbarian was preaching at a funeral service. At the most solemn moment of the ceremony, he tried to ask the widow to stand and identify herself. What he wanted to say, in proper French was: "Would the woman in mourning ("en deuil") wearing a mourning veil (called "un voile crêpe," masculine article) please stand up." Unfortunately he pronounced "en deuil" more like "andouille" (sausage). To refer to someone as an "andouille" is like calling him a "meathead." Moreover, instead of using the masculine article "le" before "crêpe," he used the feminine article and said "la crêpe," which refers to a kind of French pancake. What the pastor in effect said was: "Would the meathead with the pancake on her head please stand up". So much for the language of Robespierre.

My own ancestors are French on both sides, as far back as anyone can trace. But that didn't make me French as much as growing up in New England made me American. And as for any natural endowment that would make me God's likely candidate for missions in France, let me summarize my language aptitude this way: When I arrived at Georgetown University in September of 1971 with ten years of formal French classes behind me (I grew up in a Canuck factory town), I wasn't even able to "place out" of French 101.

After returning from my search in the East and my initial sojourn in Paris, I spent the academic year of 1974-75 at Gordon College in Massachusetts, and signed up for a course in French Romanticism in which I was the only student enrolled! That meant the privileged situation of one-on-one sessions in her office with the conscientious African-American professor Dr. Marion Carter. There is no playing hooky when you're the only student. My French language passion was ignited.

But how would I live in France where it would be legally impossible for me to work? My cousin Robert invited me to join him in the family spring water business, founded in 1858 and now booming and with infinite potential for expansion in the Boston area. He talked practically:

"You gotta be realistic in life...provide for yourself and, eventually, your family. Doesn't the Bible say that he who does not provide for his own has denied the faith and is worse than an infidel?" Robert said, not really caring what the Bible said.

"Yeah, but it also says, 'Seek first the Kingdom of God and His righteousness, and don't worry about the rest," I countered.

So my choices were laid before me.

Option A: Go into business with my cousin for a couple of years, make money, then go to France and study theology. But there were pitfalls: what if I got too settled in the U.S., too comfortable to extricate myself.

Option B: Go to France immediately with no visible means of support, and trust the Lord blindly for my material needs. Faith? Or presumption?

Robert needed an answer; time to fish or cut bait.

My whole future hung in the balance as I sat in front of the Boston Public library in Copley Square one Indian-summer day in September. Only half aware of my resemblance to the Buddha—fasting and sitting under the *bodhi* tree—I told myself I wouldn't move from that spot until I received, from God Himself, the much sought after illumination. Hours later, I was in the same spot. Nothing had happened, except that I had fallen asleep and been awakened by a derelict asking for a smoke.

I was angry with God. Why hadn't He answered my prayer? Why no word or sign from Him?

I made my way over to a local restaurant across the street and ordered something to eat.

"So ya don't want to answer my prayer?" I protested to God.

"Well so much for my useless fasting, I'm hungry. And that's at least one thing I'm sure of!"

I sat at the counter, and ordered the house special for the day, which happened to be beef stew. Because I'd already experienced life in France, I was accustomed to wine with my meals. So I also ordered a glass of the house wine to accompany the stew.

As I sat waiting for my meal, angry at God's lack of reply to my constant prayers, the waiter poured me a glass. I took a sip and almost had to spit it out. It was awful! I'm not a wine connoisseur, much less a wine snob. Furthermore, America produces some excellent wines, especially on the West Coast. But this must have been one of those lousy local productions. Whatever it was, it was undrinkable.

"That does it!" I said to myself.

"I'm not staying in a country where they serve rot-gut like this and call it wine! If you won't give me a better sign than this, than that's what I'll go on. Off to France I go!" I forsook my career selling spring water, hopped in the car and drove down to my parents' home in Woonsocket, first stop on the way to France.

Reverend Robert Lewis and BAALAM's ASS

Reverend Robert Lewis was an Oklahoma-born evangelist-pastor who had come to plant a church in my home town of Woonsocket, which he considered a mission. I cornered him in the church office one Sunday and shared my half-baked missionary vision and my fears, including linguistic limitations and financial concerns.

After reflecting a few moments, he looked me straight in the eye and stated matter-of-factly:

"You gotta go to France."

I was amazed at the clearness of his conviction and listened attentively for his biblical reasoning.

Regarding my linguistics abilities, he invoked Moses and how the Lord reminded him that He is the one who made man's tongue and he could use it how He pleased (Exodus 4:10-11). To clinch the deal, he cited Numbers 22: "If the Lord can get Baalam's ass to speak in Hebrew, then he can get you to speak in French."

Regarding finances he said that if I were truly called to the mission field, the Lord would provide for everything I need for my studies and His service.

And if I weren't truly called by God, I would just fall flat on my face and return home to the States. Nothing ventured, nothing gained. What did I risk?

"Remember the plight of Jonah," he warned. "There are still sea-monsters out there!" he added half-jokingly.

So there you have it, the theological underpinnings of my missionary vocation to France, provided in part by a glass of lousy red wine and a fundamentalist preacher from Oklahoma.

The die was cast and a couple days later, I boarded a flight for France. I was confronted by the French immigration police in Paris. I didn't have enough money to satisfy them nor proof that I would be receiving any from the States.

"Why should we let you enter the country," the policeman asked, "when we have no assurance that you will not be burden to us?"

I don't remember what I told him, but in the Lord's providence, it was enough to get me into the country. Neither did I ever lack anything, though those were some lean years—first as a student learning French in Paris, and then during five years at seminary in

Aix-en-Provence. Through it all, the Lord was faithful. As for the Holley Spring Water company which, you recall had been in operation since 1858, it folded a year after I left for France—victim of a divorce settlement between my uncle and his wife of 38 years!

CHAPTER 2

BAALAM'S ASS IN PARIS

When I first arrived in the French capital just after reading Balzac's Le Père Goriot, I was determined to become another Eugène de Rastignac, and "conquer Paris." First, I would have to find affordable housing.

Guy Pédéline

I had a variety of living accommodations that first year in Paris, not the least interesting being a fancy apartment on the left bank in the elegant 7ᵗʰ arrondissement at Rue de Beaune. I came upon the address via a posted announcement at the "Alliance Française." A French banker was looking for someone to house-sit during his frequent trips to Germany. It was a Godsend as far as I was concerned.

Mr. Guy Pedeline, a 35 year-old batchelor, was what the French call a "minet" (literally "kitten"), or one who is excessively obsessed with his appearance. An obsessive compulsive cleaner, he would spend every evening dusting and vacuuming. Except for his ritual cup of coffee and a piece of bread at breakfast, he rarely cooked as he said "that might cause odors."

Still, he was a friendly fellow and seemed pleased to have an American boarder with whom to practice English. He wasn't at all receptive to the gospel though. When I asked him why he thought he'd been put on earth, he replied "to fight dirt."

Learning French the Japanese way

I rode the metro to Blvd. Raspail and enrolled at the *Alliance Française*, the first stop for legions of foreigners who come to Paris with the goal of learning the language. The problem with this, as with enrollment in any language school, is that one spends his entire time with other foreigners who can't speak the language either. As a stranger in a not particularly friendly city, one is tempted to seek the companionship of ones own compatriots. I was determined not to speak to or befriend anyone whose native tongue was English. I curbed my desire to discuss American sports with a student from Chicago with whom I shared the longsuffering burden of rooting for a losing baseball teams! Instead I made friends with **Shuya,** a Japanese sportswriter from Hiroshima, ten years my senior.

Introverted, like many Japanese, his stated goal in coming to France was "to learn the meaning of life." During the course of the year, we would have many opportunities to exchange ideas about the gospel. Also, we talked baseball, though it would have to be in our common denominator, French! So how does one say "sacrifice fly" in the language of Molière?

The upshot of an encounter with a girl named Marie-Claude and her "Temoin de Jehovah" (Jehovah Witness) mother is that I decided I needed to study the Bible in greater depth. I would put a temporary halt to my French studies and learn more about the Word. I headed back to Swiss L'Abri, Francis Schaeffer's Christian commune and my old stomping grounds.

The French presidential election

In March of 1974, it was back to France and language study. After a brief stint at the Alliance Française, I met up with Anyck, the former English teacher mentioned in my previous book who had picked me up hitchhiking in Italy in August 1971 and who had embarked on her own journey to the East only to return to France a serious Buddhist.

She'd taken a job at the information booth at the "Gare de Lyon" railroad station, working in three languages, guiding tourists to their destinations. When she invited me to spend the weekend at her parent's home in a village 165kms southeast of Paris, I jumped at the opportunity to share the gospel with new people.

We hitchhiked out of Paris the weekend after the French Presidential elections in May, 1974, when the more conservative candidate Valéry Giscard d'Estaing defeated the socialist Francois Mitterrand in the second round of the two-phase French elections in which the two top vote-getters from among the candidates of the first round square off against each other in a run-off election two weeks after the first vote. I remember this because I had committed a major cultural faux-pas in asking the French truck driver who was giving us a lift whom he had voted for. It might be an innocent question in the States, but not so in France.

My query, was met with a pregnant silence as both the driver and Anyck looked at me in stunned disbelief before my friend blurted out: "Cela ne se demande pas!" (One doesn't ask that!).

There are many things, including politics and religion, of which one could speak freely in the States but which must be treated delicately in France. Ask a Frenchman who he voted for and you may as well ask about his sex life.

I made a significant purchase while visiting with Anyck's family near Troyes—a new Peugeot eight-speed "demi-course", with which I planned to tour the French countryside that summer. To break in my bicycle (and my legs), I decided to pedal back to Paris (100 miles) while Anyck took the train. I fully expected to be able to complete the journey in one day. To be honest, I'd never ridden a bicycle that far in one sitting. But I thought I was in pretty good shape from all the walking I'd been doing in Paris. I hit the road early in the morning from St.Parre-les-Vaudes.

It was cold and overcast and I pedaled hard to keep warm. For one not accustomed to cycling, it is a mistake to overexert oneself in the early stage of the journey. It wasn't long before I was exhausted and still had over a hundred kilometers to go! I found myself stopping more and more often in the cafés of the villages I would cross, filling myself with espresso coffee partly in an attempt to keep warm, but also for the caffeine high. Anyone who knows anything about chemically-induced stimulation knows it's short-lived. I found myself more fatigued than ever and still a long way from my destination.

It was around four o'clock in the afternoon when I pulled into Provins, about 80 kilometers from my point of departure, and halfway to my destination. My legs and buttocks were aching, and it was clear at that point that I would never have the stamina to pedal much further. But what could I do? I didn't have enough money with me to take the train, and I couldn't very well abandon my new bicycle and hitchhike. So I pulled into a service station and considered my plight, praying about what to do next.

Suddenly I had an idea as a meat-transporting truck (with a refrigerator unit) pulled into the station. I approached the driver while he filled up with gas and asked him if he was going to Paris. When he replied in the affirmative, I asked him if he might not have room in his rig for an exhausted cyclist and his bicycle.

"Désolé" (Sorry), he replied, "Le camion est rempli de viande" (" The truck is filled with meat").

So I went back to the side of the road and stuck out my thumb trying to cage a lift from one of the passing trucks. The probability that one of them would stop for a hitchhiker with a bicycle was virtually nil.

It wasn't five minutes later that the aforementioned meat-truck driver who had now completed his fill-up called me and signaled for me to come over to the truck with my bicycle. He opened the back of the truck which I could see was quite empty, lifted up my "vélo" and hung it on a meat hook. I sat in the front seat enjoying the ride to Paris as I had never appreciated a ride before! I was thankful that my prayer of moments before had been answered and that Providence had been gracious to me in spite of my foolish athletic pretensions.

The trucker brought me all the way back to Paris, even going out of his way to drop me close to my neighborhood at the "Porte de Clignacourt" not far from the Paris flea-market. I rested there for three days, my legs aching, my posterior sore from hours on the small hard seat. I used to think bicycle seats were invented by sadistic females eager to punish the male sex by inflicting pain commensurate with our phallic sins. However, since that time, I have spoken with many a female cyclist who has assured me that bicycle seats are uncomfortable and conducive to crotch pains for them too. You would think that in the hundred years that people have bicycled, someone would have designed a better seat?

I used those days of convalescence to ponder my future in France. It was becoming clear that I had fallen in love with France and I wanted to explore and become intimately acquainted with it. Driving was too fast and beyond my means, and walking too slow. Hence my decision to see the country on a bicycle. So I strapped a small pup-tent and sleeping bag to the carrier on my bicycle and set out from Paris in mid-May 1974 embarking on a three-month journey which would take me some 6000 kilometers through the French countryside.

Summer OF '74 6000 km bicycle tour of France

I headed out of Paris, and pedaled about 100kms a day down through the Loire valley, over to the Atlantic coast, down to Bordeaux and through the Garonne valley to Toulouse. I was struck by the beauty of the French countryside and was glad to be able to appreciate it by traveling at a leisurely pace. The prevailing winds were mostly north to south, so I felt I had some "pneumatic" assistance.

I was surprised to discover how much of France is consecrated to agriculture, and how much of French religious tradition is dedicated to the veneration of the Virgin Mary. There are statues of her everywhere, in almost every town and village. Most of the magnificent churches and cathedrals which dot the French countryside are called Notre Dame. I wondered if there were any correlation between the agricultural vocation of France and its Catholic veneer. Let me explain.

More than 10% of the French earn their living in agriculture (as opposed to less than 3% in the United States). This accounts for a lot about the French and has repercussions regarding metaphysics and French religious beliefs.

I remembered the theory of my Georgetown University history professor, Carroll Quigley, the "Delphic oracle of the Foreign Service School" as we called him (He was also Bill Clinton's mentor a few years before I got to Georgetown). The professor had striking ideas about the influence of nature and one's environment on his spiritual beliefs. He'd told us that in northern Europe, especially the Scandinavian countries where rainfall, trees and wild animals abound, food provision (i.e. wild animal game) was usually made by hunter-men who venerated violent sky gods. Violence is what put food on the table. The divinities of Norse tradition, "Thor" and his colleagues, are fierce and masculine, or "Dionysian," according to Nietzsche's terminology. Societies where these have been worshipped tend to be patriarchal, venerating the father/provider. Professor Quigley was fond of quoting the maxim: "Beware of men whose gods are in the sky!"

On the other hand, in southern Europe, the climate is more favorable to agriculture than to hunting. "Mother Earth", an obvious female symbol, is the provider. One plants a seed in her and eventually reaps the fruit thereof. So provision for sustenance no longer comes from above but from below. Societies such as these tend to be more matriarchal and peaceful. God is not in the sky, but in the earth. Not only that, but "She" is actually more feminine than masculine.

When Christianity replaced the pagan traditions of these nations, the northern countries had no trouble accepting the seemingly all-male Trinity, with Father, Son and Holy Spirit.

But it was different in southern Europe where matriarchal beliefs were more prevalent. The seemingly all-male Christian Trinity left a void for those who felt the need of a mother figure.

Consequently, extra-biblical myths concerning the Virgin Mary were welcomed in the more matriarchal societies which longed for a feminine element in their religion. This would explain the cultural basis for a lot of the "Mariolatry" which, to this day, characterizes the Roman Catholic countries of southern Europe.

True or not, Quigley's theory provided me with a framework for understanding much of the Catholic tradition as being derived from medieval myths which, though challenged by the 16th century Reformation, remain entrenched in countries where the Reformation principle of Solo Scriptura found no traction.

Riding my bicycle down from Paris, the first day out, I arrived in Chartres, its magnificent cathedral considered by many the most beautiful in France, yea the world. A guided tour was given by an eccentric English fellow named Malcolm, so enamored of this medieval masterpiece that he has dedicated his whole life to studying it, and has earned his living giving guided tours for English tourists. Malcolm probably knows Chartres better than anyone alive and shares his passion with all who will listen to him. He was the chief consultant for Sir Kenneth Clark who visited Chartres with a television crew for the production of the PBS series "Civilization" a few years ago.

Pointing out one of the famous original stained-glass windows, mercifully spared during France's numerous wars, the guide points to an image—based on medieval folklore—depicting the death, resurrection, and ascension of Mary, queen of heaven! Though totally unbiblical, this legend is met with easy acceptance in France. Such was one of the first 'theology' lessons of my tour of France but hardly the last one.

From Chartres I headed down through the Loire valley where the clearest, most unaccented French is spoken. The Loire valley is also home to the famous chateaux built by French kings of a bygone era, including the magnificent 800 room hunting lodge at Chambord, erected during the reign of Francois I, the 'great' Renaissance king, contemporary of Calvin to whom the reformer dedicated his Institutes in 1536 with the hope of winning Francois over to the faith of the fathers. Alas, François, whose own sister, Marguerite de Navarre was a devoted Bible-believer, became disillusioned with the true faith by the unfortunate "l'affaire des placards" of 1534. It seems that the believers, in an excess of zeal or a lack of tact, went around Paris posting anti-Catholic pamphlets or "placards" every-where. The hitherto open-minded Francois became suspicious of the 'fanatical sect' and banished them from his Kingdom. Exit John Calvin, who was forced into exile in Strasbourg and later Geneva.

From the Loire Valley, I proceeded down France's west coast through the famous Cognac region where they produce a distilled alcohol not unknown to the rest of the world. A visit to the producers of this aromatic elixir can be a welcome respite from the grind of pedaling. A tour of the producers "cave" is followed by a compli-mentary taste of this most refined liqueur. Of course, one must not over-indulge as the kilometers can seem even longer when the road zigzags.

I was eager to get to the sunny south, synonymous with vacation land in the minds of most northerners from rainy climates. After a brief swing through the Bordeaux region, I headed down the Garonne valley through Agen and Toulouse, making for sunny Provence. I tooled around Sète, Arles, and Nimes (where the "corrida" or bullfighting festival was going on, in the magnificent Roman arena).

Arles, situated near the mouth of the Rhone river on the border of the Provence region, is a quaint historic city with more Roman ruins per square meter than any other, I'm told. The museum of early Christian art is particularly interesting as a testimony to the faith of the earliest believers, which evidently included a number of well-to-do folks whose elaborately carved sarcophagi from the third and fourth centuries remain some of the most striking witnesses of the faith of that time. Surely the Church of Jesus Christ was thriving then!

Nimes is twenty kilometers from Arles. The visit there was one of the highlights of my summer. One could write volumes, à la Ernest Hemmingway, about the controversial sport of bullfighting, a spectacle which I witnessed for the first time that summer of 1974. Killing a bull is definitely an art, howbeit, with blood and guts as by-products.

As I pushed on, averaging around 100 kms. (62 miles) per day at 25 kph (15 mph), I gained a new respect for the athletic prowess of that summer's Tour de France racers who average as much as 50km/h (30mph) on some of the flatter stretches up north.

More importantly, I was beginning to learn of the Lord's magnificent provision in replacing some erstwhile indispensable earthly pleasures with others.

Like many who have been called to the mission field, I struggled with the notion of having to "give up" so many things I was attached to back home, especially professional sports. Many an American living abroad tries to placate this need via the "International Herald Tribune", incapable of weaning himself from the home ties that binds. Somehow, the fate of the Boston Red Sox has never seemed so important.

But the Lord doesn't call one to France to be talking about baseball with other Americans. If a missionary is to become "all things to all men," he must cultivate a taste for things that interest the locals. The

Lord in his goodness is capable of replacing old sentimental attach-ments with foreign equivalents. The one who thought he couldn't live without peanut butter, now acquires a taste for the 400 varieties of French cheeses. The one for whom the American league pennant race was the highlight of the year suddenly finds real pleasure and cama-raderie in conversing with French sporting enthusiasts about Richard Virenque's chances in the Tour de France. It's an indication that one has become part of the culture when his veneration for Willie Mays is replaced by an admiration for Eddy Mercx, perhaps the greatest bicycle racer of all time who, incidentally, won his last Tour de France in that summer of 1974 as I was doing my cycle tour.

Thus was confirmed in my heart, in a subtle but profound way, the Lord's promise that "no one who has left home or wife or brothers or parents or children for the sake of the kingdom of God will fail to receive many times as much in this age…"(Luke 18:28). It often takes a while to learn to trust Him; but one never regrets it when he does.

Another theological lesson awaited me when I headed up to Avignon and towards Brittany, land of my ancestors, where I spent six of the most agreeable, albeit rain-soaked weeks, in France.

To get from *Provence* to Brittany, one must travel north up the Rhone Valley towards Lyon, then Northwest towards Normandy and Brittany. It's over 500 miles from Nimes to Dieppe on the Normandy coast where I was headed. Normally, I figured this would take me about a week. But I hadn't factored in the infamous "mistral," the legendary north wind that blows down the Rhone valley for days at a time (three, five or seven consecutive days , according to lore) before it finally calms.

The mistral is at its most forceful in Avignon, the city of the Popes, where it even has caused the postponement of the famous summer theatre festival on occasion. I had it smack in my face as I struggled uproad from Avignon towards Orange, a town with a famous Roman amphitheatre not far from the heart of "Côte du Rhone" wine country. How much longer would this last, I wondered each night, as I struggled to pitch my tent in the battering winds, wondering if it could resist the tempest.

For five days and the next 200 kilometers, I virtually never got out of first or second gear as I fought against that fiendish wind that would keep me from my elusive destination. I took detours on side roads where I clung desperately, and occasionally dangerously, to passing trucks or farmers' tractors, begging them to tow me along. How difficult it is in life to "kick against the goads," or go against the movement of the *pneuma*, I thought.

Unlike a hill or mountain where one is rewarded for his climbing efforts by the view at the top and the free ride down the other side, the wind offers no consolation, no reward to him who would oppose it.

I envied the occasional cyclist who passed me on the other side of the road, heading effortlessly southward with the favorable "mistral" to his back! Life isn't fair! Thus did I philosophize for the next five days until I reached Vienne, just south of Lyon, where finally the wind let up and I rediscovered a certain coefficient of justice between the effort of pushing on the pedals and the yield such effort brings. One normally reaps what one sows, according to the proverbial wisdom. But the equation of effort to yield is influenced considerably according as the Spirit/*pneuma* is either with him or against him.

I headed north from Lyon towards the Burgundy region en route to Paris where I planned to make a stop to pick up some mail. As I pedaled, now free of my annoying adversary of the "mistral," I contemplated the solitude of any long distance cyclist. I would meet other cyclists on the road or in youth hostels where I would stay on occasion, and so it happened on a couple of occasions that we were heading in the same direction. Why not travel together a bit? Surely journeying would be more interesting with a traveling companion than alone. But it is difficult to find someone with a compatible traveling style.

Amongst the cyclists I encountered was a group of American guys I met in a youth hostel at Chartres, who were doing what I called "tourist racing." Their group (ten cyclists) was zipping through France on racing bikes, going from youth hostel to youth hostel at about 40km/h! They covered some 200-250 kilometers/day and were more interested in the sport than in the tourism. Naturally, they traveled light, carrying only a small back pack and a credit card with which to cover all the other expenses. That wasn't my style, even if I might have kept up with them.

At the other extreme was Hans, a young German cycle tourist I had met down in the "Camargue" region on the Mediterranean who had a heavy bicycle with large tires, loaded down with a tent, camping gas stove, dishes, raincoat, and even a large radio. He seemed to have everything but the kitchen sink—twenty-five kilos of gear in all! I pedaled with Hans from "St. Marie de la Mer" to Arles one day— about 25 miles. His bicycle tires even allowed him to ride on some dirt trails, unlike the tiny racing tires of the American riders who stayed strictly on the paved roads. I was neither racer nor camper, but sort of half-way between the two. Though I did carry a light tent in which I slept on most nights, I wasn't equipped like Hans.

The problem was to find a companion who would travel with me at approximately the same speed, covering the same daily distance. For a while I rode through Burgundy with an American rider I met in Dijon. I ran into John while visiting the famous Claus Sluter sculpture of four biblical prophets (Moses, David, Jeremiah, Zechariah, Daniel, Isaiah), "puits de Moïse," outside of Dijon. He invited me to stay at his camp site, some 25 kms south of the city. I agreed and pedaled the 25 kms (in the opposite direction from which I was heading) to accept his hospitality. But it was clear from the pace he kept that he would be more at home with the American racing group than with Hans the German camper.

Likewise I also traveled a bit through the central part of France with Gilles, a young French cyclist who was on his way to see family in Le Mans. We only rode together a couple of days—near Auxerre in Bourgogne as I recall—as we scarcely covered 30kms in two days! Not that there was anything special to see in that region. On the contrary, once you get out of Dijon and Beaune, the Burgundy region is mostly agricultural and rather bland. But Gilles, not a great athlete, was prone to stopping at every café of every town and village we encountered "pour boire un petit coup," as he liked to say. It was during one of these numerous café stops that I learned that Gilles was pedaling from his Burgundy home to his grandmother's place near Le Mans—a distance of only a couple of hundred kilometers— on a dare from his older brother who bet him that he couldn't do it.

"He didn't say how long it could take me," Gilles specified. "He just bet me I couldn't do it during my summer vacation."

At the rate Gilles was pedaling, I knew it would take him the major part of his summer holiday. As for myself, I was heading to Normandy where I wanted to visit the WWII landing sites, or "plages de débarquement" (landing beaches), Mt. St. Michel.

I left Gilles and headed up towards Normandy, going through Chartres again, where I tried to get as enthused about the magnificent Cathedral as Malcolm the tour guide.

Normandy visit—of armies and highway workers

Arriving in Dieppe in "Haute Normandie" (the Northern part of Normandy), I headed down the coast and thought about the events that had taken place here some thirty years earlier.

I met an elderly cyclist gentleman near the famous Omaha Beach. I had stopped in front of an old farmhouse, just a few hundred meters from the beach, when a seventy-year-old man on an equally ancient bicycle, came pedaling leisurely home from the "boulangerie" with one of the ubiquitous sticks of French bread sticking out from a basket strapped to the back of the bicycle. He turned off the road towards the farm house and stopped to greet me. He was downright delighted to learn that I was an American, come to see the famous invasion site.

We spoke of the war and that day when, as he explained, he and his family had been awakened by the sounds of Allied bombs shelling the beach in preparation for the invasion. He pointed to the spot not far from the farmhouse where he and his wife had first spotted the Allied ships coming over the horizon even as bombs were landing dangerously close to them.

I asked him if he hadn't been terribly afraid to be so close to ground zero during the invasion. He admitted that he had been afraid, standing outside, while the bombs fell close by. His fear was overridden, he explained, by the exhilarating prospect of finally being rid of the Nazis! In fact, we were jumping for joy, he told me. There are things in this life worse than death. Being enslaved is one of them.

A few miles farther down the coast I had another unforgettable encounter. I had just left for a morning visit to the famous Mt. St. Michel—the most famous tourist site in all of France after the Eiffel Tower—and was headed towards St. Malo where I hoped to spend the night at a youth hostel, as the weather was threatening. As I pedaled along on a small winding road, I caught up to a distinctive orange "fourgonette" (panel truck) of the French Highway department.

The truck was riding slowly as there was a man leaning from the open back door picking up some marking cones from the middle of the road where the lines had just been painted. I grabbed the back of the truck and struck up a conversation with the affable highway worker in the back.

After a few minutes, the truck pulled off the road to an open field. It was lunch time, the worker told me, and he invited me to join him and his colleagues for a bite to eat on the side of the road. I accepted gratefully (a cyclist is always hungry)! I thought they would be opening up a can of something from their lunch pails and sharing their sandwiches with me. I hardly expected the meal I was about to have...

After preliminary introductions during which I met three other highway workers, Lucien, J-Claude, Serge, and Yves, we took our places sitting on small stools in the back of the panel truck. In honor of the visit of an American guest, the foreman and oldest of the four broke out a bottle of chilled white wine which was kept in the van in a bucket of melting ice. I found it strange that they should go to the trouble of keeping a chilled bottle of wine for an ordinary meal, as they surely weren't expecting guests? It was a revealing insight into the gastronomical priorities of even simple French highway workers. It would be the *apéritif,* they told me, along with peanuts and crackers we nibbled on while awaiting the first course of salad which one of the colleagues was preparing as the rest of us listened attentively to the war stories of the older man whose name was Lucien. He was 55, which would have made him about 19 in 1944, my dad's age. The other fellows were all about 10 years younger. We were spell-bound while Lucien entertained us with tales of that fateful day in 1944, as Jean-Claude and Serge prepared what was shaping up to be a four course meal.

"*A table*" Serge finally called, announcing that the meal was ready, a half-hour since we'd taken the first sip of the aperitif. Meanwhile, my head was somewhat spinning from the numerous toasts of white wine we'd drunk to the U.S. army for their noble efforts. I told my hosts how my dad had been part of the Allied effort, having come over in July '44 and serving as an interpreter for the American army.

Meanwhile, J-Claude opened another bottle of white wine to accompany the *salade lyonnaise* which, in addition to lettuce, tomatoes, and endives, contained bits of hard-boiled eggs, and bacon in a mustard vinaigrette. It was delicious.

We cleaned our plates (real china, not paper) with pieces of crusty French "baguette" while J-Claude finished cooking a large bowl of "haricots verts à l'ail" (green beans with garlic) covered with butter and served with pork chops cooked over the camping gas stove they kept in their truck with frying pan and a host of other cooking utensils. This was far cry from the baloney sandwich on sliced white bread gulped down by an American worker in thirty minutes or less. We'd already been at the table for almost an hour, and hadn't even started the main course.

To accompany the pork chops and haricots, Serge opened a bottle of red wine which he poured liberally. Meanwhile, the conversation about the war continued. I asked a few questions, but was mostly content to listen to Lucien reminiscing about the war and the occupation. During all this time, I couldn't help but wonder about how long these guys normally took for their lunch and whether or not I was keeping them from getting back to work.

The main course finished, J-Claude brought out a plate covered with several kinds of French cheeses. I followed their advice, starting with the milder cheese and progressing to the stronger ones.

Throughout the entire meal, both wine and conversation were amply flowing, and I was enjoying the company of these proletariat *bons vivants*.

We finished off with the obligatory cup of strong French coffee, before Serge broke out a bottle of 90 proof "Calvados," an apple-based liqueur produced in Normandy which would serve as the *digestif* of this memorable meal.

"A plus jamais la guerre!" (No more war, ever!), said Lucien, lifting his glass in a toast.

"A plus jamais la guerre", we all repeated downing our shots of Normandy apple fire-water.

I looked at my watch. It was 14h30. We'd been sitting on tiny stools around the table in the back of that small truck for almost 2 1/2 hours! Quite a lunch break, I thought! American workers should have it so good!

I explained to my gracious hosts that I still had over fifty kilometers to pedal to St. Malo where I hoped to spend the night at the youth hostel there, and that I must be on my way. We all stood outside where I took a few photos and we exchanged addresses with a promise to send copies of the photo as soon as I had them developed.

After bidding each other adieu, I climbed on my bicycle just as the first few drops of rain began to fall, hoping it wouldn't rain too hard. I had assumed that my hosts would be getting back to work, but having noticed that it was raining, albeit ever so slightly, one of them said:

"Allez les gars; il pleut; on ne peut pas travailler; (Gentlemen, it's raining so we can't work). So as I was leaving, they were breaking out a deck of cards and taking their seats in the back of the *fourgon-nette—as* everyone knows that you can't paint in the rain.

As I zigzagged down the road, I got to thinking that I might like living in a culture where people live by the maxim: "Doucement le matin; pas trop vite l'après midi." (Easy does it in the morning; not too fast in the afternoon). One could understand why French workers enjoyed on the average 39 days of paid vacation per year, compared to the 12 days of an average American worker. Vive la France!

I finished my tour of France that summer—6000kms (3600 miles) of pedaling around what is arguably the most beautiful piece of real estate on this planet. After a brief return to the States to get a few things straightened out, I returned to France determined to master the language—a lifetime affair—and share the Good News of the Gospel with its people.

CHAPTER 3

A YEAR AT THE SORBONNE
(1975-76)

For anyone serious about perfecting his knowledge of French language and culture, the University of Paris' Sorbonne offers an excellent program for foreigners called "Cours de Civilization Française," which had been recommended to me by my mentor cousin who had done the same program in 1969. So I checked into an inexpensive hotel in the Latin Quarter (there were some, back then) and went to the Sorbonne to inquire about the requirements for enrollment. I learned that the level of study accessible to prospective students was determined by one's level of competence in French. To improve my chances of getting into a higher level for the program that started in October, I signed up for a preparatory course starting in September.

Another motivation for enrolling in the earlier preparatory course was that it afforded the student access to the Sorbonne's lodging service, furnishing a list of addresses of rooms to let. Anyone on a student budget who's ever had to find a room in Paris realizes what a precious asset such a list can be. I had already been looking for a room independently, and was discouraged to see how little was available and how expensive was even the worst hole in the wall—usually a top floor attic room called a "chambre de bonne" (maid's room). I had already visited rooms not fit for a dog whose prices would have depleted my modest budget! It would take a minor miracle to find something adequate. Still, my standards were low and I was prepared to suffer for the cause of learning French. After all, the room was only a place to sleep, and I'd slept in some pretty wretched places during my years as a vagabond.

It was with little enthusiasm that I plodded across the Left Bank from the 6th arrondissement through St. Germain des Pres to the *Rue de l'Université* address given me by the student lodging service. The building I was seeking was but a block from the intersection of the Rue de St. Pères and the "Faculté de Médicine" where a significant number of future French doctors were training.

Arriving at no. 8, I pressed on the buzzer next to the large wooden double doors through which passed both pedestrians and a few cars belonging to the residents who would park them in the courtyard of the stately 19th century Parisian apartment building of which the city abounds. Walking through the car port entrance, I was greeted by the *concierge*, a heavy-set woman of about sixty-five in a simple dress covered by an apron. Her job was to receive and distribute the residents' mail, take out the trash cans, and generally keep an eye on everything and everyone in the building. The tradition of having a *concierge* was apparently started by Napoleon as a kind of de-facto spy system for the Emperor, who wanted to keep tabs on his citizens. A concierge is one whose apartment is always strategically located at the entrance of the building, enabling her to survey everyone's comings and goings. Every Parisian knows the feeling of being watched by the little old lady spying like a weasel from behind the lace curtains to see what's going on as he tries to slip discreetly into his apartment courtyard after a late night out. Any guest of the opposite sex would be immediately suspected and taken note of. In fact, the *concierge* served as the role of a guilty conscience in the minds of many. I wonder how many adulterous relationships have been denounced by her ever-present vigilance.

A *concierge* could be a useful ally or a powerful enemy in a time of crisis or run-in with the law. Hence it was wise to stay on the good side of one's *concierge*. One must never forget to express gratitude when special services were rendered (packages held, etc.) and never forget the famous Christmas *étrennes* or gratuities destined for the *concierge*, mailman, trash collectors, etc.

As it turned out, the *concierge* at no.8 rue de l'Université, Mme. Dupont, was quite affable. Naturally, as the drop-off point of the mail, she knew everyone's business and occasionally asked me about my family in the U.S. But she was as friendly and discreet as a *concierge* can be. On this occasion—our first encounter—she merely directed me to the first floor apartment of Mme. de Joutères, the proprietor of the room I was seeking to rent.

I followed her directions and went up the impressive mahogany staircase leading up to the *1ère étage* (first floor in French, corresponding to the 2cd floor in the U.S.). I rang the bell and was greeted by a dark-haired, thirty- year-old woman with a Latino accent who inquired about my business and invited me to wait in the hallway while she retreated into the inner salons of the apartment to summon her mistress. While I waited, I was greeted by the vigorous barking of a sprightly little *caniche* (French poodle), who examined me with the same thorough curiosity of a *concierge*, save that his examination also included some sniffing.

Finally, Mme. de Joutères arrived. She was a stately octogenarian, dressed in traditional widow's solid black from head to toe. Unlike her Portuguese domestic, she spoke impeccable French. She had a regal manner and an aristocratic air becoming her family name (the preposition "de" often indicative of aristocratic origins).

"Bonjour Monsieur; je suis désolée de vous avoir fait attendre" (Sorry to have kept you waiting).

I explained my business indicating my desire to see the room which she was offering for the extremely modest sum of 200 francs per month. Based on my past experience, I imagined it would be worthy of a rat, and a not-too-fussy one at that. However, my budget being what it was, I was hardly in a position to be choosy. She began asking me some questions about myself and soon discovered that my French was not quite good enough to grasp everything she was asking. I explained as best as I could that, in spite of my last name, I spoke very little French and that I had come to France to study the language of my ancestors.

At this point she gave a command to the dog who was still excitedly jumping around at my feet. The obedient canine turned and immediately ran towards the inner sanctum of the apartment. I don't know exactly what she said to that animal but the incident impressed me precisely for that reason. The dog had very clearly understood, and I hadn't!

Mme. de Joutères sent for her domestic (Maria, who was Portuguese as I would learn) and instructed her to show me the "chambre de bonne" on the top floor where I could lodge. As I waited for Maria to accompany me, I was overcome with a sudden humbling awareness of how far I would have to go before I could claim a modicum of linguistic proficiency. For, at that point, I understood even less than a poodle. Yikes!

Maria pressed the "minuterie" (light-timer) before she and I climbed the five flights of stairs to the hallway leading to the attic rooms normally reserved for servants and domestics. On passing the hallway W.C., she apologized for the nauseous odor that reeked from therein and indicated her disgust at the dilapidated facility, reminiscent of the folkloric "bogs" of Afghanistan, I thought, peeking behind the door. I noticed it was a Turkish toilet which suited me fine as I wouldn't want to have to sit on a seat in such a setting. She stopped in front of room no. 5, inserted the key into the lock and opened the door to a spacious, clearly lit room with a table in one corner, a bed in another, a gas heater, a fireplace, and even an impressive view of the courtyard from the double windows. It was far better than anything I'd seen so far and infinitely more affordable. Alleluia! I was exceedingly grateful for the Lord's provision!

I expressed by delight to Maria and told her that I was most eager to rent that room. So we went down to see Mme. de Joutères and I immediately paid her for the first month's rent. I made no secret of my joy at finding a suitable lodging in a good location (only a twenty minute walk to the Sorbonne) and at an affordable rate. It was then that I realized that the Lord had led me to a kindly old aristocrat who, as I would discover, was a benevolent soul. Conscious of the privilege into which she'd been born, Mme. de Joutères made it a point to be generous in good works, even undercharging foreign students for the rent they paid for her *chambre de bonne*. I was delighted that Providence had made me to become the beneficiary of this rare munificence.

As I walked back across the 6th *arrondissement* to the Latin Quarter to pick up my things at the hotel in which I'd been staying, I contemplated the irony of my good fortune. For here I was walking in the very area of which Balzac spoke in the *Père Goriot* novel. At one point the hero of the story, the young Eugene de Rastignac, proclaims that "he who doesn't know the Left Bank between the Rue de St. Pères and the Blvd. St Michel knows nothing of life." I would be walking the roughly fifteen-block area between those two streets almost every day for the entire academic year. Surely I would know something of life.

One of my first lessons involved the discovery that there were some principles of the free market economy that did not apply in Paris. This conclusion came through two separate incidents in the fancier 7th "arrondissement" where my room was. It was one of those parts of the city where folks were unusually well dressed and were always prim and proper in public.

LESSONS IN FRENCH FREE ENTERPRISE

As for me, I was like Stanley Kowalski in a land of Blanche Dubois. I would often run down the stairs from my 5th floor room early in the morning before shaving or even combing my hair to get a *baguette* at the nearest *boulangerie* and some jam and butter from a local *épicerie*. The problem, I discovered, is that one tends to be treated in a less civilized manner by all sorts of people if one is ill kempt. Clothes make the man; or conversely, appearance creates prejudices. This is particularly true in Paris.

Walking around Paris at 7 AM unshaven, hair disheveled, wearing a T-shirt, I looked as out of place as a Presbyterian in hell, to paraphrase Mark Twain. As I waited in line for my morning bread, I would be passed over by the haughty saleslady who would wait on anyone in the shop before attending to me. She seemed indignant by the presence of this foreign "Ed Norton" in a part of the city with a Park Avenue clientele. Wasn't I a customer like any other, my money as good as any other? That principle doesn't apply in Paris.

The problem was compounded by my inability to articulate my needs in proper Parisian French. I was still not fluent in the language, the mastery of which is *the* important barometer of one's civility. I made the almost unforgivable error mistake of asking for "*un* baguette s'il-vous-plait," using the masculine form of the indefinite article, when anyone who is not a complete moron knows that "baguette"—its shape notwithstanding—is feminine. Hence the huffy rebuttal of the acoustically assaulted Parisian saleslady: "*UNE* baguette monsieur!"

"Yeah, that's what I said" I replied, shrugging-off my grammatical error.

It looked as if it would kill her to hand a stick of bread to this subhuman Neanderthal.

So the "baguette", in spite of its phallic form, is "feminine," while the French word "vagin," indicating a part of the feminine anatomy, is paradoxically masculine. So much for linguistic logic. I eventually learned to say "*UNE* baguette" when ordering my traditional morning fare, much to the relief of the hyper-sensitive ears of the scornful saleslady.

Dealing with her cold arrogance could be fun, so from time to time, just to get her blood boiling, I would occasionally "forget" that *baguettes* were feminine and blurt out "*UN* baguette" s'il-vous-plait," to see her reaction. It never missed. True Parisian that she was, my linguistic improprieties would make her squirm like the devil under holy water.

Since then I've concluded that one of the Lord's most severe judgments on the French for having rejected the Reformation is to have to tolerate the barbarisms and mispronunciations of legions of Anglo-Saxon missionaries who have invaded the land of Calvin, especially since the end of World War II.

Another discovery related to French business practices came one morning as I was looking at jars of *confiture* (jam) on the shelf of a local *épicerie*. For reasons unknown to me—was it my appearance? something sinister in my demeanor? the fact that I was taking too long to choose?—the store's proprietor asked me gruffly what I was doing, making it clear that he wasn't thrilled by my presence in his tiny establishment.

I was indignant and determined to educate this uncouth champion of churlishness in some of the elementary principles of capitalism.

"Don't you realize, sir," I lectured in broken French, "that I am a customer and that, in the free-market economy that is ours, I must be treated with a modicum of respect or I'll take my business elsewhere....?"

"Vas-y donc...! Je m'en fous" (Go ahead then! See if I care), he retorted.

I was flabbergasted and a bit perplexed as I walked out of the store wondering how this fellow could stay in business if he treated all his customers like that.

So for the next few weeks, I would walk several extra blocks to a more distant *épicerie* out of a self-imposed boycott of his store. I continued this inconvenience until I was a recipient of a similar discourtesy at that store as well! Conclusion; when doing business in France, unlike in the Anglo-Saxon world, the customer is rarely right. In fact, the customer is often barely tolerated by the shop owners who leave you with the impression that they're doing you a favor by selling you something. Such was my initiation to the world of commerce in the hallowed confines of the Left bank of Paris.

I might have succumbed to the vanity of it all, being a student in Paris and having the French capital as a playground. At that point in my life, it was difficult to keep one's mind focused on spiritual things. For even without money—God knows how I survived on about ten francs a day—Paris offered all kinds of tempting distractions that could easily keep a young Christian from thinking about his goal in life: to serve the Lord and Savior.

Curiously enough, it was while in class at the Sorbonne, having discussions with fellow students over coffee, or while reading some of the great writers whose works were assigned to us, that it was easiest for me to remain fixed on spiritual things.

Classes in the "Cours de Civilization Française" provided opportunity to share one's faith with students from a number of foreign countries. Our section was limited to foreign, i.e., non-French students, as we were all studying the French language and culture. That meant that the classes were comprised of students of many nationalities, including American, Japanese, Koreans, as well as a number of European countries. The only thing we all had in common was that none of us were native French speakers.

WITH BRIGITTES +"Beetter Limon" AT THE SORBONNE

The Sorbonne is also one of France's best liberal arts colleges, with a large student body, around 75% female. We foreign students could socialize with the French students during the coffee breaks between class and lunch breaks. That's when I discovered the popularity of certain French names which were in vogue then, leading to confusion on occasion. I had no less than four Parisian acquaintances named Brigitte, all born in the late to mid 50's when Ms. Bardot was at the height of her fame. Likewise, in a group of a dozen French girls born between 1950 and 1960, one was sure to find at least one Christine and a Martine.

I also learned a thing or two about the French pronunciation of English words. It happened as I was waiting my turn in one of the two lines that formed at the counter of the Sorbonne café where students would hastily grab a cup of espresso. I decided on a "Schwepps bitter lemon," and when my turn came, I placed my order saying:

"Je voudrais un Schwepps bitter lemon, s'il vous plait."

Nothing difficult about that, I thought. Yet my request was greeted with a look of bewilderment.

"Que voulez-vous?" asked the fast-working fellow behind the counter.

"Un Schwepps bitter lemon," I replied, being careful to articulate as best I could.

"Je ne vous comprends pas" (I don't understand you), came the impatient reply.

"Qu'est-ce que vous voulez?!"

"Un Schwepps *bitter lemon*" I reiterated, biting on every syllable.

"Je ne vous comprends toujours pas" (I still don't understand you), retorted the harried café employee who, until now, had been serving drinks at a record pace.

"Il voudrait un Schwepps *Beeeter Liimon*" came the reply from the fellow standing behind me.

"Oh! Schwepps *Beeter Liimon!*" he exclaimed suddenly. "Pourquoi vous ne l'avez pas dit?!" (Why didn't you say so?).

The French Café

The life of a student in Paris revolves around classes and study at the library, interspersed with visits to the café. Friends congregate there as much for the social aspect than for food and drink. In the Latin Quarter, you will see cafés patronized by students huddling around a table, sipping espresso and shooting the breeze. One might get up, leave a few books on the table—and even his unfinished cup of coffee—run to a class at the Sorbonne, and come back an hour or more later, his books and coffee still on the table. Meanwhile, some of his friends may have also gone to appointments, replaced by others now sitting at the same table. This is acceptable practice in France where in most establishments, the waiters don't push one to consume. You can literally monopolize a table all day in a French café with a simple cup of coffee.

I had a favorite café near the Blvd. St. Michel where I went when I needed to get work done, and another when I wanted to meet with friends. The former opened at 5:30 AM and I would sit there working on my lessons until class time. I spoke to no one, and no one bothered me.

Cafés in France serve an intellectual function similar to the Areopagus of ancient Athens referred to by the apostle Paul in Acts 17. They're the place where people go to exchange ideas. A couple of them ("Aux Deux Magots" and "La Coupole") on the Boulevard St. Germain were the famous haunts of the likes of Jean-Paul Sartre, Albert Camus, and the clique of intellectuals aspiring to solve the world's problems. That tradition has carried over to what is called the "cafés-philosophes" where searching souls gather religiously on Sunday mornings (no one goes to church in France) to listen to a guest speaker or simply exchange ideas. In fact, they seek some of the same things in the cafés that the Christians seek at worship: truth, camaraderie and a sense of the transcendence. All three are necessary for life, in France like anywhere else.

"LE RAT ET L'HUITRE"

The "Cours de Civilization Française" program included classes in French grammar, phonetics, and the appreciation of different French authors, using the classic "Lagarde et Micharde" anthology of French literature which is classified according to centuries. These were also relatively small classes (25-30 students) during which we would study French grammar as well as analyze the great texts of French literature. Most of our program that year dealt with "Les Fables de Lafontaine," the classic 17th century masterpiece, stories which are deceptive in their simplicity, but sophisticated in their structure and profound in their wisdom. In fact, the "Fables"—modeled after Aesop's classic, and known by virtually all French schoolchildren—is ranked near the top of the French literary pyramid for their style and profundity.

In our literature class, each of the students was given a different fable to read and analyze before the group. This provided a meaningful exercise in public speaking for most of us. If speaking in public in one's own language can be daunting, just think of what it's like to have to expose one's ignorance in another language!

Some of the "fables" were easier to analyze than others. But easy or not, the teacher, a middle-aged Catholic spinster named Mlle. Haillant, was intransigent with regards to pronunciation. Mispronunciation visibly pained her.

An American student from Chicago who was assigned to recite the fable "Le rat et l'huître" (the rat and the oyster). Alas, it was not within his linguistic capacity to pronounce the two very guttural French "r's" (in fact closer to an English "h") in that fable's title. So as 'Big John' from Chicago stood to recite in front of the class, he was interrupted at least a dozen times by the increasingly exasperated professor Haillant, who could not for the life of her understand how this American could not come close to saying *"Le rrrraaaat et l'huitrrrrre"* in a satisfactory manner. "LE RAH et RWEETRE," it came out each time.

"Mais non!" she would exclaim. "Le Raaa et l'hweetre," she would repeat, over and over.

"Etes-vous vraiment sourd! (are you really deaf?).

In fact, Big John was in fact deaf to the nuances—as many of us native English speakers are—in the pronunciation of the French "R". Even after twenty years in France, when I finally came to the point where I could occasionally pass myself off as a Frenchman, I still can't properly pronounce a French "R," which remains my shibboleth.

Any doubt about my phonetic proclivities were quickly dispelled thanks to our weekly phonetics course under the tutelage of the real life French version of *My Fair Lady's* Henry Higgins, Mr. Filiolet, who directed the Sorbonne's phonetics laboratory. Mr. Filiolet had an ear for language that would have made Professor Higgins blush. He could detect a man's accent from a mile away. He found his greatest pleasure in analyzing the political discourses of French politicians on television, attaching the deepest significance to a statesman's use of apparently innocuous words and their all-important pronunciation. What frustration must have been his over Big John and myself, for whom even hours of coaching in the art of pronouncing words like "detruire," "ouvrir," "rouler," etc., brought meager results.

VIE ET PENSEES MODERNES

Besides grammar and phonetics classes, lectures were given by noted professors who lectured to larger groups on their various specialties. My favorite was Mr. Guy-Willy Schmeltz, who gave a magisterial lecture called "Vie et Pensées Modernes" (Modern Life and Thinking) every Monday morning from 8:oo to 10:00AM. Though not a prime time for attending classes, it remained the favorite course of many and the only one I attended faithfully.

The reason was Professor Schmeltz himself. He was a man of amazing intellectual insight into modern thinking and culture. The course itself was a philosophical evaluation of the different ideologies and world views including Freudianism, Marxism, Behaviorism, Existentialism, etc. Prof. Schmeltz was adept at pointing out some of the logical inconsistencies of these different philosophies, their inherent contradictions and their shortcomings in explaining and treating the problems of individual man and society.

Concerning Marxism, for example, Professor Schmeltz professed a certain curious respect for the writings of Vladimir Lenin. He considered Lenin as a great intellectual whose opinions on most things were to be taken seriously. When it came to Lenin's views on religion however, Schmeltz said that Lenin's opinions resembled "the incoherent ramblings of a mentally retarded seven-year-old." Such was the Bolshevik's spiritual blindness with regards to the Christian faith.

What did Schmeltz himself believe? I waited months before he finally made a self-disclosure in praising the writings of the Jesuit philosopher/paleontologist Teilhard de Chardin. I was shocked. How could such a rational mind believe in the nebulous dreams of Teilhard de Chardin, with its cryptic notions of "nooesphere" and "omega point," and ridiculous belief that nature was endowed with an "élan vital" leading to the inevitable progression of humanity—in spite of all the evidence to the contrary! Teilhard was "a great poet," said fellow classmate Jaime with thinly disguised scorn, but how could anyone take his optimistic ramblings seriously?

During that time, I came across an excellent article in a Swiss evangelical review called "Chantiers," I read it in the Latin Quarter office of the "GBU" (*Groupes Bibliques Universitaires*, the French equivalent of Inter-Varsity) which I discovered about half way through the school year and where I would occasionally drop in for a cup of coffee after lunch. The article, written in impeccable French, was by a certain Henri Blocher. I'd read a number of articles by the man who, judging from his erudition, I assumed, was at least a hundred years old. Hence my surprise at discovering, during a one-day visit to the Baptist Seminary at Vaux-sur-Seine near Paris, that Mr. Blocher (born in 1937) wasn't even 40 at the time. Furthermore, he was familiar with my home town, where he had presided at worship services at the local Baptist church while a student at Gordon Conwell theological Seminary in 1959! Comme le monde est petit!

Mr. Blocher's treatment of Teilhard was a masterful application of apologetics in accordance with the truth of 2 Corinthiens 10:5: "We destroy all reasoning and lofty things that raise themselves up against the knowledge of God and bring all thought captive to the obedience of Christ." Rigorously biblical and beautifully written, his article was the most convincing analysis of the error of Teilhard's thinking. I got a copy and left it on Professor Schmeltz' desk one Monday morning before class. It wasn't until a few weeks later that I questioned him about the article, and, judging from his reaction, it had troubled him. It was a bit comical in that, in the excitement of our discussion, I forgot some elementary points of French linguistic etiquette and found myself addressing the distinguished professor in the familiar form reserved for close friends and family. He didn't take umbrage, suspecting that my *maladresse* was more a product of ignorance than disrespect.

I finished the year in Paris and enrolled at the Reformed Evangelical Seminary at Aix-en-Provence in the fall of 1976. Returning to Paris some twenty years later (1996), I stayed with an American missionary couple (Mark and Marty) who were also studying at the Sorbonne. What a surprise to learn that Marty attended a course called "Vie et Pensées Modernes" still being taught by the same Professor Schmeltz! Nothing seems to change in Paris. Surely that's why one feels perpetually young there. Even the waiter in the café where I had occasionally eaten some twenty years earlier was still at his post in 1996!

Twenty years later, I made it a point to take in Mr. Schmeltz's class on Monday morning which was now held in a different amphitheatre. Except for the change in locale, everything was the same. Professor Schmeltz had lost nothing of his verve or incisive analytical skill. The students were still spellbound by his authoritative erudition. It was "déjà vu all over again," as Yogi Berra would say.

The two-hour seminar dealt with contemporary French writers with whom I was only vaguely familiar. Though I re-introduced myself to Professor Schmeltz at the break, I didn't get the chance to learn if his beliefs had "evolved" since his Teilhard de Chardin days. The Lord only knows if M. Blocher's article eventually directed him to the Scriptures.

The academic year (1976) at the Sorbonne finished with little fanfare. I was grateful for the opportunities I had had to share the gospel with a number of classmates and even some French friends who, like sheep without a shepherd, were lost and searching, even if most of them didn't realize it..

During the course of that academic year (1975-6) in Paris, I developed a number of friendships with other students including French students studying *lettres classiques,* i.e., Greek and Latin. Most of these were female. We would meet in the student café between classes for there was high octane espresso to get us through the next period.

There was Monique, a young French literature major, looking for love in all the wrong places. Her best friend was Francine, a princess of debauchery, whose male conquests were too numerous to count. Monique—who was preparing a thesis on the 16th century French writer Joachim Du Bellay—was more concerned with finding "le grand amour," or true love, as the ultimate goal in life. She was scornful of the gospel, which she associated with a host of unbiblical traditions (she had been raised Roman Catholic) including lifelong celibacy for the truly devoted. In spite of her prejudices, she was open to discussion and we remained friends. She might have seen me as a liaison to our mutual friend Shilton, a towering American student from Oregon whose tiny room was in the same building as mine and with whom she slept on occasion.

I tried to direct Monique towards the lasting peace that only the gospel can give, but I sometimes wondered if my own personal shortcomings and longings were a counter-testimony to the message I proclaimed. Consequently, it was a surprise to me when Monique accepted an invitation to hear a Christian speaker at the "Maubert Mutalité" conference hall in the Latin Quarter one evening. When I asked her what prompted her to come, she replied: "You always seem to be happy and cheerful. If that comes from your faith in the gospel, then I want to know more."

If only she could have seen my inner struggles. For in spite of Paris' many distractions, it can be a very lonely place for a young foreign student. One can easily have *le cafard* (literally "the cockroach," it means a serious case of the blues). Fortunately for me, there was the precious fellowship of some Christians which made me grateful for my faith when faced with the millions of tragically lost souls in the city of lights. The fruit of the Spirit includes a joy that transcends our circumstances and is apparently perceptible to the non-believers. Monique's remark bears witness.

During that year, I joined a small Baptist church conveniently located on the Rue de Lille, a five minute walk from my digs. The church was comprised of about 25-30 mostly elderly folks with whom I would have naturally very little in common save the faith that united us in Jesus Christ. The pastor himself, M. Henri Vincent, was in his upper seventies and in 1924 had ministered to a French congregation in my home town! Another amazing coincidence.

The "youth" or "singles'" group was comprised of a handful of diverse students including Sida, daughter of a Romanian pastor whose congregation shared the same building with the French Baptist church. She was a precious source of encouragement to me during that difficult year. She had exceptional musical talent, which was appreciated by all. I still remember a few of the songs she taught us, including a simple, profound rhyme:

> *Sur cette terre, toute est précaire, tout est chimère, vanité,*
> *Joie et misère sont éphémères,*
> *Toi seul, O Père, tu restes à jamais;*
> *A ta lumière, ma vie s'éclaire,*
> *tous ceux qui espèrent en Toi seront sauvés. »*

In spite of its small numbers, that congregation provided a precious spiritual oasis for someone like me, in the cultural and spiritual desert of the French student world. The sincere warmth and Christian love that emanated from that group was a positive testimony even to some of my culturally diverse friends including Soliman, a Libyan-Arab, and devoted reader of Mark Twain (Who would have thought that anyone in Libya had even heard of M. Clemens?). An agnostic of Moslem background, Soliman occasionally accompanied me to church meetings and was impressed by the unabashed friendliness he found there. I remember his excitement at reading the Sermon on the Mount for the first time: "Jesus is the greatest psychologist in the world!" he exclaimed, after discovering the beatitudes.

"He's more than that," I pursued, alas without having the privilege of seeing Soliman come to the faith.

One time the folks in the church, somewhat dismayed that I continually wore the same pair of sneakers, offered me—through the mediation of Sida's brother Philippe—money to buy a pair of shoes! I was touched. For though I had no particular desire to wear anything but my sneakers, I grudgingly obliged the brethren concerned about my footwear. This was truly a practical expression of Christian love.

Sida was instrumental in finding me a weekend job at the American Church in Paris, working at the reception desk, answering the phone. This provided me with a meager but most appreciated source of income. The Lord indeed provides for His own, often through the mediation of His own people.

EPIPHANY in the shower

With the school year drawing to a close, it was time for me to be thinking about my future again. When classes finished at the end of May, I decided quite suddenly to head down to the south of France to Aix-en-Provence to check out that new seminary which had just opened and where M. Pierre Berthoud, an old acquaintance from L'Abri, was teaching Old Testament. I had learned about this seminary through a young Christian fellow who had done a brief exposé on the different Bible schools in France one night at our Baptist church youth group. I remember how during his presentation, I'd felt completely uninterested in the subject. Bible schools and seminaries were for "holy rollers" and certainly not for a sinner like me. I am not the stuff of which preachers are made, I thought.

So it was four or five months later when the decision to visit the seminary in Aix-en-Provence came to me in a "flash" of inspiration as I was down at the local public bath for my weekly shower. It was one of those deep existential experiences such as defines ones life—impossible to describe but overcoming me with the force of a mystical conviction. The fact is I just *knew* that I had to go down to Aix-en-Provence. It was that simple.

In retrospect, I see this conviction as the answer to my long-standing prayer for guidance about what I needed to be doing with my life. I find that God rarely answers with something clear-cut and definitive; it's usually the accumulation of bits and pieces of evidence He provides as we learn to walk in His ways. His Word is indeed a "lamp for one's feet." Even the best lamps don't light the pathway more than a few meters ahead.

I was unsure of myself and spiritually feeble. God in His grace took this into account as He impressed upon me with a certainty surpassing all rational explanation that I needed to go down to Aix-en-Provence to visit the Reformed Seminary there and talk with M. Berthoud, It was around 10 AM that morning in early June of 1976 when suddenly, in the middle of that shower the idea of hitchhiking down to the south of France overpowered me. Normally, it would be too late to be thinking about taking such a long trip. Aix-en-Provence is more than 400 miles from Paris! One would have to leave very early in the morning if he hoped to make the journey hitchhiking in one day. But something was moving me in an irresistible way. So I hurried out of the shower and back to my room, where I grabbed my sleeping bag and a few items of clothing before running down to the local *métro* station for the subway ride to the "Porte d'Italie" terminal, the south end of the city limits whence one picks up the *autoroute* heading south and from where I would hitchhike.

It was noon by the time I got there and, emerging from the *métro*, I headed down the street to the entrance ramp of the highway where no less than a couple dozen young men were attempting to get a lift out of the city. There would be lots of competition in finding a ride, I thought.

Knowing from experience how difficult hitchhiking could be in individualistic France, it would be natural to assume that I would be in for a long wait. Consequently, I wasn't surprised by the remarks of the first fellow I spoke to as I walked down the ramp to the end of the line. I asked him how long he'd been there.

"Depuis cinq heures et demi ce matin" (since 5:30 this morning") he replied matter-of-factly. It was already afternoon!

I was about to ask the second ones in line (two young fellows of about 18-19) when I noticed that one was scratching his name in the paint of on a roadside signpost under the inscription indicating that he had spent the previous night there! There was no need to ask these fellows about their wait as they were well into the "third stage" that all seasoned hitchhikers know well, i.e., anticipation, impatience, and finally, despair.

Humanly speaking, my hitchhiking prospects didn't look good. Nevertheless, I had one of those rare, ineffable convictions that I was walking in God's will and that He would provide a solution to my problem!

Hence my unusual peace as I submitted to the elementary rules of hitchhiker courtesy and went to the end of the line on the entrance ramp with many competitors ahead of me. Only someone who has ever hitchhiked in France can truly appreciate the hopelessness—humanly speaking—of my predicament.

Nonetheless, I tried to stack the deck in my favor. For one thing, I had made a sign from a piece of cardboard on which I wrote simply *SUD* (South). Unlike the signs of the other hitchhikers specifying destinations (Lyon, Marseille etc.), mine merely indicated a direction. In fact, I would be glad to get a lift **anywhere** so long as I was able to leave that unpromising situation. Secondly, I remembered to put into practice a tip I had learned from drivers who had picked me up in the past and of whom I had inquired as to their reason for stopping. The most important single factor, I had concluded, was the SMILE. A hitchhiker who smiles at the passing cars significantly increases his probability of getting a lift. A smile is disarming and goes a long way. The problem, of course, is that one doesn't feel much like smiling after he's been waiting in one place for hours. So the aspiring hitchhiker must be a bit of a politician and learn to force a smile even under adverse circumstances.

In any case, Providence was with me. I hadn't been there but five minutes when a small Renault "4L" slowed down to speak to some of the hitchhikers before me only to continue to the end of the line where I stood.

"Où allez-vous?" (Where are you going?) a big burly French driver asked through the open window on the passenger's side.

"N'importe où!" (Anywhere!), I replied eagerly, so long as I can get out of here, I thought.

It turned out my driver was heading for his hometown of Toulouse. He would be getting off the highway and driving through the Massif Central on secondary roads.

"C'est bien!" (That's fine!), I replied, while hoisting my bag onto my shoulder, tossing it into his back seat, and hopping in.

I was on my way: Toulouse, Aix-en-Provence, what did it matter. I'd be leaving Paris, "Du ciel ou de l'enfer, qu'importe, mais *du nouveau,»* (heaven or hell ; what did it matter so long as it was new), said Baudelaire.

I was convinced that the benevolent hand of Providence was upon me and would guide me to the desired port. So I sat back and proceeded to engage in polite chit-chat with my congenial chauffeur.

We drove hundreds of kilometers together through the beautiful French countryside. So talkative was my host that he ignored the fuel gauge and ran out of gas somewhere in the Auvergne region — the middle of French nowhere. My driver then got out of the car and hitched a ride himself to the next town with a gas container. We finally made it to Toulouse late in the evening. He was continuing on to Tarbes, so I jumped off outside the big city and walked down the road, stopping at a nearby construction site where I put my sleeping bag down for the night, grateful that the Lord had brought me safely thus far.

Arriving in Aix-en-Provence

The next day, I made it to Aix-en-Provence and was dropped off in the center of town at "la Place de la Rotonde" at the base of the famous "Cours Mirabeau," the magnificent tree-lined boulevard with its numerous fountains in the heart of this elegant, low-key town which seemed inhabited exclusively by students and bourgeois. Paris may be the crown jewel of the north, but Aix-en-Provence is the idyllic city of the south where the sun is a permanent resident. It has an ambiance that captures your heart and soul. One could linger forever at a sidewalk café under the shade of the plane trees that line the *Cours Mirabeau*, the main boulevard in the centre of town. Just outside of Aix, on rolling lavender-covered hills is the famous Mt. St. Victoire, immortalized in paintings by impressionist artist Paul Cezanne, who lived in Aix. I'll bet he savored the sweet smell of the surrounding air as much as the perpetual natural light.

All of which may explain another existential flash — a feeling that I'd arrived at my "home" for a while. For one who hadn't lived in any one place for more than a year for the past several years, this was a strange impression.

A walk through the beautiful *Parc Jourdan* led to Avenue Jules Ferry and the "Faculté de Théologie Réformée," which I'd come to visit. It was located smack dab in the middle of the student quarter, in the midst of thousands of pagans who needed the gospel, whether they realized it or not.

While walking up the driveway of the "Faculté," I was impressed to see a number of students lying around on the grass with note-books in hand, basking in the sweet *Provençal* sunshine, ostensibly studying for exams. What a change from the morose atmosphere of the Parisian student milieu with its perpetual drizzle and where a table in a local café is the closest element to leisure that one could associate with a book.

I was eager to meet students so I moseyed over to the student foyer and made a friend whom I invited to join me in a casual session with the Frisbee. He'd never thrown one, but was a quick learner. On the same lawn was a young coed sitting under a lime tree studying for her exams. Dressed in jeans and a sweat shirt, with straight brown hair and smooth skin, she appeared about 16 years old. She was in fact 21. When the Frisbee tossed by Pierre landed next to her, I took advantage of the situation and introduced myself as I stooped to retrieve it.

Hoping my introduction would be met with a smile, I was disap-pointed to be given a scowl. It was clear that our game was annoying her.

She snapped something at me about trying to study for her exams. I withdrew to a safer distance, not wishing to irritate her more than I already had. She was one to beware of, I thought. I nevertheless asked her name. It was Aline and I learned that she was from a small mining town (Alès) in the Cévennes. That's a mountainous region about 100 miles west of Aix-en-Provence.

That evening, I was invited to accompany a half-dozen students into town for a drink, a respite from exam preparation. We hit the town on the *Cours Mirabeau*, and settled in behind a table at one of the many cafés which adorn Aix-en-Provence's beautiful central artery. The students seemed relaxed as they discussed their impending exams. It all seemed far from the stressful life of the capitol. I sought wisdom and advice as I shared with them some of my background, experiences in Paris, and struggles about whether or not I might not enroll at the Seminary like them. Knowing I might soon be included in their number, I picked up the tab for the group. In fact, I had been scrimping and saving all year in Paris and was now left with just enough money to satisfy some modest needs before I would have to seek employment again.

My uncharacteristic munificence might have been motivated by ulterior motives. Maybe I was trying subconsciously to make an impression on the brown-eyed lass from the Cévennes. Maybe.

In any case, I felt much better vibes from her that evening, even a smile cast in my direction at the café and decided to ask Aline out for a pizza the following evening. She accepted!

So I spent the next day visiting classes at the Seminary where I met a young Swiss fellow who had bicycled down from Geneva to visit the Seminary. He too was seeking his vocation. Jean-Marc and I shared our concerns and both wondered if we might not enroll for the next academic year. Curiously, after attending a few classes, he and I both came to the same conclusion: seminary studies were too intellectual to be practical. Perhaps we would come for a year, but surely not more. As it turns out, we both stayed for five years and became good friends during that period. What's more, Jean-Marc eventually married Susan, an American girl from California who lived a floor below me in the same apartment building. I learned of their engagement while she and I were having coffee one morning. I knew they'd been seeing each other, but I hadn't realized is was that serious.

"I didn't' realize you were getting married," I exclaimed. "Jean-Marc hasn't said anything to me," I continued.

"That's not surprising," she added. "He doesn't know yet."

Meanwhile, I was probably under the spell of the Provençale springtime when Aline and I walked through the *Parc Jourdan* back into town from the Seminary to a restaurant pizzeria just off the *Cours Mirabeau*. I don't remember well enough the particulars of our conversation. But I do remember being left with the distinct impression that my longstanding prayer for a mate was in the process of being answered. It was a strange sensation.

PACKAGE DEAL VOCATION?

For one thing, I'd long been convinced that my vocation for France had to be a package deal. I'd been interested in a couple of girls from Gordon College as a student there, but I couldn't conceive of dragging some New England girl off to France where she might get homesick for Narragansett Bay quahogs, clam chowder, maple syrup, and the Boston Red Sox. So I made up my mind before I let myself get serious with anyone that my future spouse would have to have the same vocation as mine. In the words of the great French writer Antoine de St. Exupéry: love is not a matter of looking at each other face to face, but of standing side by side, looking in the same direction. In other words, the Lord would have to give me a French wife.

The problem was, how did one get to know a French girl? For one thing, there is no such thing as American style "dating" in France. I had platonic relationships with a few heathen girl friends in Paris who understood well that as a Christian there was no chance of my getting serious with anyone who didn't share my faith.

The situation was dramatically different in Christian circles, where true believers don't treat the search for a life-partner casually. By ironic consequence, the courting rituals among French evangelicals are subtle and filled with traps and snares which often lead to tearful misunderstandings. One must be very prudent in dealing with singles of the opposite sex. The least word can get you in a whole lot of trouble. That's surely why one French Bible school virtually forbids conversations amongst its students of the opposite sex!

Consequently, the art of interacting with members of the opposite sex was all but unknown in French Christian circles. The only alternative was the group meetings that rarely took place in certain churches. There one could get to know, albeit superficially, a potential mate by seeing how he or she interacted within the group. Still, there were great dangers even in this method as a few furtive glances at someone in the group could be easily misinterpreted.

One-on-one American style dating was foreign here. In France, one didn't go out with just one person unless one was practically engaged. So basically, one gets engaged first, and gets to know his future spouse during the engagement period. That puts a lot of pressure on the fiancés and unnecessary 'scandals' when engage-ments are broken as often happens.

In this cultural context, Aline seemed to take my simple invita-tion seriously. For her, it was considerably more than just a "date"—a foreign concept in Latin cultures. I found myself in Christian circles where suddenly, the stakes were high. .

With Aline, it was immediately clear that all three criteria for long-term compatibility were present: spiritual and intellectual compatibility and physical attraction. It was the *coup de foudre* (lightning strike). Don't ask me to explain. "The heart has reasons of which the reason knows nothing", said Pascal. Molière put it equally poetically:

"Le caprice y prend part et quand quelqu'un nous plait,
Souvent nous avons peine à dire pourquoi c'est."
[Caprice plays its role and when someone pleases us,
Often we don't know why]

But I didn't trust my feelings. Maybe it was typical male panic in the face of commitment. It would take a few months—and some illumination from unexpected sources—before that issue was resolved. In the end, I would say that things worked out for the best, notwithstanding the fact that there are special challenges in any cross-cultural marriage. Imagine waking up every morning next to someone who's never even heard of Willie Mays and who can't understand why I cry whenever I see "Field of Dreams."

For the moment, "seeking the Kingdom" meant studying the Word of God "on location" in the country of my vocation. That meant enrolling at the seminary at Aix-en-Provence.

CHAPTER 4

THE SEMINARY YEARS 1976-81

Dobie Gillis meets Einstein

This was the most trying and exhilarating period in my life. Besides the demanding study of Greek and Hebrew during that first year, there was the romantic preoccupation with Aline. Though we had been somewhat romantically involved the previous summer, I had temporarily put our relationship on hold for a while to get my thinking straight. Aline didn't appreciate my male commitment-phobia and accused me of not keeping my word. Meanwhile, our temporary rupture made for a somewhat awkward situation as we saw each other daily, but weren't really speaking. There were only fifteen other students enrolled at the "Faculté" that year and all were aware our situation. The Lord taught us both a lot during that time. Not only that, but He provided me with a good buddy with whom I could share my most intimate concerns and sentimental frustrations.

Christian R. was a new Christian, of "pied noir" (literally "black foot") origin, i.e., French who had lived in Algeria and returned to the motherland following Algerian independence in 1962. His family, like many "pieds noirs" had settled on the Mediterranean coast in the port city of Toulon. His dad was a policeman of modest academic training. Christian was easily the most academically gifted of all the students at the faculty. His brain was a sponge that absorbed everything it came into contact with. He had been a German language student at the liberal arts school before being touched by the Lord's saving grace only a few months before enrolling at the seminary. He spoke flawless English and was a terrific pedagogue.

Christian became a great friend with whom I could share every confidence during that first terrible year at seminary. We spent hours talking about the joys of our walk with the Lord and the sexual frustration of celibate life. We both had somewhat debauched pasts and found it difficult to mortify the testosterone.

We discussed the various methods of sublimating frustrations, and spent time praying for the grace to hold firm. We could empathize with the struggles of the young St. Augustin who, in his Confessions prayed, "Lord, give me chastity; give me continence — but not yet."

This led to some comical episodes, as when we visited a non-Christian girl we knew from a mutual acquaintance, with the intention of setting her straight about the Faith.

Odile was a young liberal arts coed who knew of my buddy's great intellectual prowess and hoped he might answer some of her theoretical objections to the gospel. For several hours one evening Christian addressed some of her questions.

My first impression was that Odile's so-called objections to the Faith were spiritual smokescreens that kept her from coming to the Lord in repentance. The second was that Christian and I were both struggling to avoid staring at Odile's revealing décolleté and abundant cleavage. "Pour être dévot on n'est pas mois homme," said Moliere's Tartuffe.

There were more academic battles. Linguistic zero that I am, I was studying both Greek and Hebrew, in French! My gifted buddy Christian wrestled with the hazard of being an intellectual dilettante; he was so brilliant in so many areas that he didn't know where to apply himself. He would make regular forays to the bookstores in town and buy all kinds of books on math, science, and music, determined to become an expert in whatever field was his whim.

Brilliance had its downside though. For instance, Christian had to make a conscious effort when walking out of an apartment building not to look at the names on the mailboxes in the building entrance for fear that he would remember them all and that they would "encombrer la mémoire" ("clutter up his memory"). He asked me to abstain from using proper names in any anecdotes I would tell him, for fear of encumbering his mind with useless trivia.

In retrospect, I think part of the difficulty of that first year arose from the Enemy's determination to stop us from studying the Word and to use the sins of our past to discourage us from thinking we could be of any use in the gospel ministry. Both Christian and I had been involved with eastern mysticism before coming to faith in Christ. Christian's had been more of an intellectual journey. A convinced Buddhist, he had even started learning Sanskrit to study its foundational texts in the original languages. But he had no intentions of heading off to Tibet or Nepal.

As for myself, I had rejected all intellectualism, convinced that it led only to a dead end; I didn't need all that erudition to be aware of my ignorance. I had become involved with the most radically anti-intellectual form of Buddhism, the Japanese Zen variety. Christian would chide my anti-intellectualism and remind me that human reason is "ce qui nous sépare des bêtes" (that which separates us from the animals).

Another good friend was Remi R. who, with three "r's" in his name, was impossible for me to pronounce (When I make fun of her "frenglish", Aline still retorts by asking me to pronounce "Remi R. rapidly).

Remi was a simple fellow from a modest working-class family in the Cévennes (Theology school has a greater diversity of students than the secular universities), but his family was Christian and devoid of the vulgarity one finds in lower-class folk in France. There are basically two classes of people in France: the well-bred pagans and the ill-bred pagans, the latter can be as vulgar as anything one finds in the USA.

Remi was a precious source of encouragement, a mature Christian and kind of pastor to the unstable believer I then was. He was gracious, even-tempered, generous beyond his modest means, and had a pastor's heart. His presence at the seminary was a reminder to me that the Lord hadn't called only intellectuals to serve Him in the ministry. Remi struggled even more than I did with Greek and Hebrew and yet persevered to earn his *license'* (degree) like the rest of us.

Another interesting student was Jean-Philippe W. He was an Alsatian from that part of France where they seem to have been blessed with the rigors of Germanic culture and the finesse of the French. "Our women can play the piano and milk a cow," bragged an Alsatian man, quoting a local proverb. I believe it.

I was amused by the Alsatian students, which included Jean-Daniel L. and Daniel K. They would sneak down to the seminary kitchen at night to snack on Alsatian sausage, and during the course of a conversation they would occasionally let slip some subtle scorn for what they considered the dirtier, lazier folk of the south of France.

As for Jean-Philippe, he was a model brother for me at a time when I needed a role-model: hard-working (academically and manually), generous (with time and money), cultivated, and 100% committed to the cause of the gospel. I owe my success in passing seminary Greek in large part to Jean-Philippe, who had studied classical Greek in *lycée* and helped me and others get through the less sophisticated grammar of biblical or *koiné* Greek. He would help me with my lessons while on duty as night watchman at the "Cite Abraham," one of the local student residences. He also rendered all kinds of assistance—material and otherwise—to ungrateful pagan students who took advantage of his generous nature.

Like my buddy Remi, Jean-Philippe demonstrated patience and wisdom with me and my occasional tirades against the Lord's "injustice" in dealing with me and the world. Once he exhorted me by quoting the prophet Malachi: "vous fatiguez l'Eternel par vos paroles...." (You have wearied the Lord with your words... Malachi 2:17). His rebuke penetrated my heart like a sword. Though it was not pleasant at the time, I now thank the Lord for the ministry of men like these brothers.

Curiously, one of the subjects almost never broached with Jean-Philippe was the one that preoccupied me much of the time: the fairer sex. That was hardly the case with Jean-Philippe, I came to the conclusion he was a born ascetic, totally committed to his vocation as an evangelist and Greek professor. I, by contrast, was "Dobie Gillis" of the 60's sitcom: "Same old Dobie Gillis, same old problem—girls."

Jean-Philippe and I went to Paris in February of that first year like other students taking a month off from their studies to do a *"stage"* or apprenticeship with a pastor or in some kind of Christian service. I was sent to work with a French pastor of Moroccan origin who had a ministry with the "sans logis" (homeless). Pastor Pierre Mobar, from a devout Moslem family, had come to the French capital to find work in the early 60's.

Pastor Mobar's conversion came about in a curious way. One night, a Christian evangelist had knocked on the door of his modest apartment in a working-class section of the French capital and slipped him a copy of the gospel according to Matthew. Mobar read it and was transformed overnight, His brother, a Moslem cleric in Morocco, heard what happened and came to Paris to talk some sense into this wayward Moslem. "Il n'y a rien supérieur au Coran" (there's nothing greater than the Koran) affirmed the older brother. But shortly afterwards, Pierre Mobar's brother too accepted Jesus as Savior and started a church in the north of France! Clearly, the Lord had designs on that family.

After attending Bible school, Pierre Mobar consecrated his life to sharing the good news with the derelicts—mostly alcoholics—who would come to his church-sponsored soup kitchen in Paris for free nightly meals. He would select among the mostly alcoholic vagrants those willing to improve their condition, and would take them home to the proletariat eastern Paris suburb of Gagny where he had turned a café into a dormitory for homeless men.

Those who came to stay with him were fed and lodged but had to be looking for work. Most importantly, they were not allowed even a drop of alcohol lest they be sent out into the streets, not the most appealing place on a cold and damp February night.

My "job," in addition to occasional preaching at the soup kitchen (the derelicts or "clochards" had to listen to a gospel presentation before getting their soup), was to fraternize with these men and seek opportunities to share the faith with them. I can't say I had much success, but I learned a few things about man's depravity and my own naïveté. Fortunately, Pastor Mobar was a lot more "street smart" than I was. The homeless respected him and the Lord blessed his ministry with many conversions.

The vast majority of those who came to the soup kitchen at Rue Chemin Vert were incorrigible alcoholics. They rarely if ever bathed and the stench was palpable. Some drank as many as 10-12 liters of cheap red wine per day. For these, there was little or no hope of reform. If they came to the soup kitchen, it was for their only "meal" of the day. Most wouldn't even consider the Pastor's offer of hospitality, as it entailed total abstinence from booze, impossible for most of them. However, there were some non-committed alcoholics who had only recently gotten hooked, usually as a result of trying circumstances in their lives.

One such case was Paul, a 23-year-old Basque orphan who had arrived in Paris with little money in his pocket and looking for work. Destitute and unable to find employment, he found himself sleeping under bridges with other "clochards" and hitting the bottle to forget the cold. Still, Paul wanted to work and not become a career derelict.

Thus, he gladly accepted Pastor Mobar's offer to lodge at his shelter. Sleeping in a bed was surely better than sleeping under a bridge—especially during the winter months. Paul was delighted when Rev. Mobar used his influence to find him a job unloading freight at a nearby trucking depot.

Paul was the kind of fellow Rev. Mobar was trying to help.

On my day off from the shelter, I met Jean-Philippe in town and we took a commuter train to visit his sister, who lived with her husband and children in St. Denis (a working-class suburb north of Paris famous for its cathedral, one of the oldest and most magnificent examples of early Gothic architecture). I was impressed by the gospel influenced on Jean-Philippe's entire family. His older sister, a young married woman, lived in a tiny apartment in a modest section of this proletariat suburb, raising two small children, but still found time to receive visitors. She was using her "spare" time to translate (from German to French) badly needed Christian literature. She had the manuscripts spread out on the table in her kitchen along with a dictionary and a few other reference works that we had to move out of the way to set the table for lunch.

A couple of years later I would meet Jean-Philippe's father, an unpretentious retired man who came down to the seminary to do a week of volunteer gardening on the seminary property.

It was during that brief visit with his sister that I saw the tender family side of Jean-Philippe, who clearly relished the company of his young niece and nephew as he played with them on the floor of their room. When I asked him if he would ever consider getting married and raising a family, he answered with his warm smile: "Oui......mais chaque chose en son temps" (each thing in its own time). He was clearly trusting the Lord to work out the details. The Lord did work out the details—punctually and with providential smoothness.

One day a couple of years later, Jean-Philippe and Joseline, a transfer student who had come to the Aix-en-Provence seminary following a stint as a missionary in Chad, came back together from the student restaurant holding hands (a significant gesture indeed in French Christian circles). "Ça y est" (that's done) said Jean Philippe, with a beaming smile, indicating with a gesture the position of Joseline's hand in his. I hadn't, nor had anyone else, realized that they had been speaking together seriously. Now they were a couple engaged to be married. Theirs' was the sober commitment of two people devoted to the same Cause. As of this writing, Jean-Philippe and Joseline have been happily married for over twenty-seven years.

FIDDLER ON THE ROOF

In spite of a one-year rupture, I continued to think of Aline and wondered why I had always felt elated in her presence.

Here my mind wanders to something the late Francis Schaeffer said when giving young people advice about the choice of their future mates. He traced a circle on the blackboard and explained how it represented the circle of all the Christians of the opposite sex that one would meet. Naturally, one must find his mate amongst Christians according to the clear directives of the Word (I Corinthians

7), "for what company hath righteousness with unrighteousness; what communion between the children of light and the children of darkness?"

Schaeffer's second circle, which overlaps the first, would include all the Christians one meets with whom one shares a certain intellectual compatibility. That means that illiterate peasants don't normally marry Ivy League intellectuals—at least not if they want to have something to talk about. That too seemed reasonable to me. In fact, I don't know of many successful marriages where there is a great discrepancy between the intellectual levels of the husband and wife.

Finally, there was Schaffer's third circle, which further restricted the field to those Christians with whom one shared intellectual compatibility and also physical attraction. This too seemed plausible to me. I couldn't imagine being married to someone for whom I didn't feel at least a tingle in her presence—and occasionally being "twitterpated," to borrow a Walt Disney Bambi neologism.

What produces such a tingling feeling, described whimsically in the young Cherubin's aria "Voi che sapete," in Mozart's "Marriage of Figaro"? Certainly one couldn't trust such a chimera as the basis for a relationship. I remembered a "goddess" I used to admire discretely while studying at the Gordon College library. She was a cross between a Barbie Doll and a creature on a Botticelli seashell. In fantasies, I imagined this delicate waiflike creature floating around the campus, hovering a couple of inches above the ground. She was Dante's Beatrice, with an ethereal beauty to evoke one's heavenly destination. I wallowed in this fantasy for weeks until one day I actually overheard her speaking with a fellow student outside the library. My disappointment was great. I was expecting this Beatrice to speak in Latin verse or at least iambic pentameter. What I heard from the mouth of this physical marvel, in the thickest proletariat New Jersey accent, was the sounds of a stereotypical gangster's moll from an old B movie. Whew! Welcome back to reality.

As for Aline, she had assiduously read the novels of the heart, and spoke of love with all the conviction of a French intellectual announcing the classless society. My convictions were less stable. I was troubled by the fact that my feelings—for her as for anyone else prior to that time—seemed to vacillate from ecstasy to total indifference from one moment to another. How could that be? And how does one base a relationship on that kind of psychological or emotional oscillation?

I even flirted with the idea of replacing my obsession with Aline with a new relationship, but each time I tried, I was overcome by feelings of intense physical repulsion, even nausea, at the sight of my new flame. I remembered the words of warning of a Canadian architect who had picked me up hitchhiking near Lyon and with whom I'd ridden all the way to Paris. When we got to Paris, he went to a café I recommended for dinner rather than drive immediately home to see his wife, whom he hadn't seen in a few days. I was puzzled by this, but a few drinks into the meal, he spilled his guts out to me and said that after twenty-five years of marriage, he was repulsed by his own wife! God forbid that should happen to me!

After that first academic year, Aline had gone back to work at her family's restaurant in Antoise in the Cévennes while and I remained in Aix-en-Provence.

When the new school year began in October of 1977, Aline's presence continued to preoccupy me, but I refrained from taking any action until I had a stronger conviction. That conviction came one weekend (Nov.1, 1977—it's funny how one remembers some dates) after I saw a film that had been recommended to me years before by a professor from Gordon College. The movie, "Fiddler on the Roof," is a musical 'comedy' classic about a Russian-Jewish milk farmer and his family of five daughters during the *pogroms* at the end of the 19th century. Tevye, the farmer, is concerned when his daughters want to break the sacrosanct **tradition** of the elders and marry for "love," rather than for material security. He and his wife Golda, who have been married for more than twenty years, were introduced on their wedding day. They had learned to love each other and had raised five daughters together.

One day, as Tevye's struggling with the implications of one of his daughter's romantic aspirations, he asks Golda if she loves him. Golda reacts with surprise, wondering what could have provoked such an irrelevant question. She replies in a non-committal way, so Tevye rephrases the question. Again, she makes an obtuse response. Finally, her exasperated husband questions her for the third time (reminiscent of Jesus' three questions to the apostle Peter cf. John 21) if she indeed loves him.

"For 20 odd years I have shared my bed with you, been hungry and cold with you, born you five children, prepared your meals, etc. If that isn't love, then I don't know what is. "

Golda's wisdom hit me. "Love" isn't so much sentiments as it is a covenant to stick by the other through thick and thin, for better of for worse. And it's revealed by deeds more than words.

Beyond my occasional "twitterpation" in Aline's presence, it was clear that she fell within the parameters of all three of Schaeffer's circles (spiritual, physical, intellectual compatibility), So there was no reason not to make a commitment and trust the Lord to make love grow as we went through life's adventure together. I still believe that.

So the weekend after seeing that film, I went to see Aline, who had just returned from a Christian retreat center where she had a similar conviction, and I asked her to marry me. She accepted, and we set the date for the civil ceremony: March 4, 1978.

There was still another important lesson to learn. As an American attempting to marry a French person, I would have to subject myself to a bureaucratic nightmare that would make Kafka's *Trial* look like child's play.

The French authorities don't take kindly to attempts by foreigners to 'steal' their best regional products. They oblige the would-be groom to jump through many administrative hoops, including a series of medical exams, judicial inquiries, residency requirements, etc., all determined to test the resolve of the aspirant to marriage. The worst part of the whole process, which included six weeks of regular administrative visits, bureaucratic red-tape, and all kinds of paperwork, was the fact that everything had to be done in chronological order. So if there was some delay along the way, the validity of the medical exam, for instance, could expire and the whole process would need to be re-initiated! Verily, verily I tell you, it was absolutely Kafkaesque.

As full-time students we couldn't devote much time and money to the whole process. With our wedding day fast approaching, we still didn't have a place to live. Aline had been living in a student dorm, and I had been renting a room from a fellow student for a meager 100F/month—a paltry sum even for 1977—in an old apartment building in downtown Aix.

On Friday, March 3, we still didn't have a place to live. That afternoon, we walked down to the Aix-en-Provence tourist office (we didn't own a car) where we stumbled upon an announcement about a "studio" that was available on Avenue Paul Guigou in a building called "Les Cèdres." We didn't know where that was, but we hoped it wasn't too far from the seminary, as transportation would be a real problem. Hence our delight to discover that "Les Cèdres" was in fact directly across the street from the seminary. Equally providential was the fact that the previous tenant was in the process of moving out and gladly accepted our proposition to move in immediately and so avoid paying the rest of the month's rent.

Once again, the Lord's provision was manifest to us as we moved in our few belongings that afternoon, less than twenty four hours before our civil union!

Our wedding took place, according to French tradition, at the city hall of Aix-en-Provence. I was wearing a shirt we'd bought at the market place for 50 francs ($8) for the occasion. Aline was dressed in a gown she'd bought with her mother on one of our trips to her hometown. I was indifferent to such finery, but I didn't realize how much it meant to a woman to be specially adorned for her wedding day. Aline looked great to me no matter what she wore, and thought it was superficial to be concerned with such "trivial" accoutrements. Surely there was more than a bit of Thoreau's influence in my worldview.

We had borrowed Aline's mother's car for the occasion and parked hastily in front of city hall on the morning of March 4 for what was to be the biggest day of our lives. In fact we didn't do much driving in those years as we didn't have a car nor did we need one, save for the occasional trip to visit the in-laws in Alès. I didn't much care for driving in France anyway, as the aggressiveness of the French drivers caused me to become more aggressive. It's a strange country where people are surrounded by hundreds of unwritten laws governing their daily behavior, but where traffic regulations are considered more as "suggestions." My cousin's theory was that recklessness behind the wheel of a car was the French way of compensating far all the unwritten laws that oppress them in their daily lives. Without getting too Freudian, I guess you could call it "automotive sublimation."

I remember little about the civil ceremony part of our wedding save for the fact that the city hall at Aix-en-Provence (or *mairie,* as it's called) houses an impressive marble statue of the famous 17-18th century French general "Maréchal de Villars" which we walked past in front of the main staircase on the way to the ceremony. He was the same fellow king Louis XIV had sent down to the Cévennes to squelch the Protestant "Camisard" revolt in the Huguenot persecutions in 1702. I wondered what he would think of two young Protestants strolling indifferently past him on the way to their wedding. He may have "succeeded," to some extent in stopping the Camisard offensive. In fact, his success was largely a result of buying off the Camisard leader Jean Cavalier. When 60,000 of the king's troops weren't able to defeat the 2000 Camisards insurgents in a kind of guerilla war of attrition, General Villars offered a cushy administrative job to Cavalier, who finished his days as governor of the island of Jersey. I really don't recall if that was going through my mind as we walked pas the statue depicting the general, with his elaborate attire, similar to that worn by Louis XIV himself.

Villars may have 'won' the battle, but had not completely succeeded in extirpating the Reformed faith from *Provence.* And now it would grow even stronger when the posterity of these two Protestants would add to the numbers. I couldn't help but think of the Huguenot motto: "Plus on s'amuse à me frapper; plus de marteau on finit par user" (the more one strikes me, the more hammers he wears out). Such was the determination and perseverance of the Huguenots.

I wasn't so much concerned with French history that day as that we'd arrived only in the nick of time for the wedding as we had looked feverishly for a parking place. We ended up parking illegally and earned ourselves a ticket from the local police. No big deal for most, but considering our modest budget, an unwanted expense we could hardly afford. So I photocopied our marriage certificate with the date circled and sent it to the police with the ticket. They obliged us with a word of congratulations and waived the fine. French police have hearts too.

GREAT IS HIS FAITHFULNESS

The rest is a testimony to the Lord's grace, as we discovered His faithfulness in providing for these two materially destitute theology students. We basically lived on salad, homemade yogurt, and bread during those first two years of marriage. And we weren't opposed to visiting the open-air marketplace in downtown Aix-en-Provence at closing time (around noon) when many of the "forains" or "vendeurs" (merchants) would actually throw away significant quantities of unsold, usually tainted, fruit or vegetables, which we would shovel into the wooden case on the back of my bicycle. Those were indeed days of "lean cows," when we didn't even have the wherewithal to pay our rent and when, on more than one occasion, we found money in our mailbox, obviously put there by someone aware of our struggle and eager to help us.

There is perhaps one anecdote that illustrates, more than any other, the Lord's provision. It has to do with a white dress shirt required of all those who would sing in the seminary choir. It was clear to Aline, even if it wasn't to me, that now that we were married, we would be doing everything together. That meant singing together in the seminary choir. The choir would occasionally do promotional tours, singing in churches in different parts of France and even Switzerland and Belgium.

For my first two years at seminary, I forsook the choir, having no illusions about my musical talent, nor any aptitude for musical theory or *"solfège.",*

Aline sang with the sopranos and fully expected me to join her in the choir. I persisted in declining, using as an excuse the fact that I didn't possess the requisite white shirt nor could we afford to buy one.

"If I only had a white shirt," I argued, "that would be a different story. But without a shirt...."

So my young wife threw down the gauntlet.

"If the Lord provides a shirt for you, then you'll have to join the choir," she argued.

"Of course," I concurred, hardly doubting that I would ever have the means to procure a shirt. What's more, it was our personal policy not to ask anyone—save the Lord Himself—to help us with any material means. It didn't look like I'd be swelling the ranks of the tenors or basses any time soon.

One Saturday afternoon, Aline's sister Florence came to visit us in Aix. She and Aline went shopping on the busy streets of our charming university town when Florence stumbled upon a shopping bag that had been dropped in the street and which contained an impeccable new *Pierre Cardin* white dress shirt. The receipt for the newly purchased shirt was still in the bag. So a more scrupulous person than my sister-in-law (Aline, for example) would have felt obliged to return the shirt to the boutique where it had been purchased, mindful of the possibility that the client would be returning to look for his misplaced purchase.

Florence, however, saw the shirt as a gift from Heaven and brought it home for her own husband Marcel. As it turns out, the shirt was too large for him. So on our next visit to Alès, we inherited the new "*Pierre Cardin*" shirt, which fit me perfectly well. This incident was typical of the way the Lord provided for us during those meager years and it was how my career with the seminary choir began.

Another instance of the Lord's provision followed soon after. We had been living in a studio apartment conveniently located across the street from the Seminary and adjacent to the *faculté de letters,* where Aline signed up to do modern Hebrew for the two years after she graduated from seminary while waiting for me to finish my degree and eventually my "*maîtrise*" (masters).

We'd been married a bit less than two years and had been doing our laundry in the bathtub (Laundromats were rare and expensive in France). That was adequate as we didn't have much of a wardrobe and didn't have a lot to wash. Even poverty has its advantages.

One day towards the beginning of the summer after I graduated, we received a gift of a used washing-machine in good condition from a generous Christian family of Armenian origin who owned a woodworking shop in downtown Aix. What would we do with a washing machine, I wondered? We didn't have enough clothes to wash.

CORSICA TRIP

Later that summer, after working in July and August at Aline's family's restaurant in the picturesque village of Antoise, we took a trip to Corsica to visit that beautiful island and the Lucianis, family of a student friend of Aline' who lived in the same apartment building with us. This too was the Lord's belated provision for a honeymoon that we hadn't taken, for lack of means. It was while we were buzzing around that magnificent *"île de beauté"* on brother-in-law Pascal's 125cc Suzuki motorcycle, staying with the gracious Luciani family in Ghisonnacia, that we learned that Aline was expecting our first child. So now we understood why the Lord had provided us with a washing machine.

The Lucianis were most hospitable folks who received us royally in their beautiful home, where M. Luciani managed a very successful retail sporting goods store. We ate and drank like kings, sitting around in the living room after dinner discussing religion and politics, sipping snifters of the finest *Remi Martin* cognac, while hordes of pesky mosquitoes feasted off of us! One had to wonder about the priorities of a culture where the most superfluous luxury items — fine cognac — flowed like water, but where there was no mosquito netting! I suppose if one drinks enough cognac, one doesn't notice the mosquitoes. That didn't work for me. But of more importance was M. and Mrs. Luciani fond memory of the American army which had helped eradicate the notorious Ghisonnaccia mosquito problem during the second World War. Apparently it was time for the army to return.

The island itself, with its magnificent beaches, beautiful mountain scenery, and picturesque mountain villages, some built on the edges of foreboding cliffs, is surely one of the most naturally beautiful places in the world. Yet Corsica attracts but a small fraction of the tourist trade because of the Corsicans' obstinate refusal to make their island hospitable to tourists. The Corsican "liberation" movement has been bombing the vacation homes of outsiders for decades, and a non-Corsican takes a great risk in buying property there.

What's more, the island's magnificent public beaches are often covered with refuse, broken bottles and garbage of all kinds, left behind by Corsicans as well as inconsiderate tourists, the latter probably frustrated at finding no trash receptacles anywhere. Who wants to cart his rubbish with him on vacation? I'm sure I wasn't the only one who cut his foot on a broken bottle on a beach.

Dr. Aquaviva, the Corsican OB-GYN man who diagnosed Aline's pregnancy, was an interesting fellow. He had just returned from a visit to the Untied States, his first. He was eager to impart some of his reflections on the cultural differences between his Corsican culture — more Latin than that of continental France, and the mostly Anglo-Saxon United States. He related a story about a visit to the men's room at the Washington, D.C., railroad station where he saw a man, sitting and calmly on the toilet with the door wide open calmly reading the newspaper even as he defecated. "Amazing," said Dr. A. "We Latins are a lot more self-conscious and don't like to be seen in these kinds of circumstances."

I told him that most Americans didn't either. Then he said, "Do you know the most amazing thing I saw during my entire time in the United States?"

I was thinking he was going to relate something about some American architectural or engineering marvel. For it had been clear from our discussion that Dr. Acquaviva was a very cultivated man with a scientific curiosity and a wide breath of interests. What could have amazed him? Something from the NASA and the American Space program? The Smithsonian Museum? His answer:

"While walking the streets of Washington, I saw a woman wearing bright orange pants and with a *derrière* as wide as an elephant's!"

"Many Corsican women become heavy after childbirth and with age," he admitted. "But they would dress in such a way as to hide their form and NEVER wear orange pants!" He was clearly torn between admiration and bewilderment.

The news about Aline's pregnancy cut short our "honeymoon" as the Corsican gynecologist informed us that the vibrations of the motorcycle weren't good for the developing fetus.

So we aborted our tour of the island and headed over to Ajaccio where we took the next available ferry back to the mainland and headed to Alès and Antoise to resume work at the Maurin's family restaurant.

FELIX AND MARIE-CLAUDE

Living in France exposes one to different cultures in the constant interaction with folks from the many former French colonies who send tens of thousands of students to France for university. This makes France a key mission field, as many of the world's future leaders are in the French university system. Reach France with the gospel, and you can reach a great portion of the world's people, including the inhabitants of thirty-odd former territorial holdings in Africa, S.E. Asia, etc. Ignore this potential and you allow for the rise of dictators like Enver Hoxha (Albania), Pol Pot (Cambodia), and Ho Chi Minh, illustrious products of the French university system.

Our time in Aix-en-Provence was rich in experiences with foreigners who lived in our building which was comprised exclusively of studio apartments. Many of these were inhabited by young female French university coeds living with their African boyfriends. Among our friends was a young couple in their late twenties, from Cameroun, Felix and Marie-Claude Kumba. They had come to France to allow Felix to finish a degree in economics. In fact, he wasn't a serious student and spent most of his time gallivanting with his African buddies.

We'd get together on occasion for a meal and usually discuss American Jazz, especially Buddy Tate of whom Felix was a big fan.

Aline was pregnant at the time and particularly sensitive to the way Marie-Claude was raising their own 14 month-old daughter. She was amazed to see how Marie-Claude handled virtually all the domestic chores by herself, including the grocery shopping, which she did without the benefit of either a car or a baby-sitter. On several occasions we saw Marie Claude arrive at the building carrying her daughter in one arm and an impressive number of groceries in the other, having walked over two miles from the grocery store near the town center!

Unlike her husband, Marie-Claude lacked distractions or activities. She told Aline she would occasionally spend part of the morning, when the baby was asleep, riding up and down on the elevator to relieve her boredom!

These were significant details that revealed much about the plight of women in many countries not influenced by the Judeo-Christian world view.

More revealing was an incident that happened one night when Aline and I were already in bed. It was after midnight when there came a knock on our door. It was Marie-Claude, standing there in her nightgown, crying. She explained that Felix, who was apparently out on the town carousing in the night-clubs, had given his studio key to one of his African buddies, and sent him over to his place with permission to use (sexually speaking) his wife Marie-Claude for the night!

Marie Claude was becoming Westernized enough to think she had a word to say about this. She wanted no part of this strange man and pleaded with me to speak to him—he was waiting in their apartment—so he would leave her alone.

I was half asleep but accompanied Marie-Claude to her apartment. There was a thirty-year-old African fellow there who explained to me matter-of-factly that he was a friend of Felix who had given him permission to "use," his wife, who was being most uncooperative. I was flabbergasted. More shocking than the announcement itself was the indignant tone of voice implying that she, as a woman, had absolutely nothing to say as she was merely property!

It was hardly the time and place to be going into a lesson in biblical theology about the equal worth of men and women before God and the nature of marriage and conjugal relations, so I merely asked the fellow to accept the fact that Marie-Claude did not want to sleep with him and to respect her wishes. After expressing his bewilderment at this strange culture which would grant a woman some say in this kind of issue, he decided it wasn't worth an argument and left without further incident.

Marie-Claude thanked me and I went back to the studio where Aline was still horrified by the nature of Marie-Claude's dilemma. Alas, this situation is not unique in the world. Some of the other studios at *Les Cèdres* were occupied by other young French women and their African boyfriends. Typically, they would get along reasonably well—as long as they lived in France. However, we often learned of cases of French women who would return to Africa with their African husbands, where the latter would revert to his African ways, which often included wife-beating, and polygamy.

Fed up with this kind of situation, the French women would leave their African husbands but often were unable to gain custody of children born of such a relationship, as the children—according to the laws of Moslem countries—are considered the property of the husband. The results are hundreds of French women pining away in France for their children, who are living with their fathers in Africa. A French legal association has been formed to help these women but I don't know if they've had any success.

This state of affairs is not unknown in the U.S. A relatively well-known film with Sally Fields entitled "Never without my daughter" describes a similar situation between an American woman and Iranian medical student, who start a family together in the States. Things go well with them until they returned to the Ayatollah's Iran, where life becomes a living hell for her. The film depicts her efforts to flee from that Moslem republic.

100 miles from the in-laws

Having in-laws in France could be an advantage—especially when they were just the ideal distance away. During those first few years at seminary, we would occasionally get away for a long holiday weekend, either hitch-hiking or—after our son was born—getting a lift from one of the other students who lived in Aline's beloved "Cévennes;" there were several students of the Reformed seminary from that largely protestant region of France.

We'd cross the Rhone River at Arles, a beautiful little town— Van Gogh's old stomping grounds which was about halfway to Alès from Marseille. As our children grew, we decided to take advantage of the amazing cultural riches in our proximity and stop for a visit to either Arles or Nimes on the way to the in-law's home. On one such occasion when daughter Anaïs was but four or five years old, we decided to break up our journey for a bit of tourism in Arles in hopes that our little ones would be enthralled by the Roman ruins and it would kindle their interest in European history. On that occasion, however, Anaïs was particularly eager to see her grandmother and wanted no part of any interruption for tourism. Voicing her displeasure while visiting the Arles "Arènes" (Roman Arena, still in use), she complained to us; "Vous nous amenez pour voir des bâtiments;

et ils sont tous cassés!" (You've brought us to see buildings, and they're all broken!").

From Arles westward, one leaves the sun-baked vineyards and lavender fields of Provence and heads into the more rustic, mountain area called the "Cévennes," Alès being at the foothills. In addition to the changes in climate and topography, the people are a bit different—more rugged than the *"Provencaux,"* like the land itself. We were now in the land of *"pélardon"* (goat's milk cheese) and *chataignes* (chestnuts).

Aline's home town of Alès (pop. 50,000) itself has little noteworthy to offer. In addition to the numerous *"chataigners"* (chestnut trees) which grow in the region, the area is also known for its *"mûriers"* (mulberry trees) whose leaves constitute the exclusive diet of the silkworm and the reason for the great silk industry which once thrived in the area in the days before less expensive Chinese imports. Perhaps Alès' greatest claim to fame was that it once hosted the scientist Louis Pasteur (a Christian) who took up residence for almost four years (1865-69) there while searching for a cure to the disease that devastated the silk-worm industry in the mid-19th century. The surrounding countryside is beautiful, and the nearby towns of Nimes, Arles, and Uzès are among the most charming in France.

Faire la bise

Customs change here on this side of the Rhone. We would now be doing three *"bises,"* or kisses, on the cheeks when greeting friends and relatives, rather than two as is customary in Provence (The three is probably a residual heritage from Christian Trinitarian influence. "Faire la bise" is an interesting part of French culture. Normally, one shakes hands when introduced to a complete stranger. In fact, the French shake hands all the time. Best of friends even shake hands several times per day when they greet each other in the morning and when they leave each other's company. You bring this habit back to the States, and people usually think you're running for office.

In France, in meetings between good friends of the opposite sex—or even between good friends and family of the same sex— one exchanges kisses on the cheeks called *"bises,"*, either two, three, or four depending on which part of the country one is in. A

Parisian greeting includes four "*bises*" per person. That means if twelve friends get together at one time—as in the student café at the Sorbonne—some 576 *bises* (48x12) have been exchanged before everyone has been greeted. In France, it can take a long time to say hello, or goodbye.

The ambiguity comes in when one crosses one of the "borders" between three-*bise* and two-*bise* areas, as when we'd come over to Alès from the Aix-en-Provence/ Marseille area. In the Phocéenne city (Marseille), we were used to doing two *bises* and it often took a few days for us to get used to switching to three in the Cevennes. Consequently, there would be some awkward moments when the person we were greeting would, after receiving the first two kisses on the cheeks, be leaning in for number three when we were moving on to the next person, forgetting that we'd crossed a *bise* border.

Likewise we would get into the habit of doing three *bises* in the Cévennes and bring that habit with us back to Marseille, often leaning in for *bise* number three when the person we were greeting was moving on.

Some day, someone will make a map of "La France des bises" to help everyone know the number of kisses on the check expected in each region. I think they should put up signs on the highways, reading: "Entering the Cévennes: a three *bise* area".

La Grande bouffe/ La Brunette

The best of part of visits with Aline's parents, especially during those lean seminary years, was that they spoiled us with the local gastronomical fare and we would go home with a carload of *chacuterie* (sausage*)* and *pélardons* (a goat's milk cheese) for which their region is noted. Typically, I would work up an appetite before a meal by gardening in the small plot behind the house. Even that was a great pleasure, for the soil at his *mazet* (small farmhouse) is so rich and fertile that "you could sow five-franc coins in it from which would sprout trees bearing hundred franc notes," as my father-in-law liked to brag. Tons of the best tomatoes this side of paradise came from that garden—tomatoes which were eaten in olive oil vinaigrette covered with garlic, in tomato sauces, in *ratatouille,* etc.

Mr. Maurin is a connoisseur of good eating and a great cook. He owned a restaurant which served the best beef this side of the Atlantic. He told me that it was because his butcher, Mr. Rambert, a notoriously scrupulous protestant fellow who ran a small but successful butcher shop at Antoise's *place du marché*, was an absolute master at choosing the best beef cattle. As his biggest customer, Aline's dad had been given the privilege of accompanying Mr. Rambert to the slaughterhouse on occasion where he noted with great admiration the butcher's uncanny discernment in knowing just which animals to select. The results was the best beef in the area and customers coming from as far as Alès (15 kms away) and queuing-up in front of his tiny shop.

During those student years when we survived on a diet mostly of salads and homemade yogurt, weekend trips to Alès were a movable feast; including Saturday dinner with either her sister Florence, or grandmother Brunette, and Sunday lunch at her parent's restaurant. This often involved splitting a "cote de boeuf" with my mother-in-law (Aline and her dad were not real carnivores) on Sunday before heading back to Aix-en-Provence. Those were memorable meals which I enjoyed so much that my wife would occasionally kick me gently under the table for purring too loudly as I ate.

Eating is definitely what the French do best. It's the national obsession. In fact, in our experience since we moved to S. Florida, it has never taken more than a few minutes (two minutes and 45 seconds is the current record) before any French guest has steered the conversation to food. "Oh, you just came back from a trip to Turkmenistan? How interesting! What do they eat there?"

French cultural imperialism in this regard is a welcome contribution to the world, as far as I'm concerned. In addition to the many fine chefs and restaurants in France, the best of which are referred to as "temples of gastronomy," there are a number of cooking schools which share the culinary light—spreading the gastronomical gospel if you like—to the unenlightened palates of the world. The "Cordon Bleu" in Paris is of course one of the more famous.

I had an American friend from Alaska whom I met at the L'Abri community in Switzerland. Joan had studied at the "Cordon Bleu" and was capable of conjuring up one of these great meals. We corresponded for some time after she returned home where she married a lucky compatriot who, I thought, must eat better than just about anyone in the US. Guess again. I learned from one of Joan's missives, in which I detected a hint of culinary frustration, that her husband was unaffected by her elaborately prepared sauces and was just as content eating a plain hamburger.

During one of our conversations, Joan related something of the program at the famous Parisian cooking school that surprised many of its American students. It seems that a fair amount of cooking class time is consecrated to dissecting animal innards in a way reminiscent of high school biology classes. The goal is to familiarize students with the anatomy of the animal, as a liver is not cooked the same way as kidneys, intestines, etc. Apparently, there is more blood and guts in fine gastronomy than most Americans realize. This makes it difficult for some of the more squeamish, Joan recalled.

Americans are so used to prepared foods in which all the innards have been removed that they forget what an important role butchering plays in meal preparation. It's almost as if one should forget that he is eating an animal. The tale is told of an American tourist at one of Paris' finer restaurants who ordered a fish entrée and was surprised to receive on his plate, not just a filet of flounder, but the completely cooked fish, head and all. The tourist summoned the server, explaining that he couldn't eat a fish which seemed to be staring right back at him. No problem, said the waiter who brought the plate back to the kitchen and returned it with a small blindfold placed over the fish's eyes.

Back in 1973, Italian director Marco Ferreri made a film about the French obsession with eating entitled **"La Grande Bouffe"** (the big pig-out). The film's outrageous plot concerns several successful middle-aged male friends in mid-life crisis who decide to commit collective suicide by getting together in an upscale French villa for however long it takes to eat themselves to death! The film, which starred a few serious actors, including Philippe Noiret and Marcello Mastrianni, caused a minor stir amongst the French about whom it was written. The scenarist spared no disgusting detail as the actors stuffed themselves with gargantuan portions of the most succulent foods, even as they occasionally vomited, belched and passed gas.

Even the most vulgar prostitutes the men hire to accompany them for the occasion are eventually disgusted by the whole affair. Contrasted with nightly newsreels of starving children in Africa, this was surely the most scathing critique possible of the decadence and insensitivity of the opulent Western world.

Having said that, I like to eat too and consider it one of the Lord's great blessings to enjoy a meal prepared by a French chef. There's something uncanny about the way the French relate to food. It is said that heaven is where the welcoming committee is English; the cook is French; the poets Italian; the mechanics German; and the police Swiss. On the contrary, in hell, the welcoming committee is French; the cook British; the mechanics Italian; the poets Swiss; and the police German. Still another reason to be reconciled to God, less one spend eternity eating English "cuisine."

Some of our favorite gastronomical adventures were at the apartment of Aline's late grandmother Brunette. She was a remarkable cook but, as an elderly widow, didn't often have anyone to cook for. Consequently, she enjoyed preparing gargantuan feasts for me whenever we came to visit her during the holidays. She would load up my plate with tremendous portions of *ratatouille, tomates farcies,* and any one of her numerous specialties which I would devour with gusto. When I was full, she would then ask me if the food was not good. Of course I couldn't say no, but if I dared say yes she would heap on another helping. It was my own version of the 'grande bouffe'.

During my student year in Paris, I would occasionally visit with an old French friend and English teacher. Regis taught conversational English in a couple of "lycées" in the Paris suburbs. Though a great admirer of Shakespeare and a fan of all things British, Regis was openly scornful of English culinary tradition.

"I can forgive the English for Agincourt, for Jeanne d'Arc [Joan of Arc], and for Napoleon", he affirmed. "But not for their cuisine! They have a genius for destroying food," Regis insisted. "They boil everything until there is no taste. And if there is still any taste, they take it back to the kitchen and boil it some more. C'est un scandal!"

Fortunately for Regis, he was married to Martine, a quintessential French woman who, like the majority of her compatriots, seemed to possess an innate understanding of good eating. Alas, neither Regis nor Martine knew the gospel. I tried to share something of my faith with him on occasion, usually around the sumptuous meals that Martine would prepare and to which Regis would occasionally invite me in gratitude for speaking to his English conversational classes. As he reflected on what I shared with him and savored the next bite of Martine's famous "boeuf bourguinon" he looked at me and said: "Si Dieu existe, Il punira certainement les Anglais pour ce qu'ils font à Sa nourriture" (If God exists, He will surely punish the English for what they do to His food).

CHEZ LES Mensch
"Taste and see that the Lord is good"

The priority the French put on eating was manifested to us one day as we sat down for a Sunday lunch with our friends Christian and Joëlle. Joëlle, a pastor's daughter from Lorraine, was brought up to appreciate the importance of Christian communion around the table. For her, as for many French, meals are sacred occasions—to be "set apart"—according to the etymological sense of the Hebrew word for "holy"—for the spiritual edification of all who partake. Moments spent around the table are times meant for conversation about the important issues of life such as family, faith, and politics.

From extreme left-wing to extreme right-wing, all Frenchmen agree on this issue: if on nothing else, one must never underestimate the influence of gastronomy on the soul. Hence this title ("L'influence de la gastronomie sur l'ame") of an article in the serious left-wing French magazine "Le Nouvel Observateur" a few years ago. For the French, gastronomy transcends politics. Even President Jacques Chirac's staunchest political opponents would concur with his scornful remark about English "cuisine," which probably cost the French the privilege of hosting the 2012 Summer Olympic games, as the international committee sympathetically gave London the nod.

Joëlle spares no effort in preparing food worthy of the most august occasion. She has the French gift for knowing what combination of foods go well together and an equally uncanny knack for coaxing the best flavors out everything she prepares. When she has guests, she'll even take time off from her work— managing a large printing enterprise —to prepare a special meal.

That Sunday, after the customary "apéritif" (gastronomical stimuli for the main event) which included a special rum punch with savory salmon on Melba toasts, we feasted on a tomato/mozzarella salad flavored with onions, garlic, basil leaves, olive oil and a hint of lemon. For the main course, Joelle regaled us with a special Moroccan beef dish which she embellished with her customary sense of seasoning. It was all washed down with a chilled glass of smooth Tavel rosé from the famous vineyards near Avignon.

"Moment, linger awhile," I caught myself murmuring as we camped leisurely around the table on a shady terrace discussing everything from "sailing ships to sealing wax to cabbages and kings"—and of course our incomparable blessings in Christ. I thought of the words of Ecclesiastes: "a man can do nothing better than to eat and drink and find satisfaction in his work. This too, I see, if from the hand of God." (Ecclesiastes 2:24).

Still, for Joëlle the gastronomical climax of the meal was in the dessert. For the occasion, she'd prepared a glazed fruit-based soufflé of the sort that necessitated a bit of time in the oven before serving. Alas, we were the victims of a brief power outage which struck during the middle of the meal. That was no big deal for us as our blood-sugar levels were all peaking and we were already more than satisfied. Not so for Joëlle, for whom the electric company's failure was tantamount to pulling down the curtain before the soprano's final aria and operatic crescendo.

"Vous vous rendez compte?" (Do you realize ?) she protested alarmingly. « Je ne vais pas pouvoir vous servir le désert ! (I won't be able to serve the desert !) C'est inadmissible ! "(This is inadmissible!).

Not one to easily accept failure of a sacred mission, Joëlle got on the phone to "EDF" (Electricité de France), the nationally owned French electric company, to explain her predicament. The *EDF* official replied that there was a general power outage in the area and that workers were doing their best to restore electrical service even as he spoke.

"Mais vous vous rendez compte de la gravité de la situation? » (Don't you realize the seriousness of the situation ? »), Joëlle protested.

"J'ai des invités, dont un Américain, et je ne peux pas leur servir le dessert! » (I have guest, including an Americain, and I can't serve them dessert!)

"Il faut faire quelque chose!" (Something must be done!), she pleaded urgently.

No doubt her words reached the compassionate ear of an understanding compatriot on the other side of the line. Nevertheless, the electric company official could only promise that he would contact the repair workers to inform them that there was an emergency in their sector: a group of guests sitting around a table waiting for a soufflé. I'm sure they took it to heart. Meanwhile, in lieu of dessert, we had to content ourselves with a mint-chocolate ice-cream log Joëlle kept in her freezer for such an emergency. It would have melted anyway.

Le Réveillon de Noël

The French get particularly serious about eating around the Christmas and New Year's holidays. For weeks before the holiday— from which virtually all religious significance has disappeared over the centuries—the French are assailed with advertising indicating where to get the best *foie gras*, the best caviar, the best champagne, the best smoked salmon, the best oysters—all indispensable ingredients for a "réveillon de Noel." At this time of year the French spend an exorbitant amount of money to procure the aforementioned foods. Even the soup kitchens which feed the derelicts in the streets will make a great effort to offer a special meal for the occasion. What occasion? "Noël" (Christmas), of course, though Christians are really the only ones with a legitimate reason to celebrate anything! For the others, it's "Les fêtes de la fin de l'année" (end of year feasts), as the media calls it; or even "winter solstice." careful not to say anything remotely religious.

On occasion, I have prodded agnostic French friends about what they are celebrating during this period, as they obviously don't believe in the gospel message. The answer that came from one is revealing: "Nous fêtons la fête" (We're feasting the feast). In other words, one doesn't need a reason to feast, as feasting is a reason in and of itself. The fact that most of them consider that life is "a tale told by an idiot, full of sound and fury signifying nothing"; that it's "nasty, brutish and short"; that man is a "being for death", and a "useless passion" who's born cold, hungry and wet, after which it gets worse; none of this stops the French from having a feast. In that sense, they only follow the logic of the apostle Paul who long ago wrote: "If the Christ isn't risen... then let us eat and drink for tomorrow we die" (I Corinthians 15). But how deep can the joy of such a celebration be?

SUMMERS at *LA ROCAILLE*

The Lord provided funding for our studies largely through our summer work at Aline's parent's restaurant, which her dad, a former factory worker, had started only a few years earlier. When I first met Aline, she lived in the tiniest mill-house apartment, which the ceramic factory had provided as lodging for its workers. Her dad had often worked two eight-hour shifts at slightly over minimum-wage, providing barely enough for his family to get by on. Her dad had absolutely no education, having been abandoned, as a child, as were his three other brothers, by their unworthy mother.

Fortunately, he was blessed with above average intelligence and an exceptional business sense such as one rarely encounters in France. It may seem chauvinistic to say, but I'm convinced that, with regards to the business world and the free enterprise system, there are things that the Lord has revealed to the least of the Anglo-Saxons and kept hidden from the wisest of the French. When it comes to the free enterprise system, the French just don't get it. Things like creating good customer relations, thereby insuring repeat business; offering the client good value for his money—all pretty basic stuff for the least American shopkeeper, or restaurant owner—but almost unknown in France where the client is often treated as a nuisance to be gotten rid of.

THE FRENCH ECONOMY

In general, I'd say the French economy is a masterpiece of socialist constipation. For one thing, France is perpetually plagued by strikes accompanied by intolerable acts of civil disobedience. Before we left Marseille in 1995, the bus drivers went on strike. When the government capitulated to their demands the truckers followed suit. Distraught by astronomical fuel prices or reduced government subsidies for their produce, truckers and farmers will regularly block the roads, crippling the entire country. Eventually, the government is forced to capitulate to their demands, thus encouraging other disgruntled groups to express their demands in a similar manner.

A case in point was the 1998 strike of Air France employees— already amongst the best paid in the business—just before the World Cup soccer tournament hosted by France. Naturally, they chose that moment of maximum leverage to strike as they knew the government would be too embarrassed not to resolve the issue before an event in which the eyes of the world were on France. Imagine the potential financial disaster to boot.

So the nationally owned Air France (called "Air Chance" by seasoned travelers) was, for a long time, one of the single greatest economic black holes in the French economy, losing millions of dollars ever year and only kept afloat by the generous subsidies of the government—subsidies taken in taxes from more efficiently run companies. Such are the pitfalls of a socialist economy.

Fortunately, through some kind of inexplicable grace, Aline's dad was blessed with an exceptional business acumen and understanding of human nature beyond what they teach you at Harvard business school. For one thing, he understood that if you provide a quality product at an affordable price, then you will probably do a big volume. Use better quality ingredients (more expensive oil for the French fries; better whipped cream on the ice cream) and discerning clients will notice the difference. So even if there's little profit per customer, when you multiply that little sum by 1000 people per day, then you're talking about significant figures. That may be obvious to most of you reading this, but it's a concept seems to escape most French.

Often, businesses in France seek a large profit from a relatively small number of customers. To wit, typically, French carnival rides spin around virtually empty as the exorbitant ticket prices dissuade many potential riders. So why not lower the price and have more people, you're wondering? That kind of thinking doesn't fly in France where many businesses are seeking the largest profit possible from a small number of customers. Translated roughly: more money for less work.

For instance, the main cafés in Antoise were offering ice-cream sundaes at about 30-35F each ($6-7) one summer. Aline's dad started offering better quality sundaes for half that price. When word got out (as it always does—Mr. Maurin never spent a penny in advertising, believing the best advertising was a satisfied customer's word of mouth)—he was selling tons of ice cream. This makes for a lot of work, of course. "But I have to be here anyway," M. Maurin would say. "So I might as well be busy."

Meanwhile, a family with several children would not hesitate about where to go for a meal or a sundae. Hence the success of his restaurant, named *"La Rocaille,"* where a family could eat well for a fraction of the price of other restaurants. This is possible, Aline's dad explained, by having a limited menu of fresh, top quality items which he purchased in great quantity at wholesale prices. In fact, this accounts, in a large measure, for his success: M. Maurin was a terrific negotiator when dealing with his suppliers. And he always paid in cash, knowing that this would allow them to conceal part of their profits and keep their prices low.

So that was his formula: keep the menu simple, have fresh ingredients and eliminate waste. The bottom line is that folks would queue up to eat at his place every day when restaurants offering similar menus (steak or chicken or sausage with French fries) would do a fraction of his business, basically catching the overflow when there was no more seating at *"La Rocaille."* Naturally, this created some jealousy amongst the other restaurant owners. "Ils n'ont qu'à faire comme moi" (they need only imitate me), M. Maurin would say.

Of course, the most delicate part of running the business was with the personnel. It's not easy to manage a place where there are at least a dozen unqualified summer employees—usually teenaged *"lycéens"* (high school students)—in the kitchen or waiting on tables. The boss has to be a shrewd psychologist to keep potentially unruly teenagers in line. One has to be both firm yet generous. This is another one of M. Maurin's strong points.

I remember seeing a young waiter asking him for a five franc advance on his pay in order to buy a pack of cigarettes, and seeing M.

Maurin discretely slip him a fifty franc note with a wink and instructions not to repeat it to the other waiters. The result, a contented employee who will produce. It's a matter of "casting ones' bread upon the waters," as Ecclesiastes puts it (Ecclesiastes 11:1). With time, it does return to you. Sow generously and you'll reap generously. It's a basic biblical principle, which Aline's dad has known and practiced since his youth and which, materially speaking, has paid off handsomely.

So we learned a thing or two about doing business in France even as we waited on tables in the small town of Antoise whose population swells from 3.000 in the winter to over 30,000 summer tourists, including a strong percentage of Dutch, Belgians, Germans, Swiss and English who, in typical European fashion, come to the sunny south of France for a month of camping every July. The Belgians being particularly discerning with regards to French fries (invented in Belgium), they would return often to *La Rocaille.*

Something I never got used to about French restaurants is the fact that most of them, *La Rocaille* included, allowed patrons to be accompanied by their dogs. I remember tripping over the leashes of customers whose dogs had to be held back from the waiters' ankles as we served our tables. On more than one occasion, we had to clean up for messy dogs who, sitting at their masters' feet, had been fed table scraps and slobbered all over the floor. I recall cleaning up the vomit of a dog which had eaten too much *paté!* This kind of doting on one's pets doesn't stop when they die, for Paris has a pet cemetery where some rich and not so rich eccentric folk have erected elaborate tombs to the departed domestic animals!

Some French see the Americans as comparatively cruel to their household animals. Hence the indignant reaction of a French tourist to Florida, who complained that he regularly had to leave his dog in the car in the hot sun due to the ban on canines in American restaurants.

One can learn a bit of theology from domestic animals. Your average dog thinks to himself: my master feeds me, he caresses me, he plays with me, takes me for walks, provides for my every need: my master must be God!

Whereas a cat says to itself: my master feeds me, he caresses me, he plays with me, he submits to my every caprice. I must be God.

Too many people in this world are victims of "Garfieldesque" cat theology.

Mean dogs

It was always interesting to talk with the other foreigners in Antoise to get their impressions of France and the French. For the most part, the Belgians, Swiss, Dutch, and German tourists who invade southern France in July, consider the Cévennes their summer playground, where they can let their hair down and get away with things they would never do at home.

We rarely had problems with drunken French customers, but the waiters would occasionally have to refuse requests for more beer and wine by foreigners letting it all hang out while away from home.

The western Europeans we would meet in the summer were usually enamored of the natural beauty of southern France but equally attached to the advantages they saw in their own countries where the comfort, cleanliness and standard of living is usually better, even if the food isn't.

I recall the reactions of two female German backpackers whom I queried about their overall impressions of France.

"Lots of mean dogs," they both quipped spontaneously.

I wasn't surprised by their observation. There are usually guard-dogs behind the impenetrable walls which surround the vast majority of French homes, which are almost always partially hidden from the street. This tends to make one feel somewhat like a rat in a maze as one goes through a residential area of France—a rat whose progress is announced as he walks down the street by a succession of aggressive canines following the sound of the passerby's steps with incessant barking from behind the walled properties. Get past one invisible barking dog and your peace is short lived as the mutt behind the next wall hears you approach and picks up the barking relay. French mailmen working in residential areas have it rough.

Many homes have signs warning potential intruders about the presence of a dangerous four-legged defender of the family sanctuary. "Attention: chien méchant!" (Danger: Mean Dog!). That probably helps to explain why there is so little door to door selling or evangelism in France. Even if the master of the house were to grant you access to his domain despite the protests of his canine, how friendly could *he* be? A sign on the gate of the Maurin's neighbor said it all: "Ici chien gentil; maître méchant" (Friendly dog here; mean owner).

Camisard country

Beyond the restaurant business, Antoise is a town of great historical interest. Called "la Porte des Cévennes," it was the de fact capital of Protestant France in the heart of the "département" of the "Gard," which is the only French county, outside of the Alsace region, with even a significant protestant minority—around 40%. It was near Antoise that the "Camisard" wars took place between the Protestant resistance fighters and the dreaded "dragonnades" (invading soldiers with free reign to abuse the locals) Louis XIV had sent down under the famous Marechal de Villars to forcibly "convert" the last remaining Huguenots in 1702. There are many historical markers indicating some of the famous battles between the 2000 or so "Camisard" or resistance warriors and the 60,000 royalists. Antoise is only seven kilometers away from the famous "Musée du Désert," consecrated to the period from the Revocation of the Edict of Nantes in 1685 to the promulgation of the *"droits de l'homme"* (rights of man) in 1787, during which time it was officially illegal to be a Protestant in France. *"Un roi, une loi, une foi"* (one king, one law, one faith) was Louis XIV's motto, which he vigorously enforced.

During that period (referred to as the "desert") of dreadful persecution, there was a credible resistance movement of courageous souls who would gather for the proclamation of the Word of God (Bibles were outlawed) in clandestine assemblies. The men who organized and presided over these meetings were often pastors who had been trained at the Reformed Seminary started by Calvin in Geneva. Their diplomas were referred prophetically as *"brevets de potence,"* or roughly, "hangman's degrees." After completing their studies in Geneva they would enter France surreptitiously where they would risk their lives as traveling preachers (*"prédicants"*), exhorting the faithful at clandestine meetings wherever there were protestants in the area.

It took a great deal of courage to even attend these meetings. There were often spies among the populace to denounce these believers, and the assemblies were often raided by royal troops. A preacher caught at such a gathering was summarily executed.

One such heroic preacher was Claude Brousson, an attorney from Nimes who with his family had escaped from France to Holland where he lived and was successful, before sneaking back into France to exhort the believers who had no pastors to expound the Word of God to them. Brousson lived like a hunted animal, slipping from one clandestine meeting to another for over two years before the king's forces finally caught up with him near Montpellier in 1698. His integrity was such that he didn't even attempt to escape—he had given his word— the two men charged with escorting him to his execution (at Montpellier), who had fallen asleep in the hot summer heat.

Attending one of the secret Protestant assemblies was risky business. Men caught in attendance at one of these meetings were imprisoned and often sent to Marseille, where they were forced to row in the galley ships that patrolled the Mediterranean coasts. The life expectancy of a galley slave was somewhat less than two years. Among the more famous galley slaves was the famous Scottish reformer John Knox, whom the French imprisoned for about eighteen months.

Women caught in attendance at one of these meetings were sent to prisons such as the notorious "Tour de Constance" near the mouth of the Rhone River. Here too, conditions were most inhospitable— cold and damp in the winter, stifling hot in the summer. To leave the prison, the woman needed only renounce her faith. Some did. Others, like the famous Marie Durand—arrested as a young bride when she was only fifteen—stayed locked in the same dank tower for over 37 years! She carved the word "**RESISTER**" in the stone floor of the tower which can still be read today.

The illustrious history of the descendants of the people of the Antoise region is not as well known as it should be. Most of the French and foreign tourists visiting the region have only a vague idea concerning the gospel of Jesus Christ in France, Antoise is sacred ground upon which much blood of His saints was spilled.

The history of the persecuted church in the Gard *département* would furnish multiple occasions for evangelizing customers at the restaurant. Moreover, being an American in Antoise (a rare entity, as Americans in France rarely depart from the well worn tourist Meccas of Paris and Nice), I had a natural opportunity to share the faith with anyone curious enough to ask me what I was doing there.

Though not what you would call a fervent believer (indeed he never attended worship services) M. Maurin, had enough evangelical concern to allow me to share the faith with the clients who came to 'my' tables in the semi-isolated dining overflow room. He was interested in terrestrial business, but he wasn't insensitive to the influence the gospel had began to have in his own family. In fact, he'd been indirectly responsible for Aline's conversion when he had exhorted her, in the midst of her adolescent crisis, to read the Book whence her ancestors had derived such legendary strength of character.

UNE GRIVELERIE A LA ROCAILLE

We had some interesting adventures as we worked our way through seminary those four summers at *"LA ROCAILLE."* One anecdote concerns busy Sunday evening business, when several teenagers ate and left without paying. This crime is called a *"grivelerie"* in French judicial vocabulary. It happens occasionally at busy restaurants and filling stations.

Aline's younger brother Pascal ran into the culprits in a local café after the restaurant had closed around 10:30 PM. He came back to the restaurant to inform their dad, who, in spite of his rather small stature, was a former boxing champ and a formidable adversary for anyone who crossed him.

We had often exhorted Mr. Maurin to apply biblical principles of submission to the authorities. In the case of the young thieves who'd slipped away without paying, we convinced Aline's dad to phone the local *"gendarmerie,"* located conveniently across the street from the café in question. All they would need to do is to hold the fellows until they could be positively identified, and all would be well.

So M. Maurin called the *gendarmes* and explained the situation. For the next few moments he listened to them in stunned disbelief as they told him that they didn't want to be bothered with such a concern! *"Laissez-nous tranquilles"* (Leave us in peace), they told him, *"Occupez-vous-en vous mêmes"* (take care of it yourselves).

Aline's dad was beyond furious. He was so angry that he didn't even vent his emotions, and his normally volatile temperament was deceptively subdued. I'd never seen him so resolved, so focused. He wasn't angry with the thieves but with the gendarmes who had patently refused to do their jobs. He nevertheless walked over to the café with the intention of settling up with the culprits. I'm glad for their sake that they had already left by this time, as their lives would not have been worth much. When he returned to the restaurant, he called me aside and gave me instructions. He told me that I was to forsake the restaurant work and consecrate the next day to writing letters addressed to everyone and anyone whom he assumed would need to know about the injustice of which he'd been a victim and the scandalous lack of professional integrity on the part of the Antoise *gendarmes.*

Dutifully, I penned a series of seven letters—all similar but with modifications depending on their destination—to everyone from the President of the Republic (Valery Giscard d'Estaing at the time) to the French Minister of Justice, to the local political authorities. In the letters—written from the point of view of my semi-literate father-in-law— I pleaded the case of the innocent victim of unscrupulous theft, compounded by the lack of professional conscience of those supposed to uphold the law. I was reasonably proud of my missives which I shared with Aline's dad before he placed his signature on them, having pronounced them "bien tournées" (well-composed). We then posted the letters and waited for results.

Less than a week later, M. Maurin received a phone call from Captain Jaubert of the Caserne d'Alès (regional departmental head-quarters). He called Mr. Maurin to his office for a most important meeting. Aline's dad had a satisfied grin on his face as he told me of the phone call, relating the deferential tone in the speech of the brigade captain, who was clearly upset by something.

The next day, we drove down to the caserne near the train station in Alès for the meeting with the head of the all the gendarmes in the region. It should be explained that in France, the gendarmes, unlike the police, are a branch of the military who serve a civil function. Consequently, they come directly under the authority of the ministry of Justice and operate under a military hierarchy. Which explains why the ultimate responsibility for the local gendarmes in Antoise fell upon their commander Captain Jaubert, the head honcho in Alès.

We gave our names to an armed soldier at the gate and were escorted into the office of the Captain Jaubert, a tall, thin, athletic-looking fellow of about fifty, with a no-nonsense crew cut, a steely gaze and iron handshake. He greeted us with almost somber deference. He invited us to sit down in two chairs that had been placed in front of his desk, upon which were all seven copies of the letter I had written to various officials! Clearly the buck had stopped at the desk of Captain Jaubert, who explained to us, with almost rueful regret, the consequences of our actions. Unless the matter was resolved, he would be in big trouble himself, to say nothing of the guilty gendarmes in Antoise.

Clearly the Captain had been taken to task by his superiors, who demanded that the affair be settled to the satisfaction of the plaintiff, M. Maurin—or else! It was both a revealing and pathetic experience to hear a man of such unflinching authority as Capitain Jaubert pleading with Aline's dad, a mere private citizen, to consider the consequences of his action.

"Do you realize what I'm going to have to do?" inquired the distraught Captain. "I'm going to have to severely punish the gendarmes in Antoise, who will be transferred to Lozère" (France's most rural and thinly populated *department,* with far more goats and sheep than people). That was clearly a great demotion for men who, as we were told, had been on the force for over eighteen years.

"Dix-huit ans de conneries" (Eighteen years of stupid mistakes) interjected Mr. Maurin, recalling a less-than-professional incident of the past: a case when the gendarmes had come to the restaurant to deal with a severely inebriated client, whom they escorted to the wheel of his car so that he could drive away!

Still, we couldn't help but be moved by the pleading tone and manner of Captain Jaubert, who assured us that the guilty parties would be punished, all the while hoping that the administrative military axe would spare his own head.

We left the gendarmerie satisfied and amazed by the power of the written word to produce results in France, a lesson I've taken to heart and implemented on several occasions since. Say what you will about French bureaucracy, a single well-placed letter is more effective there than a thousand petitions to one's congressmen this side of the Atlantic.

Meanwhile, back in Antoise, the Gendarmes didn't take well to their punishment and impending transfer to Lozère. They decided to exact a measure of vengeance on the Maurin family by ticketing the Maurin vehicles, which, like most in the village, were often illegally parked (Recall that the winter population of 3000 swells to 30,000+ tourists in July and August). Consequently, on any given day during those two summer months, there are always dozens of cars parked illegally. Traditionally, the gendarmes turn a blind eye to these infractions in the name of tourist hospitality. However, they were determined to get retribution on the Maurins for the *grivelerie* incident. It was no surprise to anyone when, that Sunday morning, all three of the Maurin vehicles had parking tickets on their windshields.

Aline's dad was working out in the back of the restaurant, washing salad that Sunday morning when the gendarmes stuck a ticket on his car parked in the same place where he'd been leaving it for years. He watched as the same gendarmes put tickets on the windshields of his wife's and son's cars.

"Marc, you're going to make a little trip to Alès to see our friend Captain Jaubert again," Aline's dad said to me.

"You're going to take your camera and explain to the Captain that you have some photos of illegally parked cars in the village which have not been ticketed whereas our three cars have. Ask him what he thinks they'll say in Paris when they hear about this kind of injustice."

So I drove to Alès to see Captain Jaubert, who received me promptly. I explained the nature of my visit, showing him the camera in which, I bluffed, there were photos which could be of interest to his superiors. He quite understood what I was getting at. Still, at first he didn't believe the incident about the parking tickets. I gave him a piece of paper with the license plate numbers of the three Maurin vehicles and challenged him to check with his subordinates in Antoise to see how many vehicles had been tagged for parking violations that day. So he made a call and checked while I waited.

"How many cars have you ticketed today?" he inquired.

"Tell me their tag numbers."

Then he stared in disbelief as he listened to the *gendarmes* recite the three Maruin license plate numbers.

He slammed down the phone and explained to me:

"I gave strict orders to the brigade in Antoise that there would be no vengeance taken on the Maurin family because of this incident," said the captain, noticeably angry.

"Don't worry about a thing," he reassured me.

"Go tell your father-in-law that I will straighten this matter out immediately—and please, no more letters!"

I got back to the restaurant late that afternoon in time for the evening meal service. There was some measure of consternation and bewilderment among the locals, including some of the Maurin family friends who came to the restaurant before meal hours for a traditional *apéritif* with Aline's parents. The remarks of the local *coiffeur* were typical.

He complained that he'd received a parking ticket that day from the *gendarmerie* for parking in a space where he'd been leaving his car for thirty years!

Aline's dad said nothing but grinned at me as we both understood what had happened. Not wanting to be charged with discrimination, not willing or able to retract the parking tickets inflicted discriminately on the Maurin vehicles, the *gendarmes* had decided to ticket all the other illegally parked cars in the village as well, of which there were dozens, perhaps hundreds! Thus, justice was 'inflicted' on everyone in Antoise that day when more parking tickets were handed out than on any other day in the village's history.

LE MAL FRANCAIS

Work at the restaurant, though exhausting, left me enough time to read, especially in the afternoons between the noon meal and the evening service. Unlike American restaurants with their nonstop, uninterrupted service, there are fixed hours at which one can eat in a French restaurant. At *"La Rocaille,"* we typically served between 12h and 14h30. Then we closed up until around 17h30 or 18h when the Dutch tourists would come to eat. The French typically eat at 20h. In any case, that left me time to read between 15h and 17h.

In the summer of 1974 a book was published which, in my humble opinion, is one of the single most important volumes in modern times for anyone who aspires to understand the French and French culture. Called **Le Mal Français** (The French Problem), it was written by Alain Peyrefitte, Charles De Gaulle's former press secretary, who became the "Garde des Sceaux" (roughly Attorney General) under President Giscard d'Estaing, then editor of the prestigious "Le Figaro" newspaper, and finally, member of the illustrious "Academy Française," Mr. Peyrefitte, born in 1924 (he died in 1999) was also one of France's great authorities on China. In other words, he was a man of letters and extensive international travel, including travel to the United States. His book was an indictment of some of the ills of French society, which M. Peyrefitte traced, curiously enough, to the rejection of the reformation in France!

Borrowing somewhat from Max Weber's classic, "The Protestant Ethic and the Spirit of Capitalism," M. Peyrefitte's analysis of French society compares the development of the countries that embraced the Reformation in the 16th and 17th centuries to those — France included — which rejected it.

Mr. Peyrefitte's book, which caused a furor in France when it was published, is rich in anecdotes taken from the author's vast experience and culture. Eventually, it became required reading for the seminary master's program (in 1981). In several hundred pages of history and anecdotes, it underscores the reality of the French preference for theory (vs. reality) and the abstract (vs. the concrete).

For example, in 1940 the French had attempted to protect themselves from the impending Nazi onslaught behind the security of the famous Maginot line, an elaborate system of fortified caves and bunkers which protected the eastern flank of France from the northern reaches of the Alps, along the Rhine river, and all the way up to the Belgian border near the Ardennes forests. Mr. Peyrefitte, born the same year as my own father, relates an anecdote similar to one my own dad shared with me about the tension-filled days leading up to the second world war.

Peyrefitte remembered his dad reassuring him (as my granddad had reassured my father) that the military brass had determined that it was "theoretically impossible" for an invasion force with tanks and heavy armored vehicles to enter France through the Belgian Ardennes forest (whence the Germans had already come in 1914). Hence the French had left that region virtually unprotected, save for their weakest division of soldiers.

What's more, the military commanders refused to believe the testimonies of two of their own reconnaissance pilots who, on the 11th and 12th of May, 1940, had flown over the area and spotted the advancing enemy tanks and troops. Peyrefitte concluded regretfully that the "theory of the military bureaucracy was more dominant than the facts" (Peyrefitte, p. 17).

Not surprisingly, the chapters in French history books dealing with the embarrassing defeat by the Germans in 1940, will typically blame the rout on a numerical superiority of German military equipment. Little is said of the German army's superior organization and strategy of working together, as opposed to the traditionally French tendency for individual action. As someone has said, both sides had 3000 tanks. The Germans had three packs of 1000, whereas the French had 1000 packs of three.

POTATOES

M. Peyrefitte's revealing book also tells of the cultivation of the potato in France. The magnificent tuber was imported into Europe from South America in the early 17th century and became a blessing in England, assuring a minimum subsistence for many erstwhile victims of the famines which periodically ravaged Europe when the rye or barley crop would fail.

Both Shakespeare and Francis Bacon praised the virtues of the potato, which is rich in nutritional value, easy to cultivate, and adapts to many different kinds of soil. Another advantage is that it can be conveniently left in the ground until needed so there is no storage problem.

So great was the influence of this tuber on the prosperity of England that in 1664, a certain John Forester actually wrote a treatise entitled:

" The Prosperity of England Increased by the Cultivation of the Potato".

You would think therefore that the French would jump on the bandwagon and also take advantage of this nutritional Godsend? Guess again. They refused to eat them, preferring to starve (as many of them did in one of the last great famines in 1710) rather than learn to appreciate something the English were eating. As late as 1787, the Royal Society of Agriculture in Paris considered the potato a crop "good for the cows"... and for the English.

Fortunately, a Frenchmen named Antoine Parmentier (1737-1813), eager to get potatoes accepted by his gastronomically prejudiced compatriots, was able to convince King Louis XVI of the benefits of its cultivation. He got the king to plant some in his own personal greenhouse, knowing the noble class' natural inclination to imitate the king. To win over the peasants, Parmentier had entire fields around Paris planted with potatoes and had these fields surrounded with armed guards. Parmentier understood his compatriots' desire to covet anything forbidden!

Once the potatoes were almost ripe, he had the guard withdrawn. The peasants began to steal them and eat them, which, in conclusion, is how potatoes came to be popular in France. The anecdote speaks volumes about the people I would be dealing with for years.

I wasn't the only foreign student at the Aix seminary who was baffled by the French mind. I knew a few Africans, Europeans from Belgium and Switzerland, and a Quebecois couple who complained that they had never been so cold since they moved to the south of France! Guy Dubois told me that everything in Canada was designed to protect one against the ravages of the Canadian winter, which lasts about eleven months—or so it seems. Consequently, clothing, buildings, cars, and just about everything is doubly insulated. Not so in the warmer Mediterranean countries where the cold season was viewed as a short trial to be endured. In truth, it didn't really freeze in Aix-en-Provence but for a few days in December, but it was sufficiently cold to require some kind of heat and covering from November through February.

Guy and I would occasionally joke about the things we deemed strange in France, including the French preference for theory over practice, and style over substance. This cultural tendency showed up in a very important part of our theological studies—homiletics, or the art of preaching.

Atelier de Prédication

One of our seminary courses, taught by Dean Pierre Courthial, was "atelier de predication," where the students were assigned a biblical text from which to preach. On the appointed day, the designated student would have to stand in front of his colleagues and deliver the sermon from his text, under the critical eyes of his fellow students. This could be daunting, for unlike Americans from the Bible belt, who lavish praise on each other, the French are parsimonious with their compliments.

I was shocked the first time I sat through the evaluation by his fellow students of a colleague who had just preached what I considered an excellent sermon. They harped on even the most picayune imperfections. How discouraging! What's more, they seemed more preoccupied with the style of what was said, than the contents. This pattern held consistent: a student would preach a magnificent sermon, full of grace and truth, only to be raked over the coals for having mispronounced a word along the way!

Conversely, I remember one student's eloquent, albeit semi-heretical, sermon that was well received by the student audience. This was mind-boggling.

Joking about the French bent for theory over practice, I remarked to my Quebecois buddy Guy, as we stood in the seminary hallway, that one could light the switch and run to the end of the hallway before fluorescent lights (which depended on an electrical starter) actually went on.

"Look at this Guy," I joked. "The French are so independent that even their electricity doesn't obey the normal laws of physics."

"It's not that," he replied. "The current has to go through Paris first," he joked, thinking about the French tradition of centralization.

In spite of these cultural curiosities—or because of them—I concluded that I'd made the right decision in coming to study in France. During five years at seminary I would have a precious initiation into their way of thinking. I would learn that French people don't react the same way to mundane things as Anglo-Saxons. I would learn that they are generally more proud than my American compatriots. Might this explain why they aren't as open to the gospel?

The French are not as "macho" as the Italians or Spaniards I met during the course of my European travels. But they are not completely bereft of that trait. One day as Aline and I rode our bicycles through the narrow streets of Aix on the way to the market place, I had a *"cageot"* (sort of orange crate) strapped to the back of my bicycle. At one point, near an intersection, we drove between the sidewalk and the cars on the street and I accidentally scraped, ever so slightly, a car we passed on the right that was waiting in traffic for the light to turn green. The driver began blowing the horn, pulled out into the intersection, stopped in the middle of the street, jumped out of the car and came running over screaming. I apologized briefly to which he insisted: "Tu aurais pu t'excuser!" (You could have excused yourself). I told him I hadn't stopped as I had barely touched him. What impressed me most was the fact that he was about 4ft. tall and weighed no more than 90lbs. I'm only average size (5'10", 175lbs), but I was a head taller than him and could have crushed him like a bug. Still, I admired his courage.

High heels and sneakers

One of the most obvious differences between the Americans and the French is the latter's preoccupation with style and aesthetics vs. the American preference for the pragmatic or functional. While Americans seek practical solutions for life's conundrums, the French are inclined to favor the more stylish, even to the detriment of the functional. One thinks of the line from Rostand's "Cyrano de Bergerac" in which Cyrano insists that "c'est tellement plus beau lorsque c'est inutile" (It's so much more beautiful when it's useless).

Aline and I took an October trip to Paris to revisit together some of the sites I'd taken in as a single language student. Aline's mom, sister, and brother-in-law decided to accompany us, furnishing the transportation in exchange for my services as a guide to the city of lights.

Before we left, I reminded Aline's sister and my mother-in-law that we'd be doing a lot of walking, so they should bring comfortable footwear. Alas, for *Mamie Danièle* (Aline's mom) and older daughter Florence, looking one's best matters more than being comfortable. Never does one spot Parisian women in sneakers on the Champs-Elysées, as one would see American women in sneakers on Park Avenue in New York. It would never occur to the former to sacrifice aesthetics even for comfortable feet. "Cela ne se fait pas" (that is not done!).

Only a few hours into our tourist promenades along the Seine, Florence and Mamie Danièle had to sit down as their overworked feet—beautifully shod in elegant high heels—were killing them! We stopped at the famous "Samaritaine" department store to seek a pair of shoes that both looked good (a subjective criterion) and lent themselves to usefulness in walking. My traveling companions settled on what they considered a compromise solution, each purchasing a pair of lower heels. Strike two.

By the time we got to Versailles for a tour of Louis XIV's famous chateau, Mamie and Florence had had it. The walk through the famous Hall of Mirrors was bearable. To visit the *Petit Trianon*, one had to walk a country mile through the breathtaking classical beauty of the chateau gardens, which increasingly took on the air of an opulent torture chamber to my mother-in-law and her daughter. Why did Marie-Antoinette have her simulated "peasant village" so far from the main chateau, the women wanted to know. It's a good thing they drove her in a coach to the guillotine in Paris. She would surely have expired from pain in her ankles had she been shod like her 20th century counterparts.

Le Nez de JEAN BRUN

From the opposite end of the human anatomy comes a story about a nose, that of the late Jean Brun, a philosophy professor. M. Brun taught at the state university of Dijon but, as a Christian and friend of the Aix Seminary, he came down to Aix regularly for seminars on various subjects. My first year at seminary, he took us through a whirlwind tour of the pre-Socratic philosophers on which he was a reputed expert. For all his erudition, M. Blanc was down to earth and witty. Small of stature, with dark hair and thick eyebrows, he was also possessed of a rather imposing proboscis. One might listen to M. Brun's lectures on tape and derive great benefit from his wisdom and knowledge. But it was a real treat to observe his facial expressions as he walked us through the thoughts of Parmenides and Heraclites, with a self-deprecating humor uncharacteristic of the French—especially French intellectuals, who tend to take themselves quite seriously.

Jean Brun once did an entire lecture—over an hour—on the significance of his nose. It was a philosophical comedy worthy of Cyrano de Bergerac. We always anticipated the professor's visits took advantage of his excursions to the seminary to invite outsiders to his lectures. Many French outside the family of faith have a distorted idea of what Christians are like. In the sober words of Baudelaire, "Le Verbe incarné n'a jamais ri" (The incarnate Verb never laughed). Jean Brun showed many that "it ain't necessarily so."

Birth of CALIX

Our oldest son Calix arrived in May 1980, our fifth year at seminary, while I was working on my thesis. The time of his birth was easily the happiest of my entire existence. The event started inauspiciously with Aline's pregnancy going along smoothly under the watchful eye of Dr. Victor Rieux, a septuagenarian obstetrician who had been overseeing the pregnancy since it came to light on our motorcycle trip in Corsica.

We would see Dr. Rieux for the pre-natal visits paid for by the generous French socialized medicine which, for all its shortcomings, provides its citizens with better preventive care and lower infant mortality than its American counterpart. Regular visits are required by the state, documented by the physician in a pre-natal *carnet de santé* (health log).

Dr. Rieux, who called Aline affectionately "mon enquiquineuse" (my pain in the neck) for her constant second-guessing of his evaluations, had scheduled a Cesarean section for Friday May 16, determining that Aline's pelvis was too small for a comfortable delivery.

We were in Dr. Rieux's office on Wednesday afternoon, May 14, for a last check-up, which showed nothing abnormal in spite of Aline's insistence that her labor pains had already begun. Dr. Rieux assured us that that was not the case.

We walked about a mile to a friend's apartment that evening for our weekly Bible study, during which Aline began to squeeze my hand tightly as we sat on the sofa together. "Ça fait mal," she insisted, referring to the persistent abdominal pains.

We walked home after the study (we had no car at the time) and attempted to get ready for bed, but Aline continued to complain about sharp uterine pains.

I got up and went to my desk to consult Regine Pernoud's "J'attends un enfant" (I Await a Child), a best-seller on pregnancy.

"Go to sleep," I told Aline, after reading the section that dealt with frequency of the labor pains. "These are false pains, not the real thing," I continued. "It says right here that the first labor pains are to be so far apart [I forget the frequency], followed by more contractions closer together."

" Besides, we were at Dr. Rieux's office this morning and he told us you were undergoing false labor pains; a kind of psychosomatic anticipation of the real thing."

I thought I'd presented my case well—remember the *French* preference for theory over reality?—but Aline would have none of it. She continued to moan with pain and her moans were gradually becoming louder and more persistent.

Finally at around 2AM, she could bear it no longer. I went downstairs to wake up Marc Maggio, the caretaker of our apartment building, and asked him to drive us to the clinic about two and a half miles away. Fortunately, Marc was a Christian and more understanding than the average neighbor one would wake up at such an ungodly hour.

When we arrived at the clinic it was locked up tight, save for a night watchman in the doorway. It was a holiday—Ascension Thursday—and just about anyone who wasn't indispensable was at home.

We explained to the night watchman what we were there for and he called Dr. Rieux's emergency number. That set off a series of phone calls and the crew of people involved in performing a cesarean section began arriving—the anesthesiologist, various hospital technicians, neo-natal care nurses, and of course, the surgeon himself, Dr. Rieux.

"Vous allez m'enquiquiner jusqu'au bout" (You're going to annoy me 'til the end) announced the venerable gynecologist, suppressing a yawn as he arrived at the clinic at a little after 2AM.

"Au travail!" he barked, as I was led out of the operating room, not allowed by the authorities of this particular clinic to attend the event.

I waited in an upper room where the baby would be brought after the delivery.

In the operating room, Aline was given a full anesthetic which meant that the surgeon would have to work fast to extract the baby from the mother's womb before the anesthesia went from the mother's blood to his. I didn't realize how fast it would all go. So I was only moderately curious when only a few moments later, a nurse came in to the upper room where I waited carrying a newborn baby which she proceeded to clean and dry. I could see it was a boy—a cute little tyke—and watched in a completely disinterested way as the nurse washed his eyes and ears. It several minutes before I ventured a word:

"I didn't realize there were other women giving birth tonight," I said, matter-of-factly. "Whose child is this," I inquired, wondering why its father wasn't waiting with me. I knew it couldn't be our son as we had been assured by the sonogram that ours would be a girl.

"C'est la votre" (It's yours) she said. "Le fils de la femme qui venait d'avoir un césarienne" (The son of the woman who just underwent a Cesarean).

I was speechless. Not only did I have a beautiful child, but it was a boy! I was ecstatic! I looked at my newborn son with all the intensity of an art expert analyzing a Rembrandt. It was easily the most magnificent child to have ever entered the world, with the exception of the Christ child!

When I finally got to see Aline, who had been wheeled into a room to recover from the birth, she was still sedated and in pain.

"We're parents of the most magnificent baby the world has ever seen!" I announced to her. "And it's a boy!"

She said virtually nothing. She couldn't. She was only semi-conscious. She had drainage tubes coming out of her from which flowed all kinds of blood and slimy liquids from the scar where the incision had been made. It wasn't pretty.

Finally, she mustered a couple of words: the only ones she would pronounce for the next few days.

"J'ai mal," she moaned (It hurts), referring to her post operative scar.

Unlike her later cesarean in America, where she would be given morphine to dull the pain, the French basically expected a new mother to suffer and only gave her aspirin!

I had mixed emotions. I was never so grateful to her as at that moment when she had been surgically 'slaughtered' in a most noble effort to give me that which I cherished more than life itself—a son!

But I was also concerned as the wisdom of John 16:21 (about a women forgetting the pain of childbirth after the baby is born) didn't apply to cesarean sections! Seeing the pain she was enduring, I was sure we'd never have another child, as no one in his right mind would voluntarily go through that again. This conviction made our son all the more precious as I expected he would be unique.

The next few days are a euphoric blur in my memory. I recall that didn't get much sleep for about a week. I didn't really care, as I wanted to savor every moment of ecstasy. I walked around the city of Aix-en-Provence as if I owned it, and must have been taken for the village idiot by passersby who heard me singing and dancing wherever I went.

One of the first duties of the new father in France is to make a ritual trip to city hall to officially report the child's birth. Aline and I had already agreed to name him Calix (Latin for chalice) from the root of the Greek kalos, meaning "good" or "beautiful," and close to the middle name of my paternal grandfather.

The problem was that the moniker wasn't on the official list of names recognized by the French authorities, and therefore illegal.

The law has apparently changed since then, but in 1980, one couldn't call his child anything but a name found on the official list of accepted names! The rationale for such an administrative constraint is to protect children from the fantasies of their parents. One thinks of the Johnny Cash song about "A boy named Sue," or the dubious wisdom of the likes of some rock singers who have named their posterity "Captain America" or "God."

The bottom line is that the bureaucrat at the Aix-en-Provence city hall refused to register our son under "Calix."

"You can write down anything you want," I told her. "Write Rumplestilskin for all I care. His name is Calix," I insisted.

A couple of minutes later she arrived with her superior, who explained that our choice of names would be limited to the official government list.

Once again I protested. My impatience betrayed even more than usual my foreign accent, upon which the official asked me if I weren't a foreigner.

Responding in the affirmative, I learned that I, as a foreigner, had a right to call my child anything I wanted to. And so our son's name was etched in stone, and in the annals of the French administration.

L'année de maîtrise

The birth of our son in 1980 corresponded with the writing of my seminary thesis on the abuse of mind-altering drugs. It dealt the Greek word η φαρμακεια (pharmakeia), translated "sorcery" or "witchcraft" in Paul's epistle to the Galatians. I was exploring the Bible's position on the abuse of hallucinogenic drugs. Drug abuse is hardly new; there is evidence that the Chinese used cannabis 23 centuries before the birth of Christ.

I discovered in the course of my research that various hallucinogenic agents were used as early in the ancient Near East for so-called 'spiritual' goals. The apostle Paul denounced such practices in Galatians 5:20 as among the other "works of the flesh".

Most of my time was spent in research, with only few classes to attend. That was a good thing, as Aline and I were discovering how difficult it was to get a decent night's sleep with a newborn baby.

For the first eight months of his existence, our son never slept through the night. Sleep deprivation was further aggravated by the location of our apartment building on a street overlooking a traffic light. At all hours of the day or night, we were accosted by noisy small motorcycles which, after stopping at the light, would take off in a flurry of 100 decibels like the amplified protests of a million hornets.

So frustrating were these wake-up calls that I fantasized about sitting on the apartment balcony with a rifle, popping off the guilty motorcycle riders whose mufflers had been deliberately removed. Calix's mother and I were in a state of perpetual stupor and ready to sack out any time of the day or night whenever the baby would sleep. We basically put away our watches for the year and lived spontaneously, grabbing a few hours or moments of shut-eye as the caprices of our new infant-tyrant allowed.

Infantile opposition notwithstanding, I managed to complete my thesis all the while looking for our gospel vocation in France.

It was at this period that we made the fateful visit to the frozen tundra of Quebec referred to at the beginning of this story. That option eliminated, the logical alternative was work with university students. The student milieu is largely un-evangelized in Western Europe, and we were used to sharing our faith with students from the state university which virtually surrounded the Reformed Seminary at Aix-en-Provence. It was this geographical reality which had enticed me into coming to Aix in the first place. For I discovered that my faith was fortified by the constant contact with non-Christians, whose objections to biblical Christianity were often so specious as to make the case for faith in the gospel all the more certain. This truth had been underlined by the great 17th century French thinker Blaise Pascal.

I recall how my own sister, while searching out the Christian faith, picked up Bertrand Russell's "Why I am not a Christian." written with the intentions of holding the Christian faith to ridicule. Russell's book had the opposite effect on my sister, who saw right through the anti-Christian prejudices and superficial nature of his objections which was more revealing of M. Russell's own pride and prejudices than about the claims of the gospel.

The bottom line is that "natural man will not receive the things of God, as they are folly to him" (I Corinthians 2).

Having said that, and having finished my thesis, it was clear to me that the Lord was calling me to share the faith amongst the incredulous and un-evangelized of the French university system.

It was time to put into practice the teachings of I Peter 3:15 ("Be prepared to give a reason for the hope that is within you to whomever would ask you...") as well as II Corinthians 10:5, which was the model for this aspiring defender of the faith. The only problem now was where to work.

In France, there weren't many options. We knew only of the existence of the *"Groupes Bibliques Universitaires,"* roughly the French equivalent of the Inter Varsity Fellowship. Sharing our concerns with a brother in our tiny evangelical assembly in Aix, we learned of a group called "Campus Pour Christ," which did evangelism on the university campus in Lyon. We wrote to their director, and were invited to Lyon for an interview.

We drove up to the office of "Campus Pour Christ" where we were introduced to the tiny staff, two of the half-dozen folks of an organization which aspired to evangelize the fifty university towns in France!

It was a fateful encounter. For on that day in June of 1981, we committed ourselves to the evangelization of the French university milieu under the auspices of an evangelical parachurch organization of which we knew nothing. "Campus Pour Christ" (which has since changed its name to "AGAPE") was the French affiliate of "Campus Crusade for Christ" which we had never heard of until that time. After becoming official staff members, Aline and I and our thirteen month-old baby (and one ninth of another baby whose existence we still ignored), were sent to the U.S. in the summer of 1981 to raise the required financial support for our prospective ministry.

CHAPTER 5

"CAMPUS POUR CHRIST" THE CULTURE SHOCK

W e arrived in the United States in July 1981, sent over by "Campus Pour Christ" for what was commonly called "staff-training." After a brief visit with my parents in Rhode Island with their only grandchild at the time we flew out to Colorado and were met at the old Stapleton airport and driven to Ft. Collins to the campus of Colorado State University. Though staff training and new staff initiation were annual events for Campus Crusade, this year was a special occasion, the 30th anniversary of the organization's existence. Could that have explained the up-beat atmosphere of all the staff members?

Whatever the explanation, our first impressions were mesmerizing! We were awestruck to find ourselves among so many young, zealous, enthusiastic, Bible-believing Christians, all consecrated to spreading the gospel! Remember, we'd been in France for years and didn't have any previous experience with the American evangelical world. About the only Christians in French universities were a few inconspicuous Bible nerds. Unbeknownst to most Americans, the spiritual temperatures in Western Europe have chilled to arctic levels where, to paraphrase Os Guinness, only the heartiest believers survive by huddling stoically together in their spiritual igloos. The church is all but invisible in France—and ever so timid!

The contrast with the victorious, world-conquering attitude of these American Christians was overwhelming. Our first reaction was one of envy for our French brethren: would that they all could see and experience the joy and zeal that permeated this gathering of Christian soldiers, which included a fair number of new converts, ready, willing and eager to bring the saving message to the far reaches of the world!

As enthusiastic as we were to experience such unabashed optimistic zeal, we weren't insensible to a few cultural idiosyncrasies of our American brethren, specifically with regards to their worship service with its almost *Hollywoodesque* showmanship. The choirs, the speakers, and general ambiance seemed too orchestrated and entertaining to us.

The Campus Crusade founder and President, M. Bill Bright was an unpretentious man of God with a California business background which he brought with him to the creation of an organization that had the ambitious goal of reaching the entire world for Christ within a generation. It was this kind of West Coast optimism, à la Walt Disney and Ronald Regan, which left a lasting impression and contrasted so strongly with the "peau de chagrin" (literally 'skin of sadness,' signifying "beaten in advance") attitude which prevails in the tiny French church.

Mr. Bright believed that all we had to do was to present the gospel to people, and the full number of elect—a significant percentage—would be almost instantly added to the Kingdom. Perhaps. That might be true for places like N. America or even Africa where many new people were coming to faith every day. It was hardly our experience in France where one could present the gospel *ad nauseum* with little visible results.

Beyond the cultural idiosyncrasies of the movement were a few theological peculiarities which we found more difficult to accept. Campus Crusade's aggressive support-raising policy contrasted with the more discreet—some might say hypocritical—attitude that prevails in France with regards to money.

Most French would never dare ask anyone for money, not even for ministerial work. That's partly due to the fact that the French government already takes away so much in taxes. This attitude spills over to the church where it almost seems that even the spread of the gospel should be subsidized by the government. Tithing doesn't come easily to the overtaxed French Christians.

The Campus Crusade training involved detailed instructions for raising the financial support necessary for ministry. This included a fair amount of psychological briefing for encouraging the folks we would call by phone. Years of experience had taught the 13,000 plus member "Crusade" staff to anticipate any possible objection to supporting the ministry. All reactions to fund-raising requests were analyzed in a business like manner, using a professional looking manual prepared for prospective Campus Crusade staffers.

The entire policy was, of course, buttressed by the underlying theological conviction that the support-seeking staff is not begging, but offering the faithful an opportunity to invest in the advancement of the Lord's Kingdom through their particular ministry. I believe that. Still, the whole concept was so foreign to our French experience so as to make us both apprehensive and uncomfortable. Maybe we were just lacking faith?

So it was with some fear and trepidation that, after the ten-day staff training, we began making phone calls—hundreds of them—to various Denver area churches in an effort to find those with whom the Lord would associate us in the advancement of His Kingdom in France.

J. SIDLOW BAXTER AND THE MEEKNESS
OF A BRONCO

There was one somewhat humorous incident during those heady days of initiation on the beautiful campus of Colorado State University. It makes for a good illustration of the contrast between Christian gentleness and the abrasiveness of the surrounding world.

We had just finished listening to a most inspiring lecture by a distinguished British Christian scholar named J. Sidlow Baxter who had commented extensively on the meekness of Christ. Dr. Baxter was a godly old-fashioned English gentleman with a transparent spirit and a youthful weakness for Cadbury chocolates, according to an amusing anecdote he shared with us. He had moved us almost to tears in his lecture. Jesus, who could have decimated the entire world with a word, preferred to accept the vile abuse of sinful men, even to the point of death. What an example of gentleness and self-discipline the Lord showed us in those horrendous hours leading up to the crucifixion!

Leaving Dr. Baxter's lecture, we filed out reverently through the corridors of the auditorium, treading carefully lest we step on an ant, while still meditating on the exhortation to meekness. Walking down the hall of the auditorium, we passed by one of the open doors of a projection room where a number of Denver Broncos football players (doing their pre-season training on the same Colorado State campus) had just finished watching a training film. A coach was lecturing the players — presumably the defensive linemen — on their responsibility to put pressure on the quarterback.

As the future linemen received instruction, I overheard the coach exhort his pupils in graphic terms to physically crush any opposing player who would come between them and their goal.

"Run that sucker right over and stomp him right into the ground!" said the coach, referring to the opposing player.

This was a banal and innocuous incident for anyone who knows anything about American football which, according to George Will, combines the worst two American traditions, i.e., committee meetings and violence. It was the contrast with what we'd just been learning about Christ's meekness that made it so striking. Somehow, I couldn't picture a young Jesus in a helmet and shoulder pads applying the coach's advice.

DENVER FUND-RAISING

After a couple of weeks of training we were eager to get settled somewhere where we might apply something of what we'd learned for raising the finances that would be necessary for us to return to France.

Our first stop was Aurora, Colorado, where a middle-aged Christian couple lent us their house while they went off to a training program in California for missionaries going to Ecuador.

The offer of their home — free of charge — was the first of in a long series of providential provisions on our long journey through the jungle of missionary fund-raising. Not only did they lend their dwelling, but they threw in a small Toyota, which served as our means of transportation. So we settled in their Aurora home, a couple of miles from Stapleton Airport.

The first problem we faced—one for which the Campus Crusade support-raising philosophy offered no solution—was the fact that we knew no one in the Denver area. Yet most missionary fund-raising, we had been instructed, was to be done amongst our believing friends and relatives. That presented us with a dilemma. Who could we call?

The logical first step was to call the churches, for surely there were Christian churches in the Denver area willing to partner with a young couple eager to bring the saving message to the heathen in France?

So we started by phoning all the churches—there are hundreds— in the Denver area. Fortunately local calls are free in the US, unlike in France where one has to pay for each call.

We soon discovered that not all the churches in America were enthusiastic in their support of Campus Crusade. While our appeals were most often met with polite expressions of regret explaining that the church was already overcommitted in their mission outreach, sometimes we were rebuffed for our affiliation with Campus Crusade. It appears that certain churches considered "Crusade" to be less than pure for its affiliation with Billy Graham, whose evangelistic association had allegedly allowed some theologically questionable elements to participate in its various crusades. This was shocking to us, that some evangelical brethren would have reservations about working with Billy Graham, whose reputation remains impeccable in the sight of just about anyone.

Still, I remembered the late Francis Schaeffer once affirming that he would not appear on the same panel with any known theological liberal for fear that the non-believers would confuse biblical Christianity with theological liberalism.

So our first week of missionary fund-raising was an eye-opener during which we learned the importance of associations with organizations and their reputations.

Another curious reaction came from one disgruntled pastor who told us that the French "had squandered their opportunity to hear the gospel in the 16th and 17th centuries." Thus having rejected it, God's wrath would rest upon them and their descendants forever. Once again, this kind of thinking was shocking to me, though it seems not so outrageous now, after evangelizing the French all these years. Mission work in France is not cost-effective. There is a pitifully small percentage of Christians in that county in spite of the efforts expended there by all kinds of mostly foreign evangelical groups. Surely the Lord has, to a degree "visited the sins of the fathers on the sons of those who hated Him" (Deuteronomy 5:9).

Still, we liked to think that there was a new day coming for the Kingdom of God in France. And we hoped to be part of a significant harvest that would take place in the land of Calvin. But first we had to get back there. Hence the importance of the fund-raising task at hand.

For almost a fortnight we continued phoning the Denver area churches, not realizing that many of them receive at least several calls every day from other missionaries seeking support for their work. The fact that we were absolutely unknown was a major handicap. People, even Christians, tend to support people they know and trust; it takes a while to earn that trust.

Still, we were delighted when the Lord's providence led us to two Presbyterian churches who decided to support our ministry for a least a couple of years. So our time there was not completely unproductive.

MIRACLE OF THE GASOLINE MULTIPLICATION

We got an opportunity to do a bit of tourism in the Denver area, including a drive to the top of nearby Mt. Evans (14,264'), accessible by the highest road in N. America. We drove out of Denver to the town of Idaho Springs at the base of the mountain where we arrived with the gas gauge on empty and our baby son Calix, 14 months old at the time, sleeping soundly in the back seat. We drove past a filling station but chose not to stop. For as any parent of a small child knows, one does not stop a car with a sleeping baby. Indeed we had occasionally run through traffic lights—prudently—preferring to risk a ticket rather than wake our sleeping son. Still, we could see from the warning light that we'd never make it to the top of the mountain road (about 28 miles, if I remember correctly) and back on the fumes that we had in the tank. Surely, there would be a filling station along the way, we thought. I couldn't imagine 28 miles of American road with no filling station. So we took a chance and, though we drove up the mountain for what seemed like an eternity, we never passed another filling station. We decided to carry on anyway, absolutely positive that we wouldn't make it back with the motor running. We were probably right, though we'll never know for sure. For after spending an hour or so in the cool mountain air at the top of Mt. Evans, we drove back down without the benefit of the motor—save for the one or two places near the very summit where the road actually dips and a wee bit of climbing becomes necessary. In fact, we coasted all the way back to Idaho Springs. I don't know if there's any other place in the country, indeed the world, where one can coast that far. In hindsight, I guess we could draw some spiritual inference from this experience about how the Lord has occasionally multiplied the resources of destitute missionaries on different occasions. In this case He did it a little differently. He put us on a 14,000' mountain road and let gravity do its thing.

CAROLINA Epiphany

We made it back to Aurora and left shortly afterwards, spending a couple of uneventful weeks in Philadelphia with my sister and her husband, monopolizing their telephone, beating the bushes for support there as we had in Denver. By this time, we were beginning to realize the relative impossibility of our plight. With all the missionaries around raising support for their ministries, churches and individuals would understandably give priority to their own, which only makes sense. This truth, as obvious as it seems to us now, was hidden from us till then. It was confirmed by a phone call to the late Dr. Ed Clowney, dean of Westminster Seminary at the time, and father-in-law of one of our Aix-en-Provence Seminary professors. He had always impressed us as being a man of both faith and wisdom, so we called him for advice. He told us that we would probably have to get settled somewhere, become members of a church which could recognize our missionary vocation and eventually help send us back to France.

The question: where to get settled? Dr. Clowney advised us to choose a town (in the U.S. of course) where there was a dynamic PCA church. We called "Mission to the World," the mission board of the PCA, and were given the addresses of five PCA churches—all in the southeast. The closest one was in Greenville, S.C., the next in Atlanta, another in Alabama, still another in Jackson, MS. We didn't know anyone in any of these towns, so it was all the same to us.

This was a strategic crossroads in our life, a time of testing. Little had we realized that the first and sometimes most frustrating part of missionary life was just getting to the field. We now see how the Lord allows us to go through these trials to prepare us for the exasperations of the field. At the time it wasn't that clear.

As we rode the train up to Rhode Island to see my parents, I was feeling unsure of myself and totally dependent and desperate for some miracle of Providence. This missionary support-raising business wasn't going to be easy. We hadn't realized what we'd gotten ourselves into.

I felt strongly that the Lord had called me to share the message of salvation with the French. Why else would I have invested five years in a French seminary getting to know that culture, as well as the Word?

We'd seen His hand at work in the way He led us to the only group doing full-time evangelism amongst French university students to whom we felt particularly called. But our discussions with the Campus Crusade director in France had given us the impression that our fund-raising stint in the U.S. was to be a six-week affair. Could it be that the Lord hadn't called us to be missionaries at all? If not that, then what else would I do?

The only thing I knew for certain was that I now had a wife and 1.3 children (we had just learned that Aline was pregnant) and no visible means of supporting them. Beyond that, we were in a train traveling from Philadelphia to Providence, Rhode Island, where we would stay with my parents a few days until...? We had no idea what would happen next. This uncertainty would not have bothered me in my vagabond past. That was adventure! It was great not knowing what the next day would bring—where would one sleep or what would one eat.

Now I had to make sure I could provide for my family. Suddenly, my decisions had implications that affected others. It was time to grow up—fast! What should I do?

I excluded no options, including the dreaded possibility of working in the family retail furniture store in Woonsocket with all the grief and aggravation that entailed for my longsuffering father. Should I return to France and look for secular work without the benefit of missionary support? These were just some of the things going through my mind over that six-hour train ride that late September afternoon in 1981.

Aline and I were praying to the Lord for guidance. But in times of spiritual darkness, it's not always easy to discern His response to our prayers.

As I thought about these things, our train, which was running roughly parallel to the Connecticut turnpike, went into a long tunnel. A fitting metaphor, I thought, for the predicament we were in. Is there a light at the end of the tunnel, I wondered? Tell us Lord, I pleaded, what we need to do, where we need to go.

Coming out of the tunnel we were once again moving parallel to the northbound traffic on the turnpike. The first vehicle I spotted was a semi-tractor trailer with the name "Carolina" painted on the side. I stared at the truck riding alongside us for a few moments, and wondered about its final destination as well as ours. I started humming the James Taylor song: "In my mind I'm going to Carolina:" Then it hit me—in a flash. I told Aline, we're going to the Carolinas to get settled at that church in Greenville, the first one, or at least the closest one, on the list that had been given me.

When I told her how I arrived at that conclusion, she wasn't exactly thrilled by my method of spiritual discernment. In hindsight, I would not recommend to anyone to make a decision based on that kind of "vision." But we simply had nothing else to go on.

First we would have to call the pastor of the church whose name had been given us by Mission to the World and tell him of our dilemma. That was the first thing we did when we arrived at my parents home. We phoned the church and were eventually able to speak to Pastor Paul Settle who, as it turned out, was a personal friend of Dr. Clowney as well as one of the theological heavyweights and key founding members behind the Presbyterian Church in America. After we announced to Rev. Settle that we were heading for Greenville, he assured us he would do everything in his power to make us feel welcomed. He was true to his word went beyond the call of duty of any pastor.

The next problem to which we'd given little thought was the question of transportation. Just how would we get down to Greenville, S.C.? We'd need a car, as we were discovering that public transportation in the U.S. was hardly up to European standards; it's virtually impossible to get around anywhere in America without a car.

Amazingly, I hadn't even thought of that as we'd always traveled on my bicycle or with public transportation or even hitchhiking until then. We never had a car while at seminary in France and got around easily in a pedestrian friendly town like Aix-en-Provence. It meant a bit of walking, to be sure, but we had no money for a car and therefore no choice. I eventually got a bicycle, which I used to go almost everywhere. When Aline and I were first married, I would even carry her around on the handlebars on occasion.

Likewise we couldn't afford to buy a car now.

When it was decided that we would be prolonging our stay in the U.S. to raise support, Campus Crusade provided us with a stipend of $800./month for our living expenses. That was hardly enough, even in those days, to buy a car. In France I had considered a car to be more of an expensive inconvenience than a necessity.

One day while we were visiting with my old grandmother (86 at the time) in Woonsocket, I informed her that we'd be going to settle in S. Carolina. She asked me how we'd be getting there. I told her I honestly didn't know and hadn't really given it much thought. She proceeded to hand me a wad of bills—some $1800 in all —with which to buy a car!

That was nothing short of miraculous in the light of my grandmother's reputation for frugality. This was a woman who had raised a family in the great Depression and still lived like one was going on. In fact, she'd rarely given me anything until that time.

Then there was the purchase of a vehicle at a modest price, from a garage mechanic friend of a friend in Manville, Rhode Island, who just *happened* to come upon a car that had belonged to a convent of

Roman Catholic nuns in Providence until the school they operated went bankrupt. So we got a mechanically sound 1976 Chevy Nova that had literally spent most of its life driving to and from church.

To complete the sale, I had to visit the head office of the Roman Catholic diocese in Providence for them to sign the car's title over to me. I recall my less than tactful attempt at sharing the gospel of grace with the elderly Catholic priest who signed the papers. I told him I used to be a Catholic, but that now I was a Bible-believing Christian. He wasn't impressed, and the incident—just another in the providential confluence of factors that the Lord used in my life—was an element reminding me of the delicate task ahead of us then.

Aline and I packed our few belongings and began the long drive down to Greenville, S. C., in early October of 1981. We felt like innocents abroad, like Abraham and Sarah on the way to the mysterious unknown land to which the Lord had called them.

It was fortunate that we couldn't foresee the minor hardships and frustrations that awaited us as we left the familiar surroundings of my native New England for the country south of the Mason-Dixon line.

GRIT COUNTRY

It was exciting to be off on another adventure. I had only been South once, back in 1971 when, fresh out of high school, I had hitchhiked down to Orlando, Florida to see a buddy who was working there. I had been surprised by the warmth and hospitality of the folks I'd run into, even towards , a long-haired hippie type at a time when the South was red-neck country, as far as I knew. The horrors of the "Easy Rider" movie were still fresh in my mind as I had slept by the roadside in Georgia before the interstate highway was completed and one had to drive through small Georgia towns on the way to Florida.

One morning, I had walked alone into a small Georgia town after having spent a sleepless, mosquito-bitten night by the roadside. I was apprehensive, fearing I'd be a victim of someone's dislike of long-hairs. I mustered the courage to walk into a small Georgia diner at about seven o'clock in the morning. The place was full of locals having breakfast. Would they say anything to a scraggly vagabond who just wandered in off the street? I resolved to play it safe and keep my mouth shut for fear my accent would betray a northern origin. A southern hippie might at least be tolerated, I reasoned. But a Yankee hippie wouldn't stand a chance.

I grabbed a seat at the counter, between a garage mechanic and another local clerk of some kind who was reading the morning paper. Within a couple of minutes, the waitress, a heavy-set lady of about fifty with an infectious smile and friendly manner, asked me what I wanted. I simply pointed on the menu to breakfast item "no.3": two eggs, toast, coffee, and juice. I thought that would do it, and I didn't want to give myself away. As far as they knew, I was a deaf mute. The waitress dutifully scribbled my request on her order pad before adding, with a thick southern drawl:

"Y'all want grits with that, boy?"

I had no idea what grits were. I suspected they might be some kind of biscuits or hot cakes that one might eat for breakfast, but nothing more than that. Still, the waitress waited for an answer. Timidly I answered: "Just one or two."

She burst out laughing, announcing to all within the sound of her booming voice: *"The Yankee here wants one grit!"* There was an explosion of laughter at the counter as the locals were instantly made aware of the origin of the long-haired degenerate in their midst.

The laughter was prolonged and started up again as I finished breakfast and moseyed sheepishly out the door. I didn't mind as it was a good-natured laughter accompanied by smiles. I felt reassured. This probably wouldn't be so bad. These people are okay. They just think I'm a complete idiot.

That's what I was thinking as, ten years later, Aline and I crossed the Mason-Dixon line into Virginia on I 95 heading to S. Carolina.

. Our first impression of the Palmetto State was favorable. The countryside didn't rival the beauty of my native New England. But the people seemed friendlier as far as we could tell from our stops along the way. We arrived at Second Presbyterian Church, located in a somewhat run-down area of central Greenville not far from textile mills, seedy bars, and low income housing. The contrast between this proletariat setting and the Presbyterian circles we'd soon become familiar with was striking.

Pastor Settle met us at the church. He took us to the home of the Lewis and Melissa Young, a family of his parishioners who were in the concrete business and out of town for the week and who, without knowing us, had agreed to let us stay in their home. That would never happen in France, Aline insisted. No Frenchman would lend his house to complete strangers. And what a palace it was! I assured Aline this kind of hospitality was rare for New England too. We followed Rev. Settle to the nearby town of Travelers Rest to what was surely one of the most magnificent houses we'd ever seen, much less stayed in. As it turns out, this most elegant dwelling had been featured in the "Better Homes and Gardens Magazine." We set up housekeeping at the far end of an interminable corridor and wondered if we hadn't just stumbled into the Land of Oz.

After several days of getting acquainted with Greenville, we got to meet the Youngs. Lewis was an unpretentious Southerner with a thick local accent and infectious smile. His wife Melissa was a northerner by birth who had adopted Southern ways. She may have been born in the North, as they say, but she'd come South as soon as she could. They were the epitome of Southern hospitality. They had two children, a ten-year-old boy and a thirteen-year-old daughter, who were just as charming. Aline, who was still trying to get used to the culture shock of our Colorado experience, was bewildered at the luxury of our new surroundings. Did all these people realize how differently the rest of the world lives, she wondered?

This was the beginning of our initiation into the culture of American Presbyterian circles. It is a most blessed milieu—blessed materially, because it was comprised mainly of more educated folk whose Protestant work ethic had produced a significant percentage of doctors and lawyers and successful business people. Unlike the few French Christians we knew who would make an effort to hide any conspicuous wealth, our American brethren considered it as a blessing from God—a blessing that one could hardly begrudge those who, as in the case of the Youngs, were quite willing to share it with others. It may all seem banal to American Christians reading this, but it was nothing less than revolutionary to us.

Better still was the gracious Southern positive attitude which prevailed, particularly in Christian circles. Folks down South almost always have a kind word to say. Complete strangers—from Power company personnel to Motor Vehicle employees—were invariably gracious. We hardly knew how to handle this at first. We were, in true French fashion, even suspicious of the normal kindness of the folks we'd meet. It seemed that every pedestrian I met as I walked down the street would greet me with a friendly hello. At first I wondered if I hadn't already met them somewhere until I discovered that this is how one behaved here.

This didn't' help us understand the motivation behind the prolific compliments we heard amongst the better bred Southerners. "My, what a lovely dress you're wearing child," said a aristocratic southern matron as Aline and I entered the Church for worship that first Sunday we were at Second Presbyterian Church. Aline was dumbfounded. The dress she was wearing, one of two she owned at the time, had seen its better days and was somewhat of a rag especially compared to the chic ensembles of our Southern hosts.

"Comment peut-elle dire cela?" (How can she say that?) Aline inquired.

Est-ce qu'elle se moque de moi?" (Is she mocking me?), my wife persisted.

Not at all, I assured her. It's just part of the Southern tradition of saying something positive.

Here again, the reader from the South might find this quite ordinary. For us at the time it was revolutionary. As I reflect on it, I attribute this gracious behavior to the residual grace of the gospel that has influenced this part of our great country perhaps more than any other. For the Scripture says, "Do not let any unwholesome talk come out of your mouths, but only what is helpful for building others up according to their needs, that it may benefit those who listen" (Ephesians 4:29). What a refreshing change it was from the "nattering nabobs of negativism" in France that Aline had grown up with and I had gotten used to. What a difference that would make on the psychology of raising children, as well as a contrast to the French tradition of "pedagogy by humiliation."

We saw this same philosophy applied everywhere, even on the church softball team I joined in Greenville. One is standing at third base and a pop fly drops right into your glove. Your teammates greet you with a chorus of enthusiastic "Nice catch!" If I goof up and drop the ball, it doesn't matter. They'll still say "Nice try!" What a country!

Would the American child from South Carolina come home from school with a test result of 50%, and the parents might praise him for the half of the exam he did well. A French child bringing home a test score of 50% will be humiliated for the 50% he didn't know.

This orientation of the French educational system to belittle young students contrasts with the (excessive?) tendency to compliment and encourage in the American South. Aline was particularly impressed and relished the positive atmosphere in the South, when we would return to Dixie during our regular missionary furloughs.

Another aspect of the south we were discovering was the sociological implications of ones ecclesiastic affiliation. South of Maryland, it seemed that every town we'd go through had a church on every corner (In France a neighborhood has a café on every corner).

Just as there were more than 365 varieties of cheese in France, there seemed more than 365 varieties of Christianity in the American South. There were Methodist, Pentecostal, Lutheran, and Presbyterian Churches and more Baptist churches than you could shake a stick at. For a former Roman Catholic, this was disconcerting at first. It was the homogenous nature of the Roman Church that reassured them that theirs was the real thing and that other denominations were merely splinter groups.

Moreover, there is a unity of structure in the Roman Church, with the same liturgy in the Roman Catholic Mass wherever it is celebrated around the world. No disrespect intended, but it's a bit like going to MacDonald's. No matter where you are, you can know what you're going to get in the way of food (which doesn't necessarily insure that it's of the best quality).

On the other hand, the evangelical protestant world, which knows nothing of homogeneity, is bonded together by a profound unity of the Spirit, who links all true believers in the gospel of Jesus Christ and transcends all cultural and liturgical differences. It's a unity that is almost palpable from one evangelical assembly to another, and that struck me when I first came to the faith. Sure, there are differences in the way the Lord is worshipped from one assembly to another, and such issues as music can be divisive. But there is, in most cases, a true spirit of worship among those who revere Jesus Christ as Lord.

RICH BAPTISTS

So here we were in Greenville, S.C., living in Rebel country and a tad uneasy among the ubiquitous Confederate flags, including one in a semi-rural filling station where I brought our travel-weary Chevy Nova for an oil change one afternoon.

The owner, a heavy-set, middle-aged, tobacco-chewing fellow with a thick regional accent and dirty overalls, was sitting in his "office" when I asked him if I couldn't get a quick oil change. No problem, he assured, and instructed me to pull the car into the garage. In spite of the warm reception we'd been getting from the folks of Greenville thus far, I was a bit uneasy about dealing with the locals, especially a less educated car mechanic with a confederate flag in his office.

In my youth, the only Southerners I'd had occasion to meet were the tractor-trailer drivers from whose trucks we unloaded furniture— mostly made in the Carolinas—on the loading dock at the family store. I had never heard an articulate Southerner speak until Jimmy Carter ran for the presidency in 1976. You can imagine how much prejudice still lingered in my foolish Yankee heart back in 1981.

"Where y'all from boy?" the mechanic inquired, as we watched my car going up the lift.

"Er...Rhode Island, Sir," I answered timidly, knowing the tags on my car would betray me if I tried to lie.

He just shrugged. With tobacco juice dripping on the floor, he grabbed the proper wrench to loosen the oil plug under the car, and went about his work.

"What y'all doin down here boy?" he persisted, while unscrewing the bolt, and spitting on the floor.

"I'm a missionary, sir," I replied softly, wondering about his own ecclesiastic affiliation, if any. I had no idea what the word "missionary" evoked in his mind.

"What church?" he asked inquisitively, while we stood there watching crude black oil pour out of the underside of the car into a fifty-gallon re-cycling barrel.

"Er.. Presbyterian sir...," I ventured timidly.

"*Presbyterian*?!" he said in a surprised tone, while spitting another blob of tobacco-laden saliva onto the greasy floor.

. "You know what Presbyterians are, boy?" he pursued in his slow Southern drawl, leaving me with a question I dared not answer.

"No, what?" I risked.

"Rich Baptists!" he blurted out with a chuckle.

"And you know what Episcopalians are?" he pursued.

"No," I answered.

"Rich Presbyterians!" he concluded, giving me a wink.

An interesting perspective, I thought, the humor of Bubba's filling station. But it didn't take too long for us to discover that there was more than a little truth in that simple analysis of the ecclesiastical sociology of the South.

Socialized medicine and ALINE'S URGENT "RENDEZ-VOUS"

We settled down and came dangerously close to enjoying life in the American South—a potential pitfall for one called to be elsewhere. Aline's English was improving to the point where she could almost ask for directions when she got lost on her weekly outings when I stayed home babysitting the children. One afternoon per week she would hop in the car and head for one of the malls for a badly need respite from the constraints of raising two small children. Our son Justin was born in March of that year, 1982.

Aline's legendary sense of direction caused her some grief. One time she phoned me crying that she was lost in the S. Carolina wilderness and couldn't figure out the way back home, nor could she understand the thick accents of the rural folks who would give her directions! From that point on, I always made sure she had a full tank of gas before ventured out, as her trips to the nearby mall could easily evolve into hundred mile adventures.

A more amusing episode concerned her misuse of the language when making an appointment with our pediatrician.

Aline wanted to schedule a visit to the pediatrician for our baby son Justin, who had an ear infection. It's perhaps the most banal of all childhood illnesses, according to our Greenville pediatrician Dr. James Beard (a devoted Christian and excellent physician) represented 80% of his work.

For a mother concerned about the health of her baby, though, it is an all-important matter. So Aline took it upon herself to phone Dr. Beard one morning at the local children's clinic where he worked. The telephone conversation, which I overheard while working at my desk, went something like this:

Aline (with her thick French accent and a sense of urgency in her voice):

"Allo, zis is Mme. Mailloux. I call to make rendez-vous with Dr. Bard zis afternoon. It is urgent. He is free…non? "

Aline of course did not know the American word "appointment" and used the French equivalent with its more salacious implications.

I picked up the extension phone just in time to hear my sweet wife insisting to a second secretary that it was "veeery urgent" that she have "rendez-vous" with "Ze Doctor Bard zis afternoon. He is free, no?"

Apparently, the first secretary had passed the call along to her colleague and I could overhear them both giggling uncontrollably as she, with her own thick southern twang, asked Aline to describe the symptoms.

I was going to intervene but I was laughing so hard that I really couldn't. Such are the pitfalls of a Frenchwoman in the Palmetto state.

I had to wean my wife of her of her French habit of calling the doctor whenever one of the children was less than 100% healthy. French socialized medicine is such that many in that country tend to abuse—at least by American standards—the services of their physicians. What's more, French doctors make house calls. Got a sick child? Call the doctor—even at 2 o'clock in the morning—and he'll come running over to your place. House calls cost, back then about $18. vs. the $15. fee for an office visit. And for the French, it's reimbursed by the government. I even knew a seminary student in

Aix-en-Provence who, in a bout of insomnia, didn't hesitate to call a doctor at 3 o'clock in the morning so that he would come to the dormitory and give him a sleeping pill!

It would take a whole book to elaborate on the differences between French and American medical care. For what it's worth, I offer these few generalizations:

French doctors are often amongst the most idealistic people one meets in the otherwise corrupt French society. It's not an accident that many of the noble "Médecins Sans Frontières" (Doctors Without Borders) working in dangerous conditions in third world countries are French.

In France, few go into medicine to get rich. Indeed, we have known some French doctors who—especially at the beginning of their careers—earned little more than the minimum wage! To be sure, they don't have thousands of dollars in tuition loans to repay, as the state pays for their medical studies. Neither do they have obscene malpractice insurance premiums, as French courts do not award outrageous sums to plaintiffs in the rare event of a malpractice suit. It's a different world.

"MORE LIKE A PRESBYTERIAN"

We had been in the church in Greenville for several weeks when I had the opportunity to accompany Rev. Settle and a few elders from Second Presbyterian Church to a presbytery meeting at a rural denominational church halfway between Greenville and Columbia. Presbytery meetings were most revealing to me. In my naïveté, I had imagined all church business was limited to the missionary outreach, which was the Church's main vocation: "Go ye therefore and make disciples of all nations." What else was there?

I was more than a little surprised to see how many issues were dealt with in a typical southern Presbyterian presbytery meeting. Everything is dealt with—from church disciplinary issues, to ordinations for licensure, the reports of innumerable committees, and the missions committee, to list just a few. In fact, sometimes the presbytery didn't even address mission concerns until the very end of the five-hour meeting, and even then, for only a few minutes! So the shock of discovering how much else there is to church business was enlightening to me.

Another surprising element of the presbytery meeting was its structure and the disciplined and ordered nature of the proceedings. One had to formally address the moderator and be recognized by him before speaking. One was given a limited amount of time to speak before the moderator's gavel came down and discussion was possible, followed by a motion which needed to be seconded, discussed, and eventually voted upon.

Such orderly proceedings are all but unheard of in France. The whole meeting I attended was conducted, of course, according to that other Presbyterian *"Bible"* , "Robert's rules of Order," which Pastor Settle had mastered. Indeed there were numerous occasions when the presbytery delegates, some 150-200 teaching and ruling elders from around the Palmetto state, deferred to him over procedural questions. It happened so often that I wondered how they might ever conduct a meeting in his absence! Years later, after he'd moved to a church in Texas, I visited with pastor Settle and his wife Georgia and attended a meeting of the smaller Texas presbytery. I wasn't surprised to see that here too, the elders constantly deferred to Rev. Settle on procedural questions. It was a credit to the Presbyterian tradition that so many things could be accomplished, thanks to Robert's Rules, which I had never heard of until then. It was no wonder that Mr. Henri Blocher, perhaps France's most articulate evangelical theologian, once told me that this procedural "bible" was the basis for the greatest cultural difference between the chaotic French and the organized Americans.

There was another cultural issue at hand not related to procedural questions but more to my appearance. Aline and I had come to the States with merely a backpack and a few items for the baby, expecting to stay for the six weeks of summer. We were without appropriate clothing when we began visiting the churches for financial support. My blue jeans and sweat shirts, though proper attire for the French university campus, were conspicuous amongst the Southern Presbyterians, whose church meetings resembled something of a Mormon undertaker's convention, with everyone wearing sober dark suits, white shirts and ties.

I stood out like a sore thumb at my first meeting, where I was introduced by Rev. Settle, who explained how the Lord had called us to minister amongst French university students. In fact, he was tactfully trying to cover for me for my less-than-Presbyterian appearance.

One Sunday, Ms. Jackie Wallace, a dear, sweet woman parishioner of the Church with an adventurous spirit and a heart for the Lord, approached me after worship to inform me that she had acquired a three-piece suit and some new shoes for me (I'd been wearing only tennis shoes until then).

"Y'all gonna travel in Presbyterian circles; y'all gonna hafta look a bit more like a Presbyterian!" she affirmed with good-natured insistence. I still have the shoes that Jackie gave me and I think of her whenever I wear them. So it often goes that gifts one receives remind the recipient to think of and pray for the well-being of the giver—which may explain in part why it is "more blessed to give than to receive."

FUND-RAISING FAUX-PAS

Clothing protocol settled, we still weren't getting far in raising missionary support for France. I was frustrated. Aline, on the other hand, was charmed by the Southerners and delighted that even poor Americans like us with an annual income of less than $10,000.could afford to eat at a restaurant at least once a week. In fact, there were chains within walking distance of our dilapidated rental house where we could get a salad bar family special that fed the three of us for less than five dollars! Amazing, even for 1982.

Likewise, we discovered that the most economical way to purchase the things that any family would need was at yard sales and in thrift shops. In a wealthy country like the U.S., people give away all kinds of things that most people in the third world could only dream of owning. So Saturday mornings became a regular yard-sale shopping day in search of the clothing and household items we needed.

Still, it was frustrating for me not having any idea when we would go back to France. How long did it take missionaries in the PCA to raise their support? That depended on acts of Providence. Humanly speaking, it depended on how well connected one was.

For instance, we had some friends, a young missionary couple destined to work in N. Africa (surely the most difficult mission field in the world) who were approved by the mission board at the same time as we were. Within six months, they had found all their support and were on their way to language training school. Alleluia. That was great for them. Doors had been opened for this couple by her dad who was a PCA pastor and who had intervened for them.

During the same period, we had yet to be even invited into a church to present our work, much less raise support. Meanwhile, I was painstakingly writing dozens of handwritten letters to pastors of S. Carolina PCA churches and not receiving any replies. Apparently, I wasn't going about this fund-raising business the right way. Perhaps I'd been steeped too long in the French culture, in which all serious communication takes place through personal letters. If you want something to be taken seriously in France, you write a letter to the proper authority. A personal letter is given much greater consideration there. I even received a personal reply from Mr. Alain Peyrefitte, the former French "Ministre de la Justice" (roughly the equivalent to our Attorney General) to whom I had written (while he was in office) to comment on one of his books.

Writing letters, alas, wasn't getting me anywhere in the U.S. The only return for my efforts was a bad case of writer's cramp and a growing frustration of feeling like a "voice crying in the wilderness." I should have realized from my Campus Crusade staff-training session in Colorado that, unlike the French who remain basically suspicious of telephone conversation, Americans do business—even the Lord's business—over the phone.

Still, I just couldn't get into the habit. In fact I was a bit frustrated with phone calls to Southern churches where one invariably reached a church secretary who would rarely, if ever, put one's call through to the pastor. This is understandable, as most pastors, especially in the larger churches, have more important things to do than handle calls from dozens of aspiring missionaries looking for support. This area is usually the bailiwick of the missions chairman anyway, who isn't normally on the church staff.

Having said this, I was particularly frustrated by phony promises (pun intended) from church secretaries telling me the pastor would return my call. My calls were rarely returned. That was a scandal to me. Better to say nothing rather than not keep one's word. Better still to tell the truth: explain to the naïve caller that pastors received dozens of calls every day from missionaries seeking support and have too many demands on their time to bother with returning such inquiries. That was the hard reality of the situation. Unfortunately, communicating that truth did not go well with the Southern predilection to be gracious, even to the point of dishonesty. The results were that I was often told what I wanted to hear, which created false expectations and led to a lot of frustration.

It was during one of those periods of intense frustration that I followed the advice of a brother in the Greenville church who exhorted me to take my case to some of the more influential pastors in the denomination. Surely, any flaws in the support-raising system could be overridden by some weighty personal influence?

This brother gave me a list of five of the most prominent pastors in the PCA. They were the denominational heavyweights—pastors of large PCA churches—none of whom I'd met or heard of.

I proceeded to send a letter to these estimable preachers, a missive in which I vented all my frustrations from six months of crying in the wilderness, getting nowhere. Then I violated one of my sacrosanct principles and posted the letter the same day I'd written it. One should *never* do that, because one is inclined to say or write things in the heat of the moment that one would never say under normal circumstances.

The next day with the letters already posted, I reread my rough draft and realized what a tremendous blunder I'd made. What I read was a vitriolic diatribe filled with complaints unworthy of someone pretending to trust in the workings of a Sovereign God. How I regretted sending that letter! Then I panicked. Such a letter, if it were ever read by the individuals to whom it was addressed, probably wouldn't get me excommunicated or burned at the stake, but wouldn't do much for my reputation in the PCA. I was in a heap of trouble!

In an effort to do damage control, I looked up the numbers of the churches whose senior pastors would be getting the dreaded dispatch and proceeded to make some very difficult phone calls. Naturally, the calls themselves would arrive before the written correspondence. I hoped that I might persuade the church secretaries who would be receiving the pastor's mail, to intercept the letter with my return address and destroy it before it reached its intended receiver. No such luck. In fact, my desperate attempt probably whetted their appetites. What possibly could be in this letter that its sender would want it destroyed?

Sure enough, in a few days the fallout from my literary Hiroshima began to spread. I don't recall the order in which the phone calls arrived, but I do remember vividly a least a couple of very pastoral exhortations from the likes of Rev. Frank Barker—folksy Alabama accent and all—of the giant Briarwood Presbyterian church in Birmingham, and Dr. D. James Kennedy of Florida. Both gentlemen took the time to make a personal call to express their concern with regards to the difficulties we were going through and exhorted me to persevere in our vocation. I was truly touched by their pastoral attitude and compassion, considering I was expecting a trip to the woodshed. That would be forthcoming.

A few days later, I got a call from the late Rev. Don Patterson who was then the senior pastor of the First Presbyterian Church in Jackson, MS. He let me know in no uncertain terms what he thought of my negative remarks and roundly scolded me as I deserved. I patiently listened to his reprimand and when it was my turn to reply, I didn't try to justify or excuse myself. I just reminded Dr. Patterson that he'd never taken the trouble to react, much less answer to the more pious letter I'd sent him months before when we first started on our support-raising quest. However, he found the time to scold me for my more recent missive. So I told him that, though I regretted some of what I'd written, I'd rather be berated than ignored!

I think he realized that, my tactlessness notwithstanding, there was some validity to my complaints about the missionary fundraising system. The bottom line was that Dr. Patterson arranged for us to be invited to his church which has supported our mission work ever since. Eventually, Dr. Patterson (with his wife Jeanne) was called to serve as pastor to the PCA missionaries around the world, and came to see us several times in France. He became one of our dearest friends in the denomination until he was promoted home to glory on Christmas day in 1998.

There are other tales that could be told about our 18 month stint— that's how long we were in Greenville, S.C., on that first trip—raising our missionary support. I suppose we could say that the Lord got us our support in spite of ourselves, or at least in spite of the many cultural gaffes that we committed along the way.

For instance, after the gift of the three-piece suit to make me look "a bit more Presbyterian," we were invited to visit a church in a Washington, D.C., suburb of northern Virginia. Back in those days, Aline stayed at home with our growing family. One weekend, I got in the car and drove about 500 miles (one way) to visit a church in Springfield, Va., an assembly whose address had been given to me by the Mission office in Atlanta. Not wanting to shock the faithful with my overly casual dress, I put on the suit along with a white shirt and black tie, and hit the road.

Hours later, I found myself looking for the whereabouts of said assembly in a business section of the city. I finally found the place where the Harvester Presbyterian Church" met for Sunday evening worship. It was in the basement of a bank. Curious, I thought. It must be a new church.

I knocked on the door and was greeted by a long-haired, twenty-five year old fellow sporting shoulder length hair, a long scraggly beard, cut-off jeans, and a sweat shirt. "You da preacher man?" he inquired with all the cool aloofness of Maynard G. Crebs.

"Yeah, that's me," I answered timidly. "But this suit is not really me—it's just a disguise," I protested.

In fact, much of the church, it seemed, was made up of marginal types—converted hippies. And there I stood in my three-piece suit looking like a Mormon. Moral of the story: call the mission office in Atlanta before going on speaking engagements, and ask about the sociological composition of the church to be visited. The PCA is not always a homogeneous entity!

"PAPE ROBERT" and "MAMIE DANIELE"
VISIT FROM FRANCE

We have most pleasant memories of our first stay in Greenville, S.C. In spite of frustrating circumstances, Aline loved the people in the South. She was so enthusiastic, that she persuaded her parents to come for a visit, which they did in the late winter of 1982, a few months before the birth of our second son Justin. For reasons of economy, we had them fly into Miami and drove down from Greenville to meet them, with the intention of driving up the east coast and visiting a few prospective supporting churches along the way.

There was nothing earth-shattering about that trip, but it lingers in my memory as one of the sweetest periods of bliss I have known, with a delightful carefree ambience reminiscent of Huck Finn and Jim drifting down the lazy Mississippi on their raft. Or more recently, the cross country drive of Jack Kerouac and his buddy Neal Cassady in "On the Road."

It was a long, slow (three-week) drive up the east coast starting with the tropical comfort of South Florida. Arriving suddenly in the warmth of the Sunshine state after freezing for months is a delightful experience in itself, as many a tourist can attest. One's spirit is automatically uplifted as he sheds layers of unnecessary clothing while soaking up the sun.

Aline's mom hadn't realized how warm it would be in Miami and arrived dressed in a warm woolen dress which she hastily replaced at the first clothing store we found driving up the Florida east coast. Meanwhile "Papé Robert" (Aline's dad) and I were content just to take in the sights — sandy beaches, palm trees — while drinking-in the sweet joyful music of "The Louis Armstrong Saga" on a plug-in cassette-tape player. I reached previously unattained heights of euphoria driving up the S. Florida coast accompanied by a loving family and the swinging sounds of "Royal Garden Blues." "Moment linger awhile, for thou art so beautiful and so fair!" said Mephistopheles to Faust. I caught myself saying it several times a day during that trip.

Perhaps part of the reason was that the arrival of Aline's parents meant we'd be enjoying a standard of living we had not known till then. Back in Greenville — and for years in Seminary before that —

we'd been living on salad and yogurt and very little else. Now Aline's parents, who had a bit of money back then, generously paid for the whole trip, which included stops at motels and restaurants. This was still another testimony of the Lord's munificence and a most welcomed respite from the frustrations we'd been going through.

We visited Savannah and Charleston where Aline's mother—a great fan of all things of antebellum-Dixie—thought she'd found the original Eldorado. There was even an authentic French pastry shop in Charleston so one could have the best of both worlds—old county savoir-faire, and new world friendliness and charm.

On the other hand, they were horrified by the January cold in New England! I took Aline's dad to a high school hockey game where he huddled miserably in my mother's goose down coat. He'd never experienced a New England winter and wouldn't want an encore.

We drove back to S. Carolina, stopping along the way at a church in Virginia for the missions conference of the Hopewell Presbyterian Church to which we'd been invited. The pastor there was the gifted communicator of the gospel, Rev. Tim Keller who has since moved to Manhattan where he preaches the Word with great effectiveness among the New York cosmopolitan sophisticates.

Back in January of 1982, he had ceded his speaking role at his church's missions conference to Rev. Tom Cheely, a southerner from S. Carolina who gave the keynote address that Sunday evening while I sat at the back of the church with Aline's dad—who doesn't speak a word of English—so I could translate the message for him. Most of the time, I would give him at least a rough approximation of what was being said (In the best of circumstances, simultaneous translation is extremely hard work, requiring total concentration).

This particular sermon by Rev. Cheely defied all translation. The point of the message (based on a text I've forgotten) was drawn from an illustration taken from an incident that occurred in the 1924 World Series! I could see trouble coming as soon as Rev. Cheely mentioned baseball. How do you say "sacrifice fly" or "foul ball" in French? Rev. Cheely spared no baseball idioms—all virtually impossible to translate.

There was an incident in that Series—between the New York Giants and the Washington Senators—in which a Washington slugger, a certain Goose Gosslin came to bat at a decisive moment. M. Gosslin, an excellent fastball hitter, was served a steady diet of curveballs by the opposing pitcher, which he fouled off repeatedly before hitting a drive over the right fielder's head on which he made an inside the park home run. It would have won the game for the Senators. However, Mr. Gosslin was called out for failing to touch first base. Rev. Cheely's point was that one could do everything right in life—hit a home run, so to speak—but it wouldn't count for anything if one did not know Jesus.

While I can say "Amen" to that, I was less enthusiastic in my efforts to translate baseball jargon, much less explain the rules of the game in French to my curious father-in-law, and ex-boxing champ who was pleading impatiently with me to explain to him what the preacher was saying.

"Ne comprends-tu pas ce qu'il est en train de raconter? (Don't you understand what he's saying?), asked Aline's dad.

"Bien sûr" (of course), I insisted. "Mais je ne peux pas te le dire" (But I can't tell you).

This went on for over twenty minutes during which I strained my vocabulary trying to explain arcane baseball rules before finally concluding that it can't be done.

Morale of the story: if the Lord is going to bring Aline's dad to the faith, He's going to have to use another sermon.

Une CITROEN CX

After eighteen months of frustration and, at times, encouragement, during which the Lord taught us a few things about patience and living by faith, we finally were given the green light to return to France. Our missionary support had come through—almost in spite of us—so we were finally on our way to Villeurbanne, France (next to Lyon) to share the gospel with the engineering students at the Institue National des Sciences Appliqués or I.N.S.A.

Before leaving, we spent a few days in New England with my parents, who received us royally as only parents can. In addition to their generous hospitality, reminiscent of the Lord's munificence, we received a telephone call from Aline's dad in France, one of those delightfully surprising phone calls as are rare in life.

Aline's dad rang and informed us that, in honor of our return to France, he had purchased a new car for us. Though we had always gotten along without a car, we'd surely need one now that we had two babies. We were delighted and would have been grateful for anything that moved.

"What kind of vehicle did you get?" I inquired.

"Une Citroën CX break" (Citroën station wagon) said Aline's dad.

"Super," I said, not having the vaguest idea what model it was, but assuming it was something modest enough for one working in the ministry in France, where all manifestations of wealth are frowned upon.

Most French have a hang-up about material things. Roman Catholic tradition basically equates spirituality with asceticism. Poor is holy. Rich is profane. There's a definite dualistic platonic heritage in France, which eyes wealth with suspicion. The Socialist have made hay with this idea by heavily taxing all capitalistic ventures and dissuading potential entrepreneurs. A Frenchman will have generally one of two attitudes with regards to business. If, as a businessman, you're wealthy and successful, that means you're a scoundrel who's defrauding the tax system. And if you're poor, then you're an idiot. There is very little middle ground, save amongst the liberal professions traditionally preferred by the French intelligentsia.

Getting back to my car: Aline's dad purchased for us what was, in 1983, one of the most expensive models made by the Citroën company, the CX. I didn't know that until I went down to the Woonsocket library and researched Citroëns and found the model Aline's dad had described. I was blown away.

It had hydraulic suspension (invented by Citroen and apparently copied by Rolls Royce), power everything; stereo cassette player, and even air-conditioning, which was most rare for France at that time. It costs the equivalent of $20,000. which, in 1983, was quite a piece of change. $15,000 of that was the actual cost of the car; the other $5000 (33%) was tax. That was typical in Socialist France.

A $20,000 car! I couldn't believe it. Nor could I accept it.

For I realized that no one working in the ministry in France could ever explain the ownership of such an expensive vehicle! I thought of the university students with whom we'd be working who would certainly treat me as a "capitalist"—a pejorative word in Marxist-oriented France.

I simply couldn't accept that kind of gift from anyone, much less my father-in-law who had basically spent the entire profits from his seasonal restaurant to buy it.

So the next day, I got back on the phone and called my father-in-law and tried to explain as tactfully as I could why I couldn't accept the car. I hadn't gotten but a few words in when he interrupted me with a bit of his simple peasant wisdom.

"Son-in-law" he said. "I have two things to tell you, so listen well. First of all this is not really your car. In fact, it belongs to my grandson Calix (two years old at the time). You are but his chauffeur. This way, when he comes down to see me from Lyon, I know he'll be riding in comfort and security.

Secondly, when the Lord gives you something, you simply take, give thanks, and shut up!"

With that he hung up the phone and wouldn't hear another word. That's Aline's dad.

With our transportation problems solved in advance, we left for France in September of 1983—eighteen months after arriving for what we expected would be a six-week stay. We were grateful that the Lord hadn't shown us in advance what it would take for us to get back there. But now we were ready to go about our work—His work—knowing that many would be praying for our success.

CHAPTER 6

CAMPUS CRUSADE YEARS 1983-86

We returned to France in August 1983 via Aberystwyth, Wales, where we got together for the first time with the European staff of Campus Crusade on the campus of the university of Wales. The Crusade staff (including the French, of course) was having its annual summer retreat in that town where Prince Charles once studied. The weather was exceptionally fair and this, combined with the fact that we were relieved to be arriving at our long sought destination, bolstered our morale.

From Wales we flew to the south of France where Aline's dad awaited us at the airport in Montpellier with our magnificent 1983 Citroen CX "break" (station wagon). It was even more comfortable than we had imagined, combining superior handling of a European car with American comfort.

A couple of days later in Alès, Aline's dad and I were having a drink with some of his buddies at a local café. From the terrace where we sat, we could see my shiny new CX parked in front of M. Maurin's modest little commercial van—worth about 1/4 as much.

"So how do you like that," said Mr. Maurin to his buddies at the café, pointing to our two cars.

"I bust my butt all year working at the restaurant, yet I drive that crummy little jalopy, whereas my son-in-law here, the 'prayer-merchant,' drives that big fancy Citroën! Surely there's something wrong here," he said, half in jest.

"Not at all," I protested. "It's quite normal".

"What do you mean it's normal?" M. Maurin asked.

I reached into my hand-bag and pulled-out my pocket Bible and turned to the book of Ecclesiastes.

Finding the right chapter in the wisdom literature, I read out loud:

"To the man who pleases him, God gives wisdom, knowledge, and happiness; but to the sinner he gives the task of gathering and storing up wealth to hand it over to the one who pleases God" (Ecclesiastes 2:26)."

"You're working for me," I chuckled. "Says so right here."

THE HOUSING SITUATION IN FRANCE

After a few days in the company of Aline's parents, we headed up to Villeurbanne to look for a place to live. We stayed at the empty apartment of a couple of Campus Crusade staff members and proceeded to pour over the classified ads and make phone call in search of an apartment.

Anyone who's ever been apartment hunting in France knows that a major act of Providence is required to find a suitable flat. There are far more seekers than places to rent. In a city like Paris, there are hundreds of applicants for every available flat. Of course, any American reading this would assume that the law of supply and demand would gradually rectify this situation, and equilibrium would be reached by the inexorable principles of the free market economy.

Not necessarily in socialist France. Foolish laws have been enacted in recent years which basically override the counterbalancing forces of the free enterprise system.

For instance, there was the famous "loi Quillot," passed around 1982 by the former French minister of housing which, in true Socialist fashion, would protect the 'innocent' proletariat tenants from the greedy capitalist proprietors. This law made it virtually impossible to evict a tenant from his rented flat even if he were delinquent by several months on his payments! The intent of the law was, of course, to protect the tenant against the caprices of a wicked proprietor.

Unfortunately, this law backfired in much the same way as the famous "rent controls" in California had a few years before. That law was so protective of the tenants that the proprietors, rather than risk the presence of a tenant who would damage the property, not pay the rent, and could not be evicted, preferred to leave their apartments unoccupied, or only rent them at an astronomical rate to offset the risk they were taking in renting them in the first place! Likewise the Socialist-inspired housing law in France backfired. It created a situation where major cities have thousands of empty apartments with hundreds of thousands of people wanting to rent, but unable to.

I remember a column by humorist Art Buchwald, satirizing the famous Bernard Bertolluci film "The Last Tango in Paris." The film is considered by most a heavy existentialist statement in which the protagonists (played by Marlon Brando and Maria Schneider) have meaningless sex in an empty Paris apartment they are both seeking to rent, before Brando is shot by his casual lover in an existentialist act of the will. M. Buchwald—who lived in Paris at an early period of his writing career—had a different slant on it. He joked that the reason Brando's lover killed him at the end was that she simply wanted to eliminate the competition for the apartment they were both looking at! Anyone who's ever attempted to rent a place in France knows how the endeavor can provoke one to murderous thoughts.

That's the situation we faced in the fall of 1983 arriving in Villeurbanne where we studied the classified ads for several days, visiting dozens of mostly small, dreary apartments in an effort to find something suitable. A few days of searching left us discouraged but not despairing. We were convinced that the Lord had called us to work with the French university students and that He would provide us with a place to live. Foxes have holes and birds have nests, but the Son of Man had no place to lay his head, said the Scriptures. Neither did the Son of Man have a pregnant wife and a couple of small children to house, I thought.

Acting on impulse before leaving for a day's apartment hunting in the wilds of the Villeurbanne urban jungle, I decided to stop by the office of the manager of the apartment building we were staying in just to pay my respects. I knew for a fact that there were no apartments available in this building which, because of its proximity to both the I.N.S.A. (Institut National des Sciences Appliquées) campus where we'd be working and the famous "Parc de la Tête d'Or"—a cherished refuge from the surrounding concrete—was much in demand. Even if there were any flats available, they would be awarded to tenants with references, which we, of course, did not have.

So it was with little hope that I stopped in that morning at the residents' ground-floor office and introduced myself to the manager (Mme. Bertrand) and explained our situation. She told us that there were no units available when the phone rang and our conversation was interrupted:

"Je suis désolée mais je n'ai absoluement rien de libre" (I'm sorry but I've absolutely nothing available), she explained to the caller.

She had no sooner hung up when the phone rang again and for a third time she stated that nothing was available. Our situation didn't look promising.

When the phone finally stopped ringing, I timidly continued explaining that we too, like many other people—including her callers—were apartment hunting.

"Je suis désolée pour vous" (I'm sorry for you) she lamented.

I persisted nonetheless, in an effort to make small talk with nary a glimmer of hope.

"My boss, Françis H. from 'Campus Pour Christ,' said that you might know of a place that we could rent," I ventured timidly.

"Do you too work for Campus Pour Christ?" she inquired.

"I do," I told her. "As a matter of fact, we're now staying in the apartment of a couple of the other staff members, Claude B. and Roger A".

"Pourquoi vous ne l'avez pas dit? (Why didn't you say so?), she asked.

"How soon do you need an apartment?"

We told her we needed a three-bedroom flat by September fifteenth so we could get settled before the new school year began.

She opened her ledger and told me that there would be an apartment on the eighth floor available starting on the 15th of September which she would hold for us pending the presentation of the usual documents including proof of employment with salary, references, etc.

The lodging situation in France is so difficult that proprietors can afford to pick and choose their tenants. Evidently, the "Campus Crusade's" French staff left a favorable impression, paying their rent on time and not causing any trouble. We were awarded the privilege of renting that apartment in the "residence de la Tête d'Or" when there were surely hundreds of others who might have wanted it. Though we didn't have any 'connections,' humanly speaking, we had the hand of Providence which, in this case, worked through the good testimony of our brethren and co-workers.

We were grateful for the three years we spent in that building which, like any apartment, had its advantages and its inconveniences. Though we were on the 8th floor, we could still hear the early morning bus pass by our building at precisely 5:23 every morning. It was our regular wake-up call. Also, we got to learn something about the perpetual annoyance of petty larceny that plagues life in France. About an hour after unloading our car and a small rental truck of some of our possessions, I returned to the small ground-floor storage room where tenants were supposed to store their bicycles, strollers, etc., when not in use. I was making a second trip to leave the baby carriage when I discovered that the bicycle we'd left there not an hour earlier had already been filched. Welcome to Villeurbanne.

DISARMING THE FRENCH RESERVE

It was about the only welcome one would get from the locals, amongst the most reserved in all of France. Basically, one hardly ever speaks to a stranger in France, not on the bus, in the metro, in the elevator, or anywhere else. One must first be introduced. Quite a contrast from the southern part of the United States where even complete strangers greet each other on the sidewalk as they pass by.

The French are generally suspicious of any unsolicited attempts at making conversation. One of their own—the poet, film director Jean Cocteau—defined a Frenchman as "an Italian in a bad mood." That excessive suspicion surely characterizes the Lyon area where a stranger is basically anyone who hasn't lived there all his life. This extreme reserve is hardly conducive to the evangelization of one's neighbors. Though we were there to minister to the students on the nearby campus, I couldn't imagine not having some interaction with our neighbors. Still, it took a significant effort—made somewhat easier by the presence of our small children—to get to know any of the folks who dwelt in the 128 apartments of our building.

Children can be a disarming presence capable of overriding the wariness of almost any Frenchman. One could never knock on the door of anyone's house or apartment in France and expect to be greeted with anything but suspicion. Jehovah Witnesses are about the only ones who go door to door for anything in France. However you're more likely to be well received if you have a young child in your arms.

We discovered early on that our children opened more doors for us than one would expect. There's a biblical precedent for this phenomenon. Before meeting up with his brother Esau, who had a longstanding score to settle with him, the wily Jacob sent his wife and a few of their children ahead to soften the heart of his potentially dangerous brother. Likewise, in no time, we were able to greet just about everyone in our building. Banal as this may seem to most Americans, this kind of unabashed familiarity is surely one of the most startling cultural differences between the hyper-reserved French and the normally extroverted Americans.

It takes some very un-French like boldness to initiate conversations with strangers. But the Lord has not given us a spirit of timidity, said Paul to Timothy (II Timothy 1:7). So a missionary worth his salt must learn to seek any opportunity that arises to be the Lord's ambassador. A case in point: I was riding down the elevator one day with my upstairs neighbor with whom I had yet to speak. Getting on the elevator as it opened at my floor, I normally respected the unwritten law of silence which stifles conversation on any elevator. However, I had just been reading Paul's aforementioned exhortation to the apostle Timothy and was determined to say something—anything—that might eventually lead to a discussion of the faith at some future date. It would clearly have to be just a brief word as there was hardly time for a full-blown gospel presentation in the 24 seconds it took for the elevator to get down to the ground floor from our flat.

"Bonjour Madame," I ventured, smiling at the well-dressed, sexagenarian already in the elevator when the door opened.

My neighbor was clearly shocked. "Who was this impertinent foreigner to speak to me?" she was surely thinking.

"You live on the 10th floor?" I pursued, attempting to strike up a conversation while recalling from the time we'd boarded the ascending elevator together that she'd pushed number "10."

"If ever the elevator cable snaps when you get on, you'll have about 2.0 seconds—or 0.5 seconds more than I would—to make peace with God before being crushed at the bottom," I offered. The abrupt nature of this conversation opener startled this lady who, on another occasion in the lobby of the ground floor, later admitted to me that she had lived in the building for over ten years and had yet to speak to any other resident! However, this time she was willing to speak as we were sipping an aperitif—alcohol has a way of loosening tongues—with some of the residents at a meeting that had been organized by the desperate tenants association in an effort to acquaint the neighbors with each other and hopefully curb the rampant petty larceny that was plaguing the building. This kind of problem didn't exist in older French apartment buildings where access was most often past the office or apartment of a "concierge" who was basically paid to monitor the comings and goings of everyone as a kind of in-house spy. Most modern buildings no longer have a "concierge."

INSA

We enjoyed our work with the students on the campus at INSA (Institut National des Sciences Appliquées). The head of the "Crusade" student ministry was Claude B, a brilliant, slightly eccentric chemist, who had come to the faith in a circuitous manner. A convinced agnostic as a student, he begrudgingly consented to attend a Christian meeting and returned to subsequent meetings when he discovered there were often chocolate brownies baked by Terri, the American wife of one of the campus ministers. At that point, Claude wasn't interested in the gospel, but he adored the brownies. Nevertheless, by attending the meetings regularly, Claude was being exposed to the gospel and to Christian love. The Spirit was doing His work and Claude eventually came to the faith. He brought with him a significant intellectual baggage and expertise on the creation/ evolution debate which made him a precious apologetic addition to the Campus Crusade staff.

In those days, we spent a fair amount of time on campus with a former INSA student from a staunchly communist family—died-in-the-wool Marxist from three generations—who had been brought to faith in Christ after falling in love with a young coed who had presented the gospel to him. Jean-Paul considered himself a rational man in the Cartesian tradition, with little tolerance in his worldview for anything non-rational. However, his point of view was severely challenged by his love for Françoise (who became his wife). What was love in the worldview of dialectical materialism, where even thought is only a secretion of matter? Wasn't love really nothing more than a favorable chemical reaction?

That's what Jean Paul had believed until his heart told him otherwise. His experience in this affair was not unlike that of the famous French 18th century *"philosophe"* Denis Diderot who, an avowed atheist, fell in love with an actress named Sophie Volande. Diderot was logical enough to realize that his philosophical *Weltanschauung* provided him no basis for the reality of romantic love. The apostle Paul in his epistle to the Romans says that men are "without excuse" for "holding the truth in unrighteousness." For man suppresses, by his wickedness, the truth he knows deep in his heart. With regards to his love for Ms. Volande, Diderot admitted in a moment of rare honesty: "J'enrage d'être empêtré d'une diable de philosophie que ma raison ne peut qu'affermir, mais mon coeur démentir" (I'm furious to be imprisoned by a diabolical philosophy that my reason can only affirm but my heart deny).

Fortunately, Jean-Paul drew the obvious conclusion to his dilemma. After his conversion, he married Françoise and joined the staff of Campus Pour Christ. He was my trainer assigned to instruct me in the Campus Crusade evangelistic method, which involved the use of a student survey designed for getting a foot in the door to present the gospel to the students.

Though I had some reservations about the Campus Crusade "Four Spiritual Laws" brochure (could one tell a reprobate that "God loves him and has a wonderful plan for his life"?) I remain an enthusiastic supporter of the survey method for approaching students with the gospel in a non-threatening way. When you ask survey questions, the student feels that his opinion is important. That puts you on good psychological ground for sharing the Message. What's more, he speaks first and doesn't feel as if anything is being thrown at him by some aggressive, religious sect. Most people—especially the French—are turned off by proselytizing of any kind. A correctly used survey avoids that pitfall.

Typically, we would knock on the student's door in one of the local dorms, explaining that we were with the local Christian group on campus and that we wanted only a few minutes of his time so we could learn more about the religious and philosophical viewpoints of the students. The important thing is for the student not to feel trapped. If after completing the ten minute survey, he still wants to pursue the discussion, fine. If not, we would simply leave and go to the next room. More often than not, one who had only reluctantly agreed to grant us five or ten minutes of his precious time would keep us for an hour or so discussing some key questions about the faith that had been introduced by the survey questions. This is understandable for anyone who knows what a spiritual desert France is, where one learns volumes about everything, save that which concerns God and one's eternal destiny. Our seminary philosophy professor Jean Brun, referring to his philosophy students at the University of Dijon, once quipped: "Ils savent tout, mais c'est tout ce qu'il savent" (They know everything, but that's all they know).

Naturally the survey was the key. We would start with general questions about the student's appreciation of his studies, his goals in life and the values upon which he based his life. As we progressed to the more philosophical questions, the reactions would change noticeably. The question "Do you believe in God" would often solicit a philosophical discourse from some such as: "I believe in the God of Spinoza and Einstein, the primal mover, first cause, etc..."

On the other hand, asking what students thought of the identity of Jesus Christ almost invariably got them fidgeting. Finally we'd close with a proposition: "If God offered you a way to have a relationship with Him, would you find that desirable...?" In fact, this was a loaded question: Who wouldn't want to have a relationship with a living God if it were possible?

Depending on the individual student's reaction, one would either finish the survey and go on to the next room, or attempt to discuss the gospel based on the student's answer to one of the questions. That's why it was useful to take notes while writing down the answers to the survey questions.

The goal in all of this was, of course, to make disciples by offering students an opportunity to join a "discovery group" where they would, for a small commitment of four weeks, be exposed to the basic teachings of the Christian faith, after which they would be able to make a more informed decision.

That's the theory, at least. It worked for a tiny number of students. Others would balk at making a commitment of even four weeks. More often than not, a student who had showed a real interest in the gospel while doing the survey would just as suddenly be hostile to our propositions during subsequent visits. For the Seed often falls in thin soil or amongst the thorns. Peer pressure is tremendous. I know of a few courageous students who were teased by their agnostic colleague friends for showing any interest in the faith. One of the drawbacks of the dorm room at INSA was that, unlike most student dormitories in France occupied by only one student, the INSA dorms were shared by two students. Often one roommate would be receptive to the gospel message until the other persuaded him otherwise.

So we presented the gospel to hundreds of French university students during the three years we were there. A few accepted Christ as their Lord and Savior (including a disproportionate number of foreigners). Many more remained, at least on the surface, indifferent. As the Man said: "many are called but few are chosen."

For reasons that escape me to this day, it seems that we always had more success in presenting the gospel to foreigners than to French students. Even though the INSA campus was comprised of over 90% continental French, a significant percentage of those students who came to the faith were either foreigners or from some of the French overseas *départments* or "territories" such as Martinique,

Guadeloupe, New Caledonia, Magdagascar, Réunion Island, etc. Consequently, there was always more dark skin than light skin at our Christian meetings on the campus.

There's something about the continental French that makes them impervious to the gospel. What it is, no one can say for sure, though there are many theories, including the fact that the French are generally a proud people, and the Scripture says that the "Lord resists the proud and is gracious to the humble." Whatever it is, the French resistance to the message of salvation has been the bane of many a missionary, including a brother who worked at the campus of the "Cité Universitaire" in Paris amongst the foreign students, and who personally led many Asians and African students there to the faith.

Dan L., from Dallas, Texas, had studied law before coming to France as a missionary. After a couple of years of blessed success with foreign students in Paris where many came to the faith through his ministry, he came down to join us on the campus at INSA, where in six months of effort, not a single student showed even a remote interest in the gospel. Dan was so discouraged that he shook the dust off his feet and went back to Texas where he now works with Mexican refugees in a Hispanic neighborhood of Dallas. His case is not unique.

LUC BOUVIER ET NORRIS BING

One of the more fruitful times of the week for us at INSA was Thursday afternoons when, traditionally, the students were out of class and often in their dorm rooms. It was a good time to be visiting. One Thursday, I was approached at the student cafeteria by Luc Bouvier, a spiritually sensitive young fellow from St. Malo in Brittany who was also a serious basketball fan. His sporting hero was a certain Norris Bing, the African- American star of the Villeurbanne professional basketball team, one of the best in France at the time. It seems M. Bing had consented to grant an interview for the local campus newspaper. The problem was that Bing didn't speak French, and the students, including Luc, weren't that confident of their command of English. So Luc asked me to go along as an interpreter.

I hesitated at first, not thrilled about sacrificing the only afternoon when I could visit for the sake of something of secondary importance. But I reluctantly accepted, not wanting to disappoint Luc, who seemed well on his way to the faith. After lunch, we all hopped into one of the students' cars, and headed down to a local café to meet M. Bing. The American player, who hailed from Atlanta, turned out to be an affable fellow with a big smile and a humble spirit, not exactly what I had expected from a nationally known basketball star. Luc and his fellow students were awestruck and sat around the table admiring their hero, drinking in his every word even as I translated. Naturally, he spoke mainly about basketball, the technical aspects of the game and the differences between the European leagues and the NBA. At one point one of the students asked me to ask Bing about the source of his apparent serenity and confidence.

From that point, M. Bing used the better part of our time together explaining to the students the importance of his faith in Jesus Christ! It was tremendous! I could have told them about the gospel until I was blue in the face and it would never have had the same impact as the same words coming from the mouth of their hero. So it was an afternoon well spent, one that we followed up with a meal at our apartment with the same students. During the course of that meal, the students made it clear that they wanted to maintain contact with their hero and offered to take him out to dinner after a game. Of course, they were probably thinking of their favorite pizza joint where they might occasionally splurge as a way of avoiding the student cafeteria. Norris Bing accepted graciously and they agreed on a date. When one of the students then asked him if he had any particular restaurant in mind, the basketball star said nonchalantly that he'd eaten several times at a place called "Chez Bocuse" and found it much to his liking. The faces of the students all dropped. "Chez Bocuse," located in a Lyon suburb and owned by world famous French chef Paul Bocuse, is a five-star temple of gastronomy, and one of the most expensive restaurants in France! Wealthy basketball stars might be able to afford a meal there, but it would take a university student's annual budget to pick up the tab even for a bowl of soup. Norris Bing probably had to settle for a pizza.

We didn't have a great deal of success in those years on the campus at INSA. There were always a few foreign Christian students in need of fellowship and edification. And then there were a few others (more girls than guys) who came to the faith, including a brilliant Chinese student who once spent over four hours preparing us a sumptuous Chinese meal in gratitude for hospitality.

Our Sunday night meetings on the campus were typically comprised of some 30-35 students, of which 25 or more were girls and the majority of either sex, were foreigners or non-continental French from either the West Indies, or New Caledonia, or Tahiti, etc. These were good times of fellowship as well as needed social contact between the guys and the girls.

One of the more important roles of the church in a largely pagan land like France is to facilitate social contact between believers of the opposite sex. One of the obvious consequences of the small number of Christians in France is the relatively small pool of eligible singles from which to find a spouse. Sadly, we've known many cases of single girls whose faith has been shipwrecked when they got romantically involved with non-believing men.

Les Carbet, le Père Xavier Maurier

We came to know another couple in our building, Philippe and Elisabeth Carbet who, like ourselves, had three small children, two boys and a girl. Philippe was a research scientist in one of the campus laboratories. Elisabeth, an attractive, well-educated, intellectually curious thirty-year-old woman, was a stay-at-home mom who, like Aline, was devoted to the rearing of her children. We were the only two couples in the building with three children each. It seems no one in France—save the very rich or the very poor—has that many children anymore. There's simply no place to lodge that many little ones, as most Frenchmen live in cities in apartments, and most apartments have one or two bedrooms. Finding a three or four bedroom apartment is nearly impossible. This probably explains why the French are having fewer and fewer children—not enough to replenish the population. There's simply no way to lodge them adequately. Only the immigrants from third world countries accept being confined to small apartments when they have more than two children.

Our natural affinities and common concerns led to a good friendship with the Carbets, who were practicing Catholics. Unfortunately, they didn't know the Bible well, but only the liberal theories that attacked its authority! We had a mutual friend in the person of the official Catholic campus chaplain, "Père" Xavier Maurier, a young intellectual mystic who occasionally could be found at a Catholic *aumônerie,* a sort of a Catholic student center near the campus and which served as a hang-out for the handful of more committed Catholic students in the area. I'd drop in from time to time to talk theology with Xavier. In fact, he didn't' appreciate the presence of evangelicals on campus, as he saw us as sectarian, preaching the necessity to be "born again" as a condition for salvation. This clearly made him uncomfortable. It was obvious from my discussions with him that his respect for the authority of the Bible had been sapped by liberal theories.

I tried to explain to Xavier the necessity of holding to a high view of Scripture in order to preach the gospel. The Bible was our only reliable source of communication with a transcendent God: dismiss its claims, and you logically forfeit any knowledge of God at all. He wasn't convinced.

So I told him, "Xavier, though the sign on your door indicates that you're a priest, the fact is that you're really a magician. You claim to be able to share the message of salvation with people—a message found in, and transmitted through a book for which you have apparently little respect. The Bible is the bridge across the gap that separates mortal man from the transcendent God. By undermining its authority, you've torn down the bridge in your mind, yet you still think you can walk across the gap, as if the bridge were still there. That's magic!"

The Nurse and the dying neighbor

Beyond the actual student ministry and opportunities we had to share the gospel with our neighbors, God opened other doors for us during our time in Villeurbanne where, for some unknown reason, I suffered from fairly frequent bouts of bronchitis and even pneumonia. As it turned out, this was caused by an allergy to milk products. Whenever I ate cheese and other dairy products, it would produce a lot of mucus in my lungs in which bacteria had ample opportunity to proliferate. However, before arriving at the correct diagnosis, I was put on heavy doses of antibiotics which were administered by injection from a nurse whose office was across the street from our apartment building.

Mme. Sonier was an affable, caring woman of about 45-50 who clearly enjoyed her work. Her husband was an engineer and they had no children, so she was delighted to have a job which allowed her to socialize with her clients. Her waiting room was often full as I would pop in for my brief visits to receive my antibiotic injections after each bout with bronchitis or pneumonia which I contracted three times in a space of six months.

Though Mme. Sonier's waiting room was often full, she told me that, when she deducted the rent of the office and utilities, she had actually lost money that year! Knowing the French Socialist tax structure, I'm not surprised. She explained:

"My husband said that he didn't care if I didn't earn a nickel as we don't need the money. However, I would prefer it if it didn't cost me to have you work!"

Her situation is not unique. In fact the French economy is so tax-heavy that it dissuades all kinds of private business initiative. The taxes are so excessive and human nature so corrupt that the "*fisc*" (slang for the French IRS) presupposes that the individual businessmen, artisans, and other self-employed, will hide a portion of their gross incomes. Understandably, defrauding the government out of excessive tax revenue has become something of the national sport in countries like France and Italy. In fact it may be the only way for many small businesses to survive. This presents all kinds of ethical problems for Christians in business in France.

My visits to the nurse's office were occasionally comic. After the traditional passage through the waiting-room, one would be admitted to the inner sanctum when the medical procedures would take place. Occasionally, I would be leaning over Mrs. Sonier's medical table with a needle sticking out of my butt, when one of her girl friends would just happen to drop in. Sociable that she was, Mme. Sonier would casually introduce me to her friend whose hand I would turn to shake, bent over the medical table with my drawers down!

In one conversation, I told her what I did professionally. She then told me about one of her patients, a young (37) man who lived in our building just a couple of floors below us and to whom she was administering regular morphine injections. He was dying of cancer, she said, and might appreciate a visit from someone who could tell him about God.

So I got the man's name (Jean-Jacques Levoisin) and got off the elevator on his floor where I rang the bell. A woman of about 55 answered the door. I introduced myself as an upstairs neighbor and student chaplain and asked if I might not speak to her son. She reluctantly admitted me and led me to the living room where her son lay in an adjustable hospital bed, furnished by French socialized medicine for his use during his illness.

My first impression was one of horror. It was clear by the gaunt, emaciated figure of the man that he didn't have much time left. In fact, he died three days after my visit. Consequently, I decided to go right to the essentials of the gospel, thinking I would probably not get another opportunity. I asked him if he'd like to hear a true story and proceeded to read the narrative of the resurrection of Lazarus in John chapter 11. When I reached Jesus' timeless words "I am the resurrection and the life," his mother called me aside.

"Don't talk to him about death," she pleaded. "He thinks he's getting better."

I returned to the bedside of Jean-Jacques, who looked as if he were struggling just to keep his eyes open. He hadn't said anything as I read through the Lazarus resurrection episode, probably from weakness. But now he rallied up his strength and told me, in no uncertain terms, to knock it off with my religious nonsense for he wasn't interested!

I was flabbergasted, convinced as I was that there were no atheists in foxholes or on deathbeds. Maybe I was wrong.

LYON/ Reformed Church, A Nursery, The birth of Anaïs'

When we first arrived in Lyon, we naturally sought out a Bible-believing church that we could join. There wasn't much choice, alas, not from our Calvinist perspective. The saying goes that the difference between Liverpool and Lyon is that Liverpool has three different kinds of cheese and three hundred churches whereas Lyon has three hundred kinds of cheeses and three churches.

The first step in our search involved a few telephone calls to the various Lyonnais pastors to see where— both theologically and geographically —we would best fit in. At one point we were visited by a pastor from the Reformed Church of France. Rev. Guy Mercier was an eloquent, articulate fellow, as well as the president of the council of Reformed churches in the area. Unfortunately, his church had no nursery to accommodate our small children. Worse still, he had no theology with which to accommodate anyone. It was clear after a brief discussion that he believed in neither the divinity nor the bodily resurrection of Jesus Christ. I told him as tactfully as I could that the apostle Paul—for whom the bodily resurrection of the Savior was central to the faith—would have nothing but scorn for the empty piety he preaches. If Christ is not risen (literally) then our faith is vain. Unfortunately, Rev. Mercier didn't see it that way.

We eventually joined a Reformed Church of France whose Alsatian pastor Jean-Daniel Bergmeister was a most charming fellow, even if his Barthian theology— affirming only that the Bible "contained" the Word of God—was less than rigorously evangelical.

The church itself was characterized by a general lack of vision that included the absence of a nursery for people with young children. That meant that our first year in Lyon, I attended worship alone or with the boys while Aline stayed home with Anais, whom she was breast-feeding. Eventually, I expressed my dismay to one of the older parishioners at the lack of a nursery.

"We don't need a nursery," she explained, "because we don't have any people with small children".

"And you won't have any people with small children," I insisted, "until you *have* a nursery!"

The elders were nevertheless gracious enough to lend us a room used for sewing by the ladies of the church. With a bit of tithing money we'd been saving, we altered the sewing room and made it into a nursery of sorts.

It wasn't long before word got out and a few other people with small children like ours began to attend worship. One parishioner even told us that he had attended worship as a young man, but had stayed away for some ten years when his children were born and were growing up—for want of a nursery!

As parents of three small children, Aline and I were often on duty, tending to the other children as well as our own. That was fine for a while, but we gradually discovered that we were spending far more time in the nursery than in worship. The few times we did get to attend worship, we were distraught by some things we heard from the pulpit. For instance, one Sunday near Christmas time, we came to the service with Luc Bouvier, the young INSA student to whom we'd been witnessing. That day, the pastor preached on Luke 2:2 where it speaks of the famous census taken by the Roman authorities, forcing Joseph to travel from Galilee to Bethlehem with his pregnant wife Mary. The text explains that the census was taken "when Quirinius was governor of Syria." The preacher denied the historicity of the passage inviting the congregation to consider its 'spiritual' truth.

Admittedly, this is a difficult text, as most secular records show that Quirinius ruled some nine years before. However, nothing excludes the possibility that Quirinius, like the American president Grover Cleveland, may have ruled at two different periods. That's just one of several possible solutions to this difficulty. In any case, I was distraught at being in a church where "my" students from the campus ministry might hear Rev. Bergmeister's neo-orthodox teaching. We were beginning to feel that it was time for us to be planting our own church.

When a colleague from our Presbyterian mission board visited us in Lyon with a proposal to join him in his church-planting vision in Marseille, we thought it time to be moving on. So after three years in Lyon and a year in the US (July 86-June 87), we headed down to the Marseille area for what was to be an almost ten-year stay.

CHAPTER 7

PLAN DE BOTTES (1987-94)

Plan de Bottes housing search:

One of the main practical problems any missionary to France confronts is that of housing. Before we'd left for our furlough in the States, Aline and I had driven down from Lyon to the Marseille area where we'd contacted a contractor who was building six small single family houses on a lot in the middle of the town of Plan de Bottes, our target area. As it turned out, there was one lot left in that development. After some calculation and negotiation, we were ready to sign for its purchase with the intention of having our home built while we'd be in the States on "home ministry assignment," presumably for a year.

Unfortunately that deal fell through because the owner of the land wanted 40% of what we'd agreed to pay "off the books" in order to avoid paying some hefty capital gains tax. We told the developer that we could not be a part of such overt fraud and that the owner would have to put the actual amount on the deed, or we wouldn't be buying it. At that point the developer explained that this was common practice, done to avoid paying the exorbitant taxes required by French law, and that we should not let our rigid American scruples keep us from buying our dream house. He emphasized that the other five owners had consented to this and that their homes were now under construction. What's more, we'd never be able to purchase a home in the Marseille area unless we agreed to this kind of deception.

We balked and drove back to Lyon disappointed, but knowing that we'd done the right thing. A couple of days later, we got a phone call from the CEO of the construction company who was building the houses and who told us that the problem was resolved: that he had purchased the land from the owner himself and that we could purchase the land from him at the official rate. When I asked him if he had paid part of the price to the owner 'under the table,' he admitted that he had, but that didn't matter as we would be paying the official rate. I told him that it mattered greatly for he had been part of a dishonest transaction in which we would be indirectly implicated if we agreed to go along with this. In other words, it was as if he was asking us to eat meat sacrificed to idols (I Corinthians 10:28). We couldn't do it without compromising our integrity. So we lost the deal on the house and returned to the US on furlough in 1986-87 not knowing where we'd be living upon our return. A year later, we were back in France, and looking for lodging once again.

I've already alluded to Socialist housing laws that undermine the self-correcting free-market principles. Purchase of a home was out of the question for several reasons. First, it was against our mission's team policy. Second, we couldn't have afforded one anyway. For in addition to the down-payment we didn't have, one needs an additional 18.6% for what the French call *frais de notaire* — a government tax on the purchase and sale of a house. People don't buy and sell houses in France the way they do in the States and rental are difficult to find.

Consequently, it was with little hope that I drove from Alès to Marseille in search of housing one hot July day in 1987, leaving Aline and the children at her family's home. A quick look at the real estate market in Plan de Bottes — an independent "commune" (town) of some 11,000 people sandwiched between Allauch and the Marseille's 13th "arrondissement" — was not promising. There were only three "villas" (single family houses) available for rent in the entire sector, and two of them were way out of our price range.

So it was with little hope that I arrived at the "Bd. du Vauban" address where I had an 11 AM appointment with M. Cohen, the real estate agent. I discovered a charming little villa on a large, somewhat unkempt property, bordering the "Canal du Midi" which snakes its way through the area.

I was instantly smitten, even though I'd yet to set foot in the house itself. When I did knock at the door, I was greeted by Mr. Cohen, a stocky, middle-aged Jewish man from Marseille who had arrived a bit earlier to turn on lights and open shutters to show the house to its best advantage.

I was already salivating at the idea of closing the deal on the rent of such a well situated property with a magnificent southeastern exposure and plenty of room for the children to play—notwithstanding the ominous presence of the canal which, I learned later, has claimed the life of more than one local, swept away by its swift, unforgiving current. However, we weren't the only ones looking for a place to rent. I'd no sooner arrived than two others prospective tenants—a young, well-dressed, professional looking couple, and a distinguished sexagenarian woman with a haughty demeanor—also turned up to inspect the villa. Obviously, M. Cohen was taking the greatest advantage of the law of supply and demand which was already well stacked in the landlord's favor. All I could think about, as we toured the villa which, like all French homes, was more beautiful than practical, was the confrontation that would surely arise at the end of the visit when all three perspective tenants would be vying for it. How would the landlord decide which tenant to accept? Did I even have a chance as a foreigner? Both prospective lessees were French, and apparently more financially qualified. What chance did I have? Humanly speaking, almost none.

Then—in the middle of the visit—I had an epiphany, a flash: an overwhelming sense of peace resulting from the ineffably delightful conviction whereby I simply *knew* that we'd found our house and the answer to our prayers of the past few weeks!

I'm by no means a mystic. Indeed, the Calvinist tradition, to which I subscribe, is skeptical of most so-called mystical experiences. However, while M. Cohen was giving us a tour and touting the merits of the house, a Bible verse popped into my head. It wasn't a verse that I had been reading on that day, nor at any time in the recent past. It was one of those obscure passages in the book of

Deuteronomy from Moses' discourse to the Hebrews before they entered the Promised Land. In chapter 9 we read how Moses reminded the Jews that their impending possession of the promised land of Israel was not merited, but a gift of God's pure grace. The text reads: *"After the Lord has driven them [Canaanites] out before you, do not say to yourself: 'The Lord had brought me here to take possession of this land because of my righteousness.' No, it is on account of the wickedness of these nations that the Lord is going to drive them out before you"* (Deuteronomy 9:4).

Likewise, I was convinced, against all reason, that the Lord was going to answer our prayerful request for adequate housing by chasing these two "Canaanite" competitors away.

Consequently, I was perfectly serene at the end of M. Cohen's tour of the house when the dignified elderly woman told the agent: "Il n'y a pas de problème, M. Cohen, je la prend" (No problem M Cohen, I'll take it") completely ignoring the presence of the other two parties, while explaining self-assuredly that her physician husband would call him to close the deal that evening as soon as he came home from work. She then walked confidently out the door. What nerve! I thought. Who does she think she is?

My reaction was obviously shared by the young couple who, after the older lady's departure, explained more humbly, but with equal conviction, that they too were interested in renting the house. M. Cohen, a shrewd businessman, simply handed them one of his business cards with instructions to call him at his office in the afternoon. The couple looked at him hopefully and departed.

I was left alone with M. Cohen who was closing the shutters he'd opened before the visit. I told him that I too was interested in renting the coveted villa. I was seriously wondering how he'd react to my request as the youngest—and easily the worst-dressed—of the prospective tenants. Naturally, he asked me about my profession, a legitimate question for one wanting to know if I would have the means to pay the monthly rent (4000F = ca.$800).

I explained that my "boss" (God) would be providing through the brethren of the Presbyterian Church in America. We chatted on and eventually began discussing theology. Two hours later, I found myself in M. Cohen's office in downtown Marseille, signing the three-year lease.

As it turned out, M. Cohen was a God-fearing Jew, with a better-than-average knowledge of the Old Testament Scriptures. He had, in Hebrew script, the Ten Commandments, under the glass desk-top in his office. I ventured to tell him about my existential 'illumination' of that morning when the aforementioned verse from Deuteronomy had popped into my head. He was amused but kept mum about what had prompted him to choose us over the others. Whatever the human reasons for his choice, we knew that the Lord had work for us to do in Plan de Bottes and was thus confirming it to us, providing us with good lodging where we could invite our children's friends and their parents.

Aline and the children were pleased when I phoned and told them the Lord had provided us with a magnificent place. I was thinking, of course, about the house's location, surrounded by a big field which offered all kinds of room for the boys to run around. Aline was more interested in the house itself which I couldn't adequately describe. How many bedrooms did it have? What was the lay-out? How about closets: were there any? French houses don't always have closets. I couldn't answer any of these questions. I hadn't paid attention to these details. I did tell my wife that the house had a nice balcony with a view facing east towards the morning sun. I'm not very observant.

Sobering phone call

A few weeks later (in early September, 1987) , we were in Plan de Cuques, still unpacking our things when we received a phone call from some dear friends in the States whose daughter used to ride to school with our son Calix during the year we were in Greenville, S.C. It was the kind of call one dreads receiving. Merlin M. told me that their seven-year-old daughter Anna had taken ill and died quite suddenly from some rare form of leukemia.

Although shocked by the news, I was amazed at the serenity in Merlin's voice as he described how Anna had gone to bed that fateful night and how Robin, Merlin's wife, had prayed with their daughter before turning off the light and leaving the room.

Uncharacteristically, Anna had called her mother back and asked her to "thank Jesus because He's here with me." Though Robin had found this request a bit unusual, she nonetheless complied, praying: "Thank you Jesus because you're here with Anna." Then Robin left the room and Anna went to sleep.

In the middle of the night, Anna woke up, began spitting-up blood, and went into a coma. She died the next day in the local hospital from some rare form of leukemia which kills with lightening speed.

While losing a child is as painful a trial as one can face, Merlin and Robin found reassurance in knowing that the Lord had given their daughter an ineffable sense of His presence in the hours before He took her home. For never before had Anna sensed nor insisted with such conviction that Jesus was there with her.

Equally amazing to me was the tone of Merlin's voice as he related the events. Though not one given to crying easily, I couldn't hold back the tears upon hearing this. Merlin, on the other hand, related the events with a calmness and serenity that one can only describe as supernatural. It's amazing the way the Lord gives grace to his children in their time of greatest need. Meanwhile, Robin and Merlin have since given birth to a Down's syndrome child named Daniel. The supernatural love and serenity they've displayed in the midst of these trials has been a great testimony to many people. While not quite able to walk on water, Merlin and Robin, like others who have suffered greatly, have learned some deep truths about the mysteries of suffering through which many have been edified.

Gardening in *Provence*

After settling in our new digs, I decided to take advantage of the temperate climate of *Provence* to do some gardening. I was thrilled at the idea that I could be tilling the soil in February while my dad back home in New England was still waiting for the snow to melt. I wrote home and asked for a few packages of *Burpee's* sweet corn, determined that I would introduce my neighbors to the delights of corn on the cob—virtually unknown in France. I rented a tiller and plowed about 200 square yards in the back yard and planted about a dozen rows of Burpee's "golden bantam." It wasn't long before, under the warm *provençal* sun, the seeds began to sprout. The plants were no more than a few inches high when one of our neighbors, Michel Uderzo, a fisherman of Italian origin and himself an amateur gardener, asked me what I was growing.

"Du maïs" (corn), I announced proudly.

"Pourquoi?" he asked. "Vous n'avez pas de poules à nourir" (Why? You haven't any chickens to feed).

No, I told him. This was eating corn, for people.

He looked at me amazed. No one eats corn in France. It's feed for cattle and chickens. Although I tried to explain that it was a type of corn that was meant for human consumption, he remained skeptical. Crazy American, he must have thought.

"Il faudra bien attacher les plantes pour qu'elles resistent au mistral" (You'll have to tie the plants well so they'll withstand the effects of the north wind"), he warned. Although I was skeptical, it didn't take me long to get the message. The plants were only a few inches high when we were battered by the ferocious north wind, which blows down the Rhone valley for days on end with gusts of over fifty miles per hour. When the mistral blows, anything that's not nailed down gets blow away, and glaziers do a booming business replacing broken window panes resulting from slamming French doors.

As it turned out, M. Uderzo was right. My corn was decimated by the *mistral*, which blew away fully half the plants. Those that survived suffered from the drying effects of the wind. To satisfy the corn's great need for water, I had the garden hose running almost continuously. With water at over ten francs per cubic meter in parched *Provence,* it didn't take much math to calculate that each ear would end up costing me a small fortune. People have killed for water in the South of France, as anyone familiar with the great Marcel Pagnol novels ("Jean de Florette" and "Manon des Sources") can tell you. Worse yet was the fact that the clay soil of *Provence,* baked under the hot sun, soon became as hardened as the bricks for which it is used. Iowa need never fear competition from *Provence* as the Corn Belt. I learned the hard way.

In despair, I went to see my other neighbor—M Razanno, a seventy-year-old amateur gardener from Sicily—to ask him what my soil was good for. He scooped up a fist full and began sifting it in the palm of his hands.

He then pointed to the roof of the house. "You can make excellent roof tiles with this clay," he said matter-of-factly.

"Roof tiles!" I exclaimed. "Is that all it's good for?"

"No", he shrugged. "You could also make '*santons*' with it," referring to the clay statue figurines for which *Provence* is famous.

I was discouraged but stubborn. I made a couple more attempts at growing peas and tomatoes with middling success before abandoning any hope of growing my own vegetables. If the Lord was going to feed us, He was going to have to do it some other way than through my feeble attempts at husbandry. Meanwhile, there were other fields to harvest.

Invitation to an apéritif

Many of the homes in Plan de Botte had been built by Italian immigrants from Marseille who had vegetable garden plots outside the city limits on which they had constructed small weekend getaways that they gradually turned into permanent homes.

When we first arrived in our town we were determined to do everything possible to acquaint ourselves with our neighbors. We decided it would be a good idea to invite them for an *apéritif*—a late afternoon drink served with chips and *Amuse-gueule* snacks (literally, "playthings for one's beak"). Such a thing is not normally done in France. One invites his friends to "*faire la cremallière*," i.e., inaugurate new lodgings with a party. But one does not invite strangers into his home. It can take years before a Frenchmen feels comfortable enough to invite you into his home.

We made up a friendly-looking cartoon drawing of the family, explaining we were new in the area and would love to make their acquaintance. I walked around the neighborhood with our four-year-old daughter and literally stuffed our friendly looking homemade invitations into about forty mailboxes. French mailboxes are often too small to hold all the junk mail one receives and often the postmen literally have to crumble it up to stuff it in. We were hoping that our invitations would serve as an evangelical ice-breaker, that some might wonder what brought this American to the south of France. This could be a natural stepping stone to presenting the gospel.

How many people did we expect? We had no idea, but were convinced that some would come if only out of curiosity. On the scheduled day, we got everything ready and waited, and waited, and waited... Finally, our next door neighbor, Mr. Razanno and his wife, dropped-in. They were the only ones to accept our invitation. Our idea had failed miserably, so it seemed.

At first we were discouraged by the lack of response. But even several years later, when we would occasionally speak to neighbors, they would remember the invitation to which they had dared not respond—because one doesn't enter the home of a stranger in France.

Attacked by "VICKS"

Our immediate neighbors in Plan de Bottes, Pierre and Chantal Ferrat—both pharmacists—moved in about a year after we arrived. They bought the small house next to ours, which had been for sale at what we considered an astronomical price. As pharmacists, they could afford it. Physicians can be poor in France. But in a country which consumes the greatest amount of pharmaceuticals per capita of any—mostly reimbursed by the government—pharmacist is a most lucrative profession. French physicians traditionally prescribe numerous pharmaceuticals for any reason. Visit the doctor for a cold, and you leave with a list of things to pick up at the pharmacy, including antibiotics, cough suppressants, expectorants, and a host of other products of doubtful necessity or effectiveness.

Why such a plethora of medicines, I asked our family physician, Dr. Lenzini?

"Tradition," he told me. "The French believe that the doctor hasn't really done his job properly unless he's prescribed a number of remedies to treat ones symptoms."

Ironically, even a small French bathroom typically has a giant medicine cabinet stocked with all kinds of pharmaceuticals. Because the state pays for the medicine, the French have no economic reason to refrain from purchasing them. This, of course, suited the likes of our pharmacist neighbors, the Ferrats.

As soon as they moved in, they had the large fence surrounding their property covered with a tarpaulin to hide the yard from outside. Behind that fence lived their ferocious German shepherd named "Vicks" who barked incessantly at any irregular noise. He was a huge, mean looking animal who would clearly have devoured anyone foolish enough to penetrate or even approach the gate. Every morning at around 11:30, we could hear his aggressive barking at the mailman who had to approach the gate next to which the mailbox was placed.

Mr. Razanno, whose home bordered the Ferrat property on the other side, bore a scar on his arm from the time Vicks leaped up the fence between their properties and chomped on his arm as he was trimming the bushes abutting their properties. Likewise, his son-in-law Serge Siliviano, a Marseille taxi driver and occasional *pétanque* partner, was once forced to take refuge by standing on the roof of his cab when pursued by Vicks, who had managed to escape.

We lived in subconscious fear of what would happen to our children if the beast ever escaped the confines of their yard, or what would happen should they ever be invited to "fortress Ferrat" to play with their daughter Aurélie, who was the same age as our second son and who was often at our house. "Fortunately" the Ferrats were not hospitable and never returned our repeated invitations to get together socially, nor ever invited our children. In other words, they were about as friendly as their dog.

One day, our worst fears came true. I had gone jogging with our eight year old son Justin, who followed me on his bicycle. As we turned the corner onto our street, I could see that Vicks had somehow escaped from his yard and was standing in front of the gate of the Ferrat residence where we had to pass to get home. As soon as he saw me running, he took off in my direction and attacked, clamping his snout onto my posterior, ripping my jogging suit, and drawing blood. I hit the ground face first, covered my head and wiggled around while the dog continued to bite me. Meanwhile, Justin heeded my warning and pedaled away in the opposite direction.

After Vicks withdrew from me, I ran into the house, my butt bleeding (I still have a scar) and my adrenaline pumping profusely. I grabbed a baseball bat and ran back out the door towards the Ferrat's gate where Vicks sat waiting to be let in. I was grateful that the dog had gone after me and not my son. I was also grateful that I hadn't been bitten in another more sensitive part of my anatomy. But I was still furious and seriously contemplated beating the dog to death with the bat lest he finally kill someone.

As I stood there ten meters away from the growling beast, I wondered if I could successfully inflict a lethal blow to him before he was able to bite me. Frankly, I wasn't sure. Then I also wondered how it would look for the local pastor to be savagely pummeling one of God's four-legged creatures with a baseball bat. It probably wouldn't have helped our testimony in the neighborhood. I hesitated long enough for my adrenaline production to slow down and reluctantly went back in the house.

Naturally, I reported the incident to the Ferrats when they arrived home. Their cold-hearted indifference was distressing. They insisted that by running, I had provoked the dog, and that the whole incident was therefore my fault! Mrs. Ferrat even snickered when I told them about my bloody posterior.

Most Americans would wonder why we didn't file a suit against the Ferrats and force them to do something about their menacing beast. But French law does not work the same way as ours. People don't easily sue each other in France. Their legal system simply doesn't encourage the proliferation of suits as in the U.S. Moreover, French courts don't normally award punitive damages significant enough to cover the costs and aggravation that a suit entails, much less the obscene amounts occasionally awarded to plaintiffs in the States.

A case in point: a Marseille high school teacher sued an angry parent who had punched him in the nose over a dispute about his son's academic performance. The local newspaper, "Le Méridional," carried a big headline when the teacher was awarded what the press deemed the "astronomical" sum of 5000F (about $800 at the time) for the incident. $800 for a broken nose? That might have netted one $8. million in the U.S! It's hardly worth all that trouble for $800. Consequently, the French rarely sue.

As for Vicks, I actually flirted with idea of giving him some poisoned meat. That advice was given me by a friend who had occasionally been attacked by dogs as he jogged through residential areas. I might even buy the poison at some local pharmacy—sweet irony. The Ferrats would of course be suspicious of the cause of the illness or death of their guard dog. And then we might have a law suit on our hands. So we never did anything save pray that the Lord would protect us from the beast next door.

Au Bar des Roubauds

In the continued effort to get acquainted with neighbors, I started visiting a local café called "Bar des Roubauds" just down the street from us, stopping in after lunch for an espresso. Plan de Bottes was not like most French towns which boast, on the average, one café for every thousand residents. Typically, in a town of 10,000 people like Plan de Bottes, one should expect to find at least a dozen cafés. Not so with Plan de Bottes, whose former mayor considered cafés to be breeding grounds for drunkards and wastrels—his pretext for having most of them closed down. The only one left was a *café-tabac-PMU* (where coffee and tobacco products are sold and horse-racing bets are placed) at the center of town opposite the church.

A mile up the road towards our house sat the tiny, uninviting, "Bar des Roubauds". This bar was run by Clementine, a sixty-year-old widow whose husband, I learned, had committed suicide the year before we arrived. Clementine herself feigned indifference to the gospel. I had occasion to speak with her privately but she invariably retreated behind her distant Roman Catholic heritage when confronted with the doctrines of grace. Tell her about Jesus being the "Way, the Truth, and the Life," and she's suddenly a devotee of the Virgin Mary!

It's not an unusual reaction, as I've seen it numerous times. Talk about the gospel to Catholics who haven't set foot in a church in years, and they are suddenly Catholic.

I would drop in on Clementine from time to time in an effort to fraternize a bit with the motley group of people who frequented her establishment. For a while I began to hang out there at night, sitting in the corner with a newspaper and an opened Bible, seeking opportunities to share the Good News with some of the bar's denizens. These included less than academically serious high school students as well as young working people wanting a place to smoke cigarettes, listen to rock music, and socialize with members of the opposite sex, away from the surveillance of their parents.

One of the main attractions at the Bar des Roubauds, as at other bars, was a "baby-foot" (Americans, like Germans, call it *"fussball"*) or game-table-soccer at which some French youth develop an amazing mastery. One of the best players, a veritable virtuoso of "baby foot," was a twenty year old auto-body worker named Olivier who could score a goal virtually every time he gained possession of the ball. With a prodigious display of dexterity, he could even do a number of trick shots, shooting the ball with a backwards flip from one of his defensemen. It never ceased to amaze me to see how skillful he had become at that game, which is serious business in French proletariat circles.

I made a couple of good friends at the bar: Emile, a retired baker who lived above the bar; and Victor, a crippled, retired cobbler who would drive his electric wheelchair from down the street to the bar at precisely 13h30 for an extra-sweet cup of espresso, which he would habitually wash down with a glass of red wine.

Both Emile and Victor died within a year of my arrival. I had the opportunity to speak to both of them about the gospel while they were in the local nursing home. Neither of them, however, made a clear profession of faith. Victor even went so far as to forbid me to pray for his recovery, as he insisted that he was ready to go. I clearly remember reading to him from the gospel according to John while I visited him in the hospital, only to have him interrupt me by saying that he "knew all that" and was ready to meet his Maker. I never knew what to make of that.

As for Emile, the only feedback for my efforts came from his daughter who, after his funeral, came to thank me personally for visiting him in the hospital in the days before he died.

Such is the work of an evangelist, in France or anywhere else. One shares the Word of eternal life without ever knowing whether or not the Word has penetrated the hearts of those who hear it. For many are spiritually blind and do not see what is evident to anyone enlightened by the Holy Spirit to his own sin and his need of a Savior.

The natural man does not receive the things of God as they are folly to Him (I Corinthians 2:14).

Joel's Martians

Speaking of folly, this is a logical place to share an unforgettable experience with a man who was a permanent fixture of Plan de Bottes. His name was Joel, and I don't think it uncharitable to say that he was considered to be the village simpleton. Joel could be seen hanging around the local café in the center of town, mooching cigarettes from the locals and striking up rambling conversations with anyone who would listen. Of North African origin, Joel's parents had, like many foreigners, given him a French name to facilitate his assimilation into French society. He was in his early 40's, well-groomed and often sported a cowboy hat—most unusual in France. He also wore an American university ring, though he couldn't tell me where he'd gotten it. Apparently, he lived in an apartment in "La Rose," a largely proletariat neighborhood of Marseille, a few bus stops south of Plan de Bottes. Why he spent his days loitering around the café at Plan de Bottes remains a mystery to me. It was clear from all accounts that the Plan de Bottes café owner, a M. Clamart, didn't appreciate Joel's presence. This was understandable as Joel, in spite of his proper, albeit eccentric attire, was without income, save for a modest government stipend. On more than one occasion I saw M. Clamart scold him for ordering drinks at the café when he couldn't pay for them. I once saw the local priest bailing him out, paying for the coffees he'd ordered for both himself and another patron. Likewise, when he came to speak to me, it was usually for a handout.

Our church sponsored a regular Christian literature table in the Plan de Cuques marketplace every Saturday morning. One had to get there early, as the "forrains" (ambulant merchants) arrived around 6AM and jockeyed for the limited number of places on which to display their wares. So after setting up our literature table, I would usually go across the street to the café and nurse a cup of espresso while waiting for the local shoppers to make their rounds.

This particular morning, as I sat there reading the Bible, Joel came by and asked if he could join me at my table. He was used to being rejected by most people, and was appreciative when I invited him to sit down. Though intellectually he wasn't "playing with a full deck," there was nonetheless a certain "method to his madness," as Polonius said about the raving Hamlet. He once asked me, out of the clear blue, if I thought there had ever been a bridge across the Bering Strait. The suddenness of his inquiry startled me, but I had to admit it wasn't a bad question for an "idiot."

I was aware of the limited scope of any conversation with Joel. One could hardly proceed with him logically from one point to another. Yet this time, as we sat there for over half an hour together in front of my opened Bible, he looked at me with the forlorn look of one ripe for the Word. So I began to explain the gospel to him, going ever so slowly, looking for signs of understanding on his part. He seemed to be following closely, not interrupting as he usually did, but rather absorbing every word. Could it be that the Spirit was working in his confused heart to open it to the good news of salvation? I was hopeful—as any evangelist— that I was going to have the privilege of ushering him into the Kingdom.

Then suddenly, he looked at me straight in the eye and, with a serious expression, asked if I would answer one question, one that had been bothering him. Naturally, I assumed it pertained to the faith. I looked at him expectantly and asked him what he wanted to know?

Looking both sincere and troubled at the same time he blurted out:

"Pastor, do you think that if Martians existed, they would eat mushrooms?"

I was flabbergasted. Had I really thought that I was going to have a sane discussion with Joel? What could be going through the mind of one who could ask such a question? It would take a miracle to really communicate with Joel. There are precedents of course. Still I wondered what it might be like on Joel's planet.

Chez Papé Robert

To break our routine, we made periodic trips to visit Aline's parents in Alès, which is about 100 miles west of Marseille—just the right distance to have between oneself and one's in-laws. It's not for nothing that God ordered man "to leave his mother and father" and cling to his wife (Genesis 1).

Conversely, if one lives too far from his in-laws, they might be frustrated at not being able to see their grandchildren often enough. Worse, when they did visit, they might have to stay overnight. One hundred miles is just about right.

While we worked in the Lyon area during the Campus Crusade years (1983-86) we would visit Aline's parents about every other month. On those drives down the French *Autoroute* (interstate highway) at 140 kmh (ca. 85 mph) I was always grateful for our "son's" car which carried us in comfort and relative security.

On one such visit, as we sat in the family kitchen sipping our morning coffee, Aline's Dad asked me to choose one of the fatter chickens from the chicken coop behind the family home in the hills overlooking Alès. He explained how he would be doing errands for the family restaurant and how it would therefore be my job that day to prepare the meat for the family meal.

The death of a chicken

I was raised more as a city boy than a country boy, so the idea of killing and cleaning a chicken was a difficult one to swallow at first. But one couldn't easily refuse any request from Aline's dad, a former boxing champ. And I'd seen him do it on several occasions so I knew what was involved.

The first step was to choose a chicken from the hundred or so fowl he kept in his chicken coop. Already that was more than I could handle, as I scarcely knew how to grab a chicken the right way, assuming there was a right way. So it was with considerable apprehension that morning, just after my father-in-law left for his errands, that I gulped down a glass of wine (though it was 9 AM) for a bit of artificial "courage," and climbed up the hill behind his house to the chicken coop. I'm sure I looked more than a little ridiculous chasing around the coop trying not to upset the birds, who were as nervous as I was.

When I finally did catch one of them, seizing it by the neck, I was so tense that I practically strangled it and the chicken passed out. I guessed I had killed it as it lay there motionless. Good, I thought, breathing a sigh of relief. This way I won't have to cut its throat and bleed it—a task I anticipated with even more dread.

But as I carried the bird down the hill to the kitchen where I was heating a kettle of water to scald it in preparation for plucking off its feathers, it occurred to me that my method of chicken-slaying might not be very kosher. I got to thinking about the Old Testament interdiction against eating animals "étouffés dans leur sang" (suffocated in their blood). I began to wonder if there might not be a legitimate reason for removing the animal's blood before eating it. Talk about the practical implications of theology.

I didn't know what to do with my comatose chicken. Should I slit its neck and bleed it or not? Would it make any difference? , I wasn't sure and didn't want to risk it. I had occasionally observed Aline's dad preparing a chicken by slitting its throat, then holding it upside down while the blood poured out. If it were that easy just to strangle the bird, then why go to all the trouble of bleeding it?

Not wanting to take a chance, I looked at the motionless fowl on the ground which was now beginning to show signs of life. My chicken wasn't dead after all, so now I had to do something. I picked it up and waited until the semi-conscious bird began to revive. When it looked as if it were ready to start running around, I grabbed the knife and, holding the struggling bird between my knees, seized it by the neck and slit its jugular vein. I then held it up-side down until all the blood dripped out and the struggling fowl finally gave up the ghost.

This may not sound like much of an exploit for any country folk reading this, but for a hopelessly squeamish city-slicker like me, it had to rank up there as one of the more difficult things I'd ever done.

The chicken finally dead, I took my 'victim' into the kitchen and put the body in the sink and poured a full kettle of boiling water over it, which helps considerably in removing the feathers. Then I grabbed a kitchen knife and performed surgery, removing the intestines and all other manner of foul-smelling innards. I still wasn't quite sure what to remove and what to leave in, so I followed the advice of a surgeon friend who told me: "When in doubt, cut it out."

By that time, the courage-inducing or fear-anesthetizing effects of the glass of wine had long since worn off and I was proceeding strictly on guts, both mine and the chicken's. The job over, I put the bird onto a large open pan and left it on the stove where Papé Robert, ever the master chef, would take care of the cooking.

LES OLIVES

My father-in-law's *mazet* or farmhouse was on a few acres of land on which were twenty olive trees. These produced somewhere between 80 and 400 kilos of olives each year, depending on the season. One year they would produce much, the next year there would be very little. The "cueillette" or harvesting of the olives was normally done around the Christmas holidays. That was one of my favorite annual activities. I liked to spend the afternoons meditating on my next Sunday's sermon while standing out in the sun picking olives. It wasn't the kind of work that most Frenchmen would bother doing for it's hardly a cost-effective use of time. "Un travail de moine" (a monk's work), Papé Robert called it scornfully. It would take us over an hour to pick the seven kilos of the tiny *patchouli* olives, which one would exchange at a nearby olive press for one liter of olive oil. One could buy a liter of oil on the open market for around 30 francs (or $6.00) at the time. That's why most Frenchmen don't pick olives, but buy them from other Mediterranean countries—especially Italy, Greece and Spain—where labor costs are lower and the olive production proportionately greater.

But for me it wasn't for money as much as the pleasure of working in the December sun with my head in the olive tree branches where the mind can wander. I came to consider every full branch of olives a reminder of the Lord's blessings. So who are we to ignore the Lord's blessings? Also, there's a great satisfaction in seeing the fruit of one's labor—a privilege not given to many evangelists in France—and enjoying the oil from ones own olives. Monk's work or not, I looked forward to these visits in Alès and the therapeutic escapism afforded me by the olive harvest.

JUNE 93 PETANQUE TOURNAMENT

Another favorite French activity concerns a game I've come to love which also happens to be the national pastime of millions of French. The name is "pétanque," which comes from a contraction of the *provençal* French "pieds tanqués" (literally "feet planted"), and distinguishes the game from another version (called "jeu provençal") which allows the players to take a few steps before throwing. What one tosses—underhanded, of course—is in fact a steel ball or "boule" about the size of a baseball but weighing anywhere between 600 and 800 grams (1.3 to 1.7 lbs. for you metrically challenged).

The game was invented in the south of France in the early part of the 20th century in a town called La Ciotat, about twenty kilometers east of Marseille. *Pétanque*, the feet-planted variety of the game, was supposedly invented for the sake of a crippled fellow who liked to play but obviously couldn't run.

Pétanque is much the same as Italian *bocce* save that the distances are shorter and the terrain surface is not necessarily smooth. In fact, one can play on any dirt surface (not grass or pavement) with either two, four or six players for a match.

One traces a circle of approximately 50 centimeters (ca. 18"), in which one stands. He then tosses a small lead ball or jack called a "bouchon" or "cochonet" (little pig) six to ten meters away. The first player, standing in the small circle, then attempts to get one of his "boules" as close as he can to the "*bouchon*." The second team's first player then attempts to toss one in even closer, for it's the ball closest to the "bouchon" which scores the point. The second team plays until they can get a ball in closer to the "bouchon" than any of the adversaries' "boules."

Often the opponent's "boule" is simply too close to the *bouchon* to be beaten in the part of the game that's called "pointing." That's where the "tireurs" ("shooters") come in—the players whose job it is to shoot (on the fly, preferably) the adversaries' *boule* out of the way. Shooting a pétanque ball from ten meters away is a real art. However for experienced players, it can be almost as routine as shooting a free throw for an NBA sharpshooter where the success rate of over eighty percent is not extraordinary. The more rough terrains favor the shooters (vs. the pointers) as it becomes difficult to approach the *bouchon* on a bumpy surface and virtually impossible to roll one's *boule* into the adversaries. That's why the hot-shot *pétanque* players prefer rough, irregular terrains.

My first exposure to the game was in 1974 while I was in Paris and used to watch the retired folks playing *pétanque* on the big open unpaved surface near the *Hotel des Invalides*. Even then I could tell from the accents and dramatic gesticulations of the participants, typical of the south of France, that this was principally a southern game. In fact, the first time I ever played *pétanque* was at my brother-in-law's wedding in 1979 near Avignon. At that time, we'd played in a bumpy parking lot and I'd been impressed to see how adroit my father-in-law was at reading the terrain, like a golfer reading the putting green to determine the trajectory of the ball. But I didn't start playing regularly until we moved to Marseille in 1987 where I discovered that playing *pétanque* afforded me a great opportunity for social contact with locals. It was almost like being a soccer or bicycle racing fan in that it permitted one access to a whole segment of the population for whom interest in these activities was significant. I only started getting serious about the game when we moved to Plan de Bottes and my old buddy and I (Jean-Pierre Tran, son of a Vietnamese communist), began to play fairly regularly on Saturday afternoons.

The first real test of my *pétanque* proficiency came in June, 1993, when Jean-Pierre and I entered a local tournament in town. It was a Saturday afternoon affair with several dozen locals gathered behind the café where there was a large dirt parking lot which would serve as the *pétanque* terrain. The tournament was organized by the local *pétanque* club (every town in France has at least one) but open to anyone willing to plunk down the ten-franc entrance fee. First prize would be about 300 francs for the winning team or 150 francs (about $30 at the time) per player. But no one really entered the tournament for the money. It was more for the glory of winning at a game at which many excelled. This particular tournament was organized "*à la mélée,*" which means the names of the participants were thrown into a hat and paired at random. That meant that I probably wouldn't be playing with my buddy Jean-Pierre. That was too bad, as I always played better with him as a partner. This barely educated brother (he came to the faith though our ministry) was a real "son of encouragement" and knew how to instill confidence in his partner. Confidence is indispensable in *pétanque*, especially for shooting. The psychological element is imperative. The fact is if you think you're going to hit your opponent's ball, then you probably will. Likewise, if you lack confidence, the results can be catastrophic. Without comparing oneself to the elite shooters who rarely miss, a decent shooter must hit at least two thirds of his shots to be successful in tournament play.

Because this tournament was "*à la mêlée,*" one could as easily be paired up with a skillful partner as with a hacker who thinks he's skillful. I had prayed at home before going to the tournament that somehow the Lord would afford me an opportunity to share the Word with some locals as "one of the guys" who happens to have faith in Jesus Christ.

I was hardly expecting to win the tournament, in which there were some 24 teams competing in a one game elimination. In other words, after the teams were chosen, and the adversaries paired off, one played until he lost. Lose and go home.

I wasn't optimistic either as we warmed up a bit before the actual tournament started, for I noticed some terrific shooters hitting perfect shots (called "*carreaux*") from as far as ten meters away. One gentleman in particular whose name I never learned really stood out.

In the draw, I was paired-up with a sullen, chain-smoking grouch named Curbello, who had something of a reputation amongst the local *bistot* crowd. It was obvious that he wasn't pleased to have been linked up with me in the draw. What could this foreigner possibly know about playing *pétanque,* he must have thought. He was right,

Our first game would be against the "*tireur d'élite*" (sharpshooter) who'd so impressed me while we were warming up. I assumed we were going to get clobbered: probably be skunked 13-0 and forced to "*baiser fanny*" (literally kiss fanny) in local jargon. Incidentally, that expression comes from *pétanque* lore, apparently from the town where the game was invented. The consolation prize for being skunked 13-0 was that you slept with "Fanny"—the attractive waitress of the bar where *pétanque* was invented and on whose terrain the game was first played. That bit of folklore is revealing.

We did not "*baiser fanny,*" Au contraire, my grouchy partner, a left-hander, was a better than average shooter. As for me, the exceptionally heavy *boules* I was using for the match were perfect for the sort of terrain we were playing on. Still the biggest surprise was the counter-performance of our erstwhile sharp shooting adversary who, for some strange reason, wasn't nearly as accurate as he'd been while warming up. So we won the game 13-7 and were on to the second round. So far so good.

It continued going well for M. Curbello and myself through the second, third, fourth and fifth games against some progressively serious adversaries, until we found ourselves heading for the final. Throughout it all, I was having a grand time but my partner, ever sullen and grumbling, never cracked a smile. Mr. Curbello was practicing what I later discovered to be standard *pétanque* etiquette which, when played by connoisseurs in tournaments, was a very serious affair with few spoken words, almost like chess. It's a kind of psychological warfare; one should never say or do anything, save play ones *boules*, stand still, and offer an occasionally disparaging remark in an effort to discourage one's adversaries. It took me a while to learn that; I was having too much fun.

When we won the final game handily 15-7 (the final game is always to 15 points), we were presented with the trophies and prize money. While we were having our photos taken, someone in the small crowd suggested that we all head back to the café to celebrate the occasion. It sounded good to me. Meanwhile, the grumpy Curbello slipped away and I found myself the center of attention at the café where some 20-25 individuals had come to talk about the tournament, all hoping that the winners would buy a round for everyone. So that's what I did. It came to 135 francs, but it might have been one of the best investments for the Kingdom that I'd ever made. As host of the occasion, I had an opportunity to speak to many folks who would never darken the door of a church. What could I tell them?

I had my cue when one suggested that Curbello and I had been more than a lucky to win all seven games. I didn't disagree, of course, but I reminded them that ultimately there was no such thing as "luck," and that the Sovereign God who controls the trajectory of the stars in the skies might surely intervene on occasion to correct, with a providentially placed pebble, the trajectory of a *boule* as it rolled along the ground—especially if it suited His purpose. And His purpose that day might well have been to let me win the tournament so that some folks in Plan de Botte could hear the message of salvation in Jesus Christ.

I can't say that my brief sermon that late Saturday afternoon in June 1993 in the south of France produced much fruit, as I don't recall ever seeing any of the gentlemen from the café present at our worship services. Still, the Seed was sown. And I went home joyful, albeit only five francs richer than I had come, after subtracting the ten franc entrance fee and the 135 francs for the round of drinks from my 150 franc winnings.

The victory had afforded me entrance into a new confraternity of local *pétanque* aficionados, where it was now easy to be invited to play with the serious players.

With Bubba Furman vs. the Marseille masters

I became a dedicated *pétanque* fan from that time on and spent many a Saturday afternoon with my old buddy Jean-Pierre Tran and whoever came by the courtyard of the church under the plane (*platanis vulgaris*) trees which are ubiquitous in France and provide cool shade from the hot *provençal* sun. When we moved to the southern part of Marseille with the prospect of planting a new church there, I found myself looking for a place where there were regular *pétanque* games. That wasn't difficult in Marseille, the *pétanque* capital of the world. In every park where there was a flat piece of land, one could hear on any given afternoon the unmistakable sound of *boules* clanging together, an acoustical identification of France in the same way as the crack of a bat (in the days before aluminum bats) could be heard in most American towns in the spring and summer.

One place where there were regular games was at the Place Carli where the Marseille conservatory was and where Aline and I brought our children for their music lessons every week. On one occasion, I was escorting a visiting American guest around Marseille when we went past the park at the Place Carli and stopped to watch some men playing *boules*. Our guest, Bubba Furman, was a thirty-year-old country boy from the tobacco fields of eastern North Carolina who had won a trip to France as a representative of the Kiwanas or Rotary Club (I forget which) and who had looked us up in Marseille. Prior to that, he'd never even been to Atlanta, let alone overseas.

His rural simplicity was striking as together we strolled down the "Canebière," Marseille's main artery. "Golly, look at all the cars!" he exclaimed with disarming, Gomer Pyle naïveté that one imagined had disappeared from the earth.

Brother Bubba was obviously intrigued by the French national game, so the next day, I took two sets (six *boules*) of *pétanque* balls with us and went down to the park near the Place Carli where some men play regularly. After a bit of preliminary explanation and practice, my friend Bubba and I were ready for a game. Playing one on one against a novice player wasn't all that appealing to me, so I asked a couple of the local hot shots if they wouldn't mind accommodating us for a game. I explained that, until that day, my guest had never even seen a *pétanque* ball before, let alone thrown one. Consequently, we were no threat to beat anyone and just wanted to have fun initiating my American visitor to the sport.

So just to amuse themselves, a couple of regulars decided to take us on, thinking, no doubt, that the game would be over in a flash. Much to everyone's surprise, my friend Bubba turned out to be an amazingly adroit player, perfectly able to transpose his well-honed skills as a softball pitcher to the *pétanque* terrain. Our opponents watched incredulously as Bubba placed virtually every one of his *boules* right on the *bouchon*, forcing the other team's shooter to raise his game to new levels so as not to be overwhelmed. It was prodigious!

Not only that. As the shooter for our team, I hit more of my shots than I normally would. So the game finished with Bubba and I handing two experienced Marseille players a 13-12 defeat! It felt almost like the U.S. hockey team's defeat of a clearly superior Soviet adversary at the 1980 winter Olympics. It was almost as sweet as Greg Lemond's victory in the 1989 Tour de France—another story worth re-telling.

The 1989 Tour de France;never say never

For millions of fans around the world, the Tour de France bicycle race (held in July) is the sporting highlight of the year. Before the well-publicized heroics of Lance Armstrong, another American rider, Greg Lemond, won the tour on three separate occasions, including the 1989 Tour in what was arguably the one of the greatest athletic triumphs of the century.

For those not familiar with the famous Tour de France bicycle race, a word of introduction is in order. Participants endure for three weeks hundred mile climbs up the steepest mountain roads in the Alps and Pyrenees, and downhill chases at up to 65mph, followed by 150 mile stretches through the sun-drenched plains. Only the fittest of athletes can even attempt it. Only a handful of the 180-190 cyclists who do participate (usually eighteen or nineteen teams of ten riders) have a remote dream of winning. Most simply hope to win a single one of the twenty legs, perhaps finish the race, and facilitate the efforts of their team's lead rider.

Tour de France champions are a different breed from the average rider. Consider the case of five-time winner, Spaniard Miguel Indurain, a soft-spoken superman whose seven-liter lung capacity (twice that of an average man), exceptionally slow heart beat (ca. 30 pulses/minute at rest), and steel thighs earned him the nickname "the Extra-Terrestrial." Likewise, American seven-time champ Lance Armstrong was blessed with exceptional natural physiological capacities, including a larger than average heart. These guys are well-trained thoroughbreds.

Greg Lemond, a young cycling talent from Nevada, won the tour de France for the first time in 1986, riding on the same team with the great French champion Bernard Hinault. In fact, Hinault won the last of his five Tour de France victories in 1985 only because his teammate Lemond, who was obviously more fit that year, basically let him win.

But in 1986 it was Lemond's turn to win the Super Bowl of cycling. Then, his career and his life were almost snuffed out in a hunting accident in the winter of 1986-87.

Lemond returned to cycling in the spring of 1989 but no one thought he had a chance of getting back to his old form. For one thing, he still had a lot of buckshot in his body from the near-fatal shotgun blast. Only the prestige of his '86 victory afforded him entrance in the race. Unfortunately he was accompanied by a mediocre team whose members would mostly abandon him during the course of the race.

In the summer of 1989, the man to beat was the Parisian Laurent Fignon, two-time winner of the "Tour" (1983+1984), fresh from his victory in the almost as prestigious "Giro" (Tour of Italy) in May. No one considered Lemond a serious contender as he'd simply been away from that level of competition for too long.

As the race went along, Lemond managed to stay close to the leader Fignon—so close, in fact, that Fignon complained he was fed up with hearing Lemond breathing down his neck every day. But Lemond had no choice as he had no teammates left to ride in front of him so he could ride in their slipstream (That's what teammates are for in cycle-racing. The lesser riders basically escort their team leaders to the foot of the mountains, conserving the leader's energy, whereupon the more rested leader charges up the mountain where races are either lost or won).

In 1989 the "Tour" was run counterclockwise around France with the Alps at the end and an unprecedented time-trial race into Paris. As the racers struggled through the last determining days in the Alps before the long flat stretch into Paris, it became clear that Fignon was the superior rider that year. For on the last mountain leg in the Alps, he had managed to pull away from his major adversaries, including Lemond, and the Spanish rider (and 1988 winner) Pedro Delgado, pulling ahead of them even as he raced by himself with no one assisting against the wind. It was a formidable effort.

Like millions of others in France and around the world, I followed the race religiously and watched the highlights (if not the actual race) every day on national television. At that time, we were staying with Aline's parents in Alès along with her Parisian cousin Dominique. It was a vacation period during which I basically read and did some gardening. On the weekend, I had to drive in to Marseille to preach for our tiny congregation on Sunday morning. Though many churches in France close their doors for the summer, we thought it better to maintain the regular worship service for even a few faithful. It's not as if God goes away on holiday!

In Alès, Dominique and I would watch the daily television coverage of the race together, with him rooting for his fellow Parisian Fignon, while my allegiance was with Lemond. For three weeks it wasn't clear which of the two was the stronger that year. But when they reached the Alps towards the end of the race, I was forced to concede—much to the glee of Dominique—that Fignon was the "le plus fort" (the stronger). He'd built up a virtually insurmountable lead in the Alps before the last stage into Paris, which now looked to all like a mere formality. Fignon was a full fifty seconds ahead of the second place Lemond, with only a 24 kilometer time-trial left. It was mathematically most improbable, if not impossible, that Lemond or anyone could make up fifty seconds on such a relatively short run. By way of comparison, a previous time trial of 75 kilometers had produced only an eight second difference between Lemond and Fignon. Theoretically, over 24 kms the best Lemond could expect was to arrive a few seconds faster than Fignon. Even then, Fignon, as the first place rider, would have the advantage of leaving last, and knowing how fast Lemond had ridden, he could pace himself accordingly. Fignon was clearly in the driver's seat on that last day of the race.

With almost a minute to make up, Lemond was the second to last rider to leave the starting-gate that Sunday afternoon for the relatively short sprint into Paris. Short of breaking a leg, the race was virtually won for Fignon. Before the time trial even began, he was accepting congratulations from the other riders and even shook Lemond's hand congratulating him for his second place finish! In football terms, it was as if Fignon were ahead by four touchdowns at the two-minute warning.

Likewise, the French press was already congratulating the Parisian hero for his performance which, following his victory in Italy, was a second major triumph for French cycle racing. The French sportswriters were proud of their national hero, who would be the first French winner of the "Tour" since Bernard Hinault's last victory in 1985.

I left Alès for Marseille early that morning—about a two-hour drive—for the worship service where I preached for the few faithful who weren't on vacation. After the service, I turned around and drove back. When I got back to Alès at around 14h30, the in-laws were still at the dinner table savoring lunch. I sat down to eat and then announced that I was going to lie down for a nap as we'd be driving back to Marseille that evening.

"Aren't you going to watch the final stage of the Tour," Aline's cousin Dominique asked teasingly?

"The race is over," I conceded. "Fignon is the strongest," I reiterated as Dominique gloated.

"After you come down from your nap, we'll go play some *pétanque* if you like," suggested Dominique.

"That way, when I beat you, it will be *double* humiliation day for the Americans," he laughed.

Tired and sleepy from the food and wine and the summer heat, I headed up the stairs to our bedroom to lie down for a nap with the radio softly playing in the background. Dominique settled down in front of the television in the living room determined to savor the victory of M. Fignon in Paris. There were 136 riders left from a field of some 190. At 14h30, some of the lesser riders were still going through the time trial while all of France waited impatiently for the last two, Greg Lemond, followed by Laurent Fignon.

I drifted off to dreamland with the radio on next to me. About an hour later, I awoke and was in a semi-conscious state when I heard the announcer say something about an exploit of Greg Lemond. Was I dreaming? Surely he couldn't have won the Tour. I thought. Did Fignon fall and break a leg?

I hurried down the stairs and saw Dominique sitting in front of the television, his mouth wide open, starring in disbelief at the screen as if he'd seen a ghost.

"Lemond a gagné" (Lemond won) he announced dumbfounded. I couldn't believe it myself, but it was true. Greg Lemond had indeed won the leg by sprinting at the incredible speed of 54kms/h (ca. 32mph) over the entire 25 kilometers (the fastest speed ever recorded in a Tour de France time trial), beating Fignon's time by 58 seconds and winning the Tour de France by eight seconds, the slimmest margin of victory in Tour history! The French journalists were in a veritable state of shock. Never had I seen so many normally loquacious commentators suddenly at a loss for words. Lemond has done something that no one, not even his biggest fans, thought could be done. It was truly an amazing victory!

"Ready for that *pétanque* game now?" I asked Dominique.

He was only too eager to get away from the television. We headed down the steep Maurin driveway to the flat area of the parking lot of the "Mine Témoin" (a coal mine display) where we usually played and where I proceeded to beat him three straight games.

The drive back to Marseille couldn't have been sweeter.

CHAPTER 8

LIFE IN THE MARSEILLE AREA

Buck the garbage collector and the Jehovah's witnesses.

Since she could talk, our daughter regularly begged me for a pet. An affectionate girl, Anaïs loved to play with Papé Robert's dogs, a male boxer named "Pilou" and his female consort, "Poupette," whenever we went to visit the in-laws. I had told her it was impossible to keep a pet animal in an apartment building in Villeurbanne. I promised her that we'd get an animal if and when we ever lived in a real house with a yard. Women, even at that age, are like computers; they have memory. She held me to my word when we moved to Plan de Bottes.

At first she wanted a horse, pointing out that we had a property big enough for him. I tried to explain to her something of the obligations entailed in caring for an animal that size, but with little success. If I didn't want to look after her horse, then it could stay in her bedroom, she argued.

I eventually got her a canary, which we kept in a cage in the kitchen. But that didn't last long. She released it one day as she felt bad that it was caged when it obviously wanted to fly around.

We settled on a dog, which we acquired when "Poupette" gave birth to a litter of a half-dozen pups, one of which we claimed. "Buck," named by son Calix after the hero of Jack London's "The Call of the Wild," was 100% mongrel, with his mother's exceptionally long tail and his father's impressive jaw. "Pilou," like many boxers, I'm told, had such powers of compression in his muzzle that, on two occasions, he actually punctured the tires of the mailman's car when he ventured up the Maurin driveway to deliver a package! He was perfectly disciplined and harmless with small children including our own who, as toddlers, would jump on his back and even attempt to insert pebbles in his nostrils!

Likewise, Buck was basically stupid but very protective of our children, whom he would even defend if I were foolish enough to spank them in his presence!

Unfortunately, Buck had one nasty habit: He was a garbage collector. He'd roam the neighborhood at night (our property wasn't fenced in) when we let him out, and go around collecting every accessible garbage bag for miles around. He would bring them to a spot near the field not far from our house and on the side of another neighbor's home. This must have gone on for months until one day the neighbor in question learned the identity of Buck's owner. He gave me a call and informed me that there was a small mountain of garbage in his back yard where our mutt had been bringing his prizes every night for months. And would I kindly come and pick up Buck's trash.

I grabbed a few 100 liter trash bags and a pair of gloves and spent the better part of an afternoon gathering up dirty diapers, broken bottles, tin cans and all manner of foul things such as my dog had reportedly brought to the neighbor's yard from all around the town. Naturally, I wasn't pleased with Buck and dragged him over to the scene of his crime where I stuck his snout in the trash before giving him a sound thrashing with a whip-like *martinet.*

When a few weeks later, the neighbor called me again with the same complaint, I was livid and dragged Buck back to the neighbor's, where I once again stuck his snout in the garbage and gave him the thrashing of his life, even breaking the *martinet* in the process.

Later on, I felt bad about the way I'd whipped my dog and wondered if he might not even be innocent of the charges against him. I hadn't actually seen him do it. How did I know if the neighbor wasn't lying in a scheming way to get some sucker to come to his house and pick up all his trash periodically?

My doubts subsisted until a few nights later when I was cycling into the center of town on the way to municipal choir practice. Who should I cross on the main road about a mile from our home but Buck, trotting merrily along with a trash bag hanging from his jaw. He was probably headed over to the neighbor's yard where he would, by custom, scatter his 'treasure.'

Surprised to run into his master far from home, the dog at first seemed happy to see me and started running towards me with his long tail wagging profusely. But then, as if suddenly realizing that he's just been caught red-handed in a despicable crime, he just as briskly bolted in the opposite direction, apparently remembering the reasons for his beatings.

One day we heard him barking as he usually did when someone approached the yard. His was an impressive, resonating, even threatening bark, uncharacteristic of his friendly 'personality.' As he persisted, I went outside to see two middle-aged women standing near the entrance to the driveway, petrified in fear before our imposing looking pet.

"Don't worry ladies," I shouted as I approach. "He's perfectly harmless."

Then, suspecting the identity of the ladies and wanting to have some fun, I added: "He only bites Jehovah's Witnesses."

The women looked even more terrified:

"But, we..we..'re Jehovah's Witnesses," one of them stuttered.

"You needn't worry," I joked. "He already ate one of your colleagues for breakfast."

MEAL TIME IN FRANCE;

The life of a pastor-evangelist in France involves taking advantage of every possible opportunity to develop friendships, with the ultimate goal of sharing the faith with whomever will listen. One of the best traditions of French culture, the two hour lunch, is also one of the most favorable for sharing what's in one's heart. Someone calculated that 65% of Jesus' words, as recorded in the gospel, were uttered in the context of a meal. The fact is, if you spend an hour or so sharing a meal with someone and you're not able to eventually veer the conversation to spiritual concerns, then you probably don't have the gifts required for a missionary vocation. It's that simple. For there is something most propitious about discussing serious topics with folks who are convivially seated at your table and whose blood sugar level is peaking after a fine meal. Notice well that important qualifying adjective before the last noun.

French gastronomical standards are very high. One doesn't get invited to meals as often in France as one would in the States, where a simple hamburger or hotdog grilled over the back-yard barbecue is socially acceptable. In France, an invitation to dine means an occasion to sample the hosts' best spread or homemade specialties. Consequently, one must consider the investment of time, energy and expense before inviting someone to dinner. It's costly and time-consuming, but what better venue for sharing the good news?

When we first arrived in Plan de Bottes, both fresh and zealous in our new vocation, we took it upon ourselves to set aside every available Sunday to invite guests to our home. That included everyone from our children's friends' parents to the municipal employee with whom I casually spoke as he was cleaning the street in front of our house one day.

These weekly ministry meals involved heroic efforts by my wife on a regular basis. The long-term results were not apparent. Such is the plight of anyone who would share the faith with the French. We act on the premise that the Word of God is powerful and never without effect (Isaiah 55). Some day in glory we hope to meet at least one Frenchman whose presence there will be at least partly attributable to Words he heard while savoring Aline's special salad dressing and "gigot d'agneau à l'ail." Never underestimate the influence of gastronomy on the soul!

The cuisine is of course very different from one region of France to another. In the north, especially in Normandy and Brittany, it tends to be very rich, with many sauces, all made from butter. In the south of France where the Mediterranean diet prevails, olive oil is the main ingredient. I'm speaking of the region south of the French "Mason-Dixon" line which crosses the Rhone valley around the Montelimar area, down to the "Cote d'Azur" around the Mediterranean. It's in Montilemar and south that the olive trees and the sunshine begins.

Then there is the incredible number of cheeses—more than 400 varieties at last count! Cheese in France can be a most telling food item. Each variety is revealing of the mentality of the ones who prefer it. You have your mild-mannered people who lean towards camembert, brie, etc. Then you have your more assertive, not to say dominant, personalities—people who, like my father-in-law, tend to gravitate towards Roquefort or the strongest goat's milk cheeses. It's been said that every French cheese corresponds to a different personality type. Charles De Gaulle reportedly lamented that it was impossible to govern any county which produced over 365 varieties of cheeses.

With all the cheese and butter consumption, one often wonders why there isn't more heart disease amongst the French, who ingurgitate astronomical quantities of cholesterol. It's a fact that baffles medical science that the French have one of the lowest incidences of heart disease of all industrialized countries. This has been attributed to the beneficial effects of red wine consumption, which apparently keeps the nasty LDL cholesterol in check. Referred to familiarly as "the French paradox," it proves that one can still enjoy dairy products and not die from clogged arteries. But to enjoy the mountains of butter and cheese produced by the French dairy industry, one has to patronize the wine industry and do his part in consuming some of the oceans of wine produced by French *viticulteurs*. That's a challenge many accept willingly.

PLAN DE Botte open air market

When we weren't entertaining guests, one of our regular activities while living in Plan de Botte was to tend a Christian literature table in the Plan de Botte market, the town's main activity every Saturday morning. One had to arrive early to be assured of having a spot to display his wares. For the other merchants, that meant essentially food or clothing. Our status as an officially recognized *association* allowed us to set up a book table promoting our "wares."

I would go to the marketplace on Saturday and place a number of Bibles, New Testaments and devotional books for sale to the public. In the four or five years that I did this, I don't think I sold more than a couple of books, both by Dr. Martin Luther King, who is seen by many French people as something of a folk hero, with his militant action against American racism—at least that's how he's perceived in France. While a certain racist heritage is, in my opinion, the most shameful element of our U.S. history, racism is not limited to America. Occasionally, I would find myself defending the United States against the simplistic pronouncements of some typically anti-American Frenchman for whom racism encapsulated the whole story of U.S. history. This conviction is of course largely promoted by the liberal media that harps *ad nauseum* on the oppression of the African Americans for the first 200 years of our history. The presence of a number of notable African-Americans (especially jazz musicians) who took up residence in France because of perceived racial injustice also reinforces this idea. One cannot broach this subject without encountering some smugness among Frenchmen convinced that their own country is devoid of the horrors of "Uncle Tom's Cabin." Rather than contradict them, I would usually agree that there was a shameful amount of racism in the U.S. Then I would remind them that those African American slaves had been abducted from Africa and brought to the New World as prisoners by European (including French) slave-trader ships! To hammer home the point that no one nation is exempt from this sin, I would remind them of the plight of many *Magréhbins* (Arabs from Maghreb region of N. Africa) in France and conclude by saying that I would still rather be black in Mississippi than Algerian in Paris. That last remark silenced most detractors of American history and culture.

I would stand at our literature table for hours every Saturday morning in an effort to get to know the locals, hoping to dispel the suspicion that naturally surrounds any non-Roman Catholic religious group in France. At first, most people would shy away from our table as if we had the plague. As we became better known in town, acquaintances we met through our children, for example, would stop to chat, if they weren't even remotely interested in the Gospel.

Our goal, at that point, was to be sensitive listeners, to show our neighbors a congenial face of "protestants." As people would see us from week to week, they became more accepting. Still, it's a long term process in France and there are no shortcuts. It's been calculated that it takes an average of seventeen years to plant a church in

France, and even that would most often be a small assembly of fifty or less with more black skin than white as the middle class French "Duponts" and "Durands" remain largely unaffected by the gospel.

The local Catholic priest

In a country like France where religion knows no higher authority than that of "tradition," the opinion of a Roman Catholic priest can carry significant weight in the minds of the pious few. The local priest can be a powerful enemy or a useful ally in the proclamation of the gospel. Consequently, it's probably good form for the minister of the gospel to try to establish cordial relations with the Roman prelate if there's one in the area. That's not always the case, as the number of Catholic priests has shrunk drastically in France in recent decades, even as their average age has risen (over 63 years old at last count). There's a crisis of vocations amongst the Catholics in France, with fewer and fewer Catholic seminary graduates. Typically, a local priest might serve several parishes concurrently, saying Mass in the morning at one and in the evening at another.

The church building itself is used primarily for funerals, weddings, and baptisms. Most Frenchmen go to church only on these three occasions: when they're "hatched, matched, and dispatched," as the saying goes.

The priest's basic role has been reduced to that of an underpaid religious functionary with very little time devoted to teaching or even studying the Word.

It was important for the sake of our testimony before unbelievers to establish at least a *modus vivendi* with the "rival" Christian forces. With this in mind, I met with the only Roman Catholic priest in Plan de Botte, Abbé Briscoles. An elderly man (75-80), he presided over a parish where scarcely a handful of mostly elderly women even bothered to attend the weekly Saturday evening Mass. According to one survey, only 6% of French are considered "practicing" Catholics, and these are defined as those who attend church at least once a year!

After I introduced myself to Abbé Briscoles, I told him about our project to evangelize the area with the intention of planting a Bible-believing church. Our first meeting seemed to go rather well and he was amenable when I suggested that we have a brief moment of prayer together before parting. I left him with a copy of the survey questions we were using to learn about the religious and philosophical beliefs of the local people and asked him for his opinion.

A few days later, we met again in the sacristy at the back of the church. By this time, he had answered all the survey questions including the one indicating his belief that "all religions lead to God." When I gently protested that these were not the teachings of the Scriptures nor even the Roman Church, the conviviality that had characterized our first encounter suddenly vanished. He even threatened to "preach against" us unless we modified our views.

"Why don't you enter the Catholic Church?" he scowled, obviously disgruntled that the only religious activity in town was escaping his control. So I tried to explain tactfully that we had some rather fundamental theological differences with the Church of Rome including the authority of the Bible vs. tradition, the co-redemption of Mary, etc.

He rebutted by explaining with casuistic reasoning worthy of Pascal's Jesuit opponents, how all men are their own co-redeemers. In short, it was clear that his beliefs and teachings were light-years away from the absolute limits of the biblical faith as expressed in any of the universal Church's (Catholic included) traditional creeds. Fortunately, *Abbé* Briscoles did not stay long in Plan de Bottes after our arrival. He was replaced by a somewhat younger priest, le *Curé* Gauvin, with whom we would enjoy a friendly relationship.

The terrace of the local café

As the pastor of the only local protestant assembly, I realized the importance of leaving a good testimony to the locals. Any *faux pas* on my part could be a source of scandal to someone. I was made aware of that after we'd been in Plan de Botte for a couple of years. One day when I was running late and eager to get home, I drove through the center of town. Making a left turn, I hurriedly passed through the main intersection rather than stop for a couple of elderly ladies who stood on the sidewalk waiting to cross. As we went by with our window open, my daughter Anaïs and I heard one of the ladies say to the other: "Tu as vu cela! C'était le Pasteur, et il ne s'est même pas arrêté pour nous!" (Did you see that! It was the pastor who didn't even stop for us).

A similarly 'scandalous' incident occurred one day as I sat on the terrace of the town's lone café near the same intersection. Having set up my literature table at the marketplace at 7 o'clock, I was left with an hour or two to kill before the locals would arrive for their Saturday morning shopping. As was my custom, I would read the Bible and the Marseillais newspaper while savoring a cup of espresso. This was often the best opportunity to chat with some of the local *forains* who would also take advantage of the brief lull in activities between their set-up time and the arrival of their customers.

However, on this occasion, there was no one to speak to, so I lit up a Cuban cigar that my mother-in-law had given me as a birthday present (I never bought them myself, just on principle). This partic-ular Saturday, as I read through the Word with an occasional puff on my *Cohiba* (they're not illegal in France), a middle-aged gentleman whose presence I had not noticed came walking past me. Observing my Bible and cigar, he looked straight at me, and asked in a most judgmental tone:

"Ton livre, ne dit-il pas que tu ne te souilleras pas?" (Your book; does it not say that you should not defile yourself?).

Stunned by the abrupt nature of the question from a total stranger, I replied somewhat defensively:

"Not exactly; though it does say right here that you should not judge others."

The gentleman, whose identity I never learned, simple walked away without another word. The bottom line and moral of the story is the confirmation of the truth enunciated by the apostle James, who warns that they should not be numerous who teach the Word "for we will be judged more severely."

Occasionally, I had the opportunity to speak with M. Clamart, the grumpy forty-five year old owner of the café. Hard, cynical and impa-tient, he wasn't a fellow you would want to cross. In fact, I'd seen him refuse to serve some people on a whim, his café being the only game in town, unless one headed to Allauch, the next village some two miles up the road. Like many French businessmen, he made you feel as though he were doing you a favor by waiting on you.

Once as I sat there, enjoying my espresso, M. Clamart came by and sat down at my table. He began to express his disapproval of the local Catholic priest, the Curé Henri Gauvin, who, theological differences notwithstanding, was a dear friend of ours. It seems that the Curé Gauvin, who had recently arrived in Plan de Botte, had taken some independent action with regards to the town's annual feast of Marie Magdelène, for whom the church was even named. According to tradition, this famous gospel character came to *Provence* after the resurrection of Jesus and took up residence in a grotto in the hills of "La Sainte Baume" not far from Marseille. According to tradition, she would have crossed Plan de Botte on her journey from the coast to the grotto.

Of course there is strictly no historical basis for this legend. Still, the town celebrates it once a year with a horse drawn float carrying a statue of Marie Magdalene through the town center. Usually, the local priest participates in this curious mixture of religion and folklore by dressing in his most elaborate ceremonial vestments, sprinkling holy water on the horses and the statue, and pronouncing the requisite (Latin?) incantations as the procession goes by.

This time, however, *Curé* Gauvin refused to reschedule his habitual morning Mass just to participate in this ceremony. This break with sacrosanct tradition was upsetting to some of the locals.

Personally, I wasn't surprised by his decision. Only a few days before, he and I had met at the St. Mary Magdalene presbytery for one of our regular discussions. At that time, I had chided him in a friendly sort of way for the traditional participation in this event which owed more to folklore and to commerce than to the gospel.

Many of the townspeople, including M. Clamart, were indignant by *Curé* Gauvin's defiance. Clamart was hoping to find a sympathetic ear for his complaints in the protestant pastor who, he assumed, was the "adversary" of the Catholic priest. The priest's refusal to participate was going to cost the café owner some lost revenue if the procession did not stop, as it normally would, in front of the church opposite M. Clamart's café.

"How about that new priest", M. Clamart complained to me as we sat on the terrace. "He won't even be part of the procession!

What nerve! Why that's his job, isn't it, to participate in local 'religious' functions. Don't you think?"

"Not necessarily," I replied. "I don't know of any article of the Catholic faith which obliges a priest to sprinkle holy water on a horse drawn float once a year for any reason."

M. Clamart was startled by my reply.

"So you're siding with the priest!" said the increasingly disgruntled café owner.

"It doesn't happen every day, does it?" I smiled.

"Boff!" Mr Clamart grumbled, as he got up, leaving in a huff.

Solomon and "Falcoche"

A major part of any missionary's life has to be raising his children. The French are particularly sensitive to the testimony of the home life. An ill-mannered child scandalizes the French, who have fortunately escaped the ravages of the influence of Benjamin Spock. Until recently, the French have tended to adhere to old school methods which implicitly, if not explicitly, recognize the biblical truth that "folly is attached to the child's heart, and that the rod of correction will chase it from him" (Proverbs 22:15) .

We were careful about the way we raised our children knowing their behavior was a reflection on our homelife and our ministry. Fortunately, they were fairly compliant children, though far from perfect.

A memorable incident came when our two boys saw a film based on a novel called "Vipère au Poing" (Viper in the Fist) by the French writer Hervé Bazin. A family saga, it includes a mother named "Falcoche" who treats her small boys badly to the point of inciting them to seek vengeance on her. In her absence, they plot their revenge while repeating incessantly "vengeance à Falcoche" (vengeance on Falcoche).

Impressed by the film, one of our sons wrote with a pen, "vengeange à Falcoche," on the wall of our bathroom. This was unacceptable, as even the younger one knew it was forbidden to write on the walls. The problem was we didn't know which one had done it—Calix, who was eight at the time, or his six-year-old brother Justin. When accused, both denied it. I was stumped. Then I had an idea.

I explained my dilemma to the boys: someone had to be punished for the crime which they both denied. As I didn't know who was to blame, I would therefore resolve the issue by punishing both of them.

This announcement was met with vigorous indignant protest from our older son Calix and curiously revealing acquiescence from Justin. Their reactions, like those of the women in the famous Solomon caper, revealed the truth. Justin was the culprit who needed to be punished. And I had a rare opportunity to play Solomon.

Roger Valmet in Plan de Botte

One day we received a visitor to Plan de Bottes, a fellow Aline's dad had known, by reputation at least, in their hometown of Alès. Roger Valmet was the type of man who—in the words of "Papé Robert"— if you saw him walking down the sidewalk towards you, you would do well to cross the street to avoid him. Valmet had a history of drug-dealing, and all kinds of felonies and shady dealings, including robbery and racketeering. Even his physique inspired fear. He was only 5'8", but weighed over 300 pounds. He sported a bushy black beard, and had multiple scars on his face from numerous brawls. He limped on his prosthetic leg, his right leg having been severed by a fall from a train while in a drunken stupor. He was a larger than life version of Bluebeard.

Then, something happened to him. In one of his many incarcerations, Roger had become a Christian and his life was thoroughly transformed. Not only that, but he even got married, to Véronique, a former Marseille hooker who had also become a Christian. Now they devoted themselves to social work and essentially lived off a small government pension and the sale of paintings done by Roger. He had taken up painting in prison.

We met them in Alès, but Roger and Véronique came to stay with us one weekend in Marseille. He accompanied me to the market-place one Saturday morning on a day when local French politicians were campaigning for office. One candidate was M. Bertrand Tardif, a wealthy young industrialist who, as owner of the "Olympique de Marseille" soccer club, had used his considerable finances—à la George Steinbrenner—to turn the team into a European soccer powerhouse in the early 90's. However, that all ended abruptly in 1994 after M. Tardif was caught bribing opposing players and virtually fixing games. His trial was a major media event in France. Among the trial's more memorable aspects was his unforgettable defense after he'd been caught in a lie about his illicit activities. He eventually admitted that he'd lied, but "in good faith" ("Oui, jai menti, mais j'ai menti de bonne foi"). That line of defense has prompted interesting theological discussions ever since.

Mr. Tardif got off with a relatively light sentence and eventually went to work producing movies. A protégé of the late French president Francois Mitterand—he was still highly regarded by a large segment of the local Marseille population for his role in bringing a champion soccer team to the city. Hence he was campaigning for one of the congressional seats of the district, which included our town of Plan de Botte.

He was making his way through the local market place that day, shaking hands and smiling at the people, telling them "I'm Bertrand Tardif, and I would like your vote for the forthcoming election..."

We were standing near the table as Tardif approached our direction. Suddenly Roger Valmet jumped out from behind the table and placed himself squarely in front of M. Tardif, who offered a perfunctory hand to the former gangster.

"Mr Tardif, I'm not from here, but I know this town well as I once spent three years in Les Baumettes [Marseille's infamously overcrowded prison]. But now I'm no longer a gangster as my life was changed by an encounter with Jesus Christ."

"Interesting" said the politician thoughtfully. "I'd like to have an encounter like that too" said the well-known figure of French political circles, not really knowing what to say.

"You can, M. Tardif!" insisted Roger Valmet, pointing a finger directly at M. Tardif. "In fact, you must!"

The sudden nature of the confrontation was no doubt shocking to the politician, who scurried away from the "pirate evangelist" like a frightened mouse surprised by the light. It was the last we saw of M. Tardif that day.

The town of Plan de Botte

Notwithstanding this rare visit from a celebrity, Plan de Botte is a rural, almost provincial town with a mainly white population. There weren't many *Magréhbins* living in this area which had only a small number of high-rise, low-income houses. In fact most of our neighbors were of Italian origin. I used to tease the folks on our street that, with a name like mine, I was the only Frenchman there. One didn't hear any other language save French, and occasionally a bit of Italian, on the streets of Plan de Botte.

In an effort to maintain our children's familiarity with English, I would try to set aside time every week for chatting with them in English. For our daughter Anaïs, that meant weekly Sunday morning trips to the café where we would sit on the terrace speaking to each other in English.

One Sunday morning, I'd come into town with my daughter to purchase bread from a local pastry chef for our church's weekly communion celebration. That day it was raining so we had to sit inside the café. Seated inconspicuously in a corner, we rambled on about different things when suddenly there was a heavy silence in the café. Though we'd tried to be as discreet as possible, it seemed that some of the locals overheard us speaking in English.

A local loudmouth was present, a forty-five year old soccer fan who spent every spare moment in the café when he wasn't working at the municipal pool.

His loud critiques of the Saturday night performances of the beloved "OM" soccer team were a regular feature of our Sunday morning visits to the café. Suddenly he blurted out:

"Moi, je n'aime pas tellement les étrangers ici." ("Me, I don't appreciate foreigners here") .

Anaïs and I were taken aback by this roughneck's remarks. Coincidentally, on the day of his xenophobic outburst, I happened to glance at the Marseille sports page where I learned that both of the Marseille team's goals in a 2-1 victory over the rival Parisian team had been scored by a certain Chris Waddle, an Englishman, and one of the stars of the team.

So as Anaïs and I walked out of the café, I stopped at the table where our loudmouth fan did his regular café "broadcasts." Pointing to the photo of the hero of the day in the Marseille newspaper, I chided him: "It's a good thing we have a few foreigners here, isn't it?

Embarrassed, he just smiled sheepishly and mumbled under his breath.

A Night at the OPERA

One of the highlights of our years in Marseille was our annual trip to the opera. The Marseille opera house is an imposing building downtown near the "Vieux Port," and the red-light district. Obtaining seats to the opera in an *Italian* town like Marseille was no mean feat, for the Italians love their opera even more than soccer, if that's possible. Consequently, buying tickets involved queuing up for hours at the ticket window months in advance of the actual performance. As soon as the program was announced, the tickets were sold out. One had to be perseverant to be an opera fan in Marseille.

We became regular patrons of the Marseille Opera from the time we first brought our children, all three of them, to see Mozart's "*La Flute Enchantée*" (The Magic Flute) back in 1989 when they were 5,7, and 9 years old. We had familiarized them with the libretto, with the help of a record which narrated the Masonic tale. They were familiar with the characters and were thrilled when they could identify them as they came on stage. The children's understandable excitement brought us some rebukes and sustained "hushes" from the mostly elderly patrician crowd in attendance that Sunday afternoon, which was about the only time one could bring small children to the opera.

It was a different story a few years later when Aline and I got tickets for a Saturday night performance of Verdi's "*Rigoletto.*" What an amazing contrast! On Saturday night, the crowd was a lot younger, and more convivial. Not content to sit there and applaud politely after each act, the audience jumped up and down in their seats and screamed and whistled with delight after each aria as the singers performed their various roles. Some numbers were so well received that the enthusiastic throngs would insist the actors do an encore, and even a double encore, applauding and cheering louder at each reprise! The singers themselves obviously loved it. I'd never seen such enthusiasm, save at the soccer stadium. Such is the appreciation of even the working-class Marseille folk of Italian origin for the art of the opera.

Claude R., Le Santonnier d'Allauch

Among the more interesting characters we met during our years in Marseille was a fellow whose boutique I stumbled upon one day while looking for a birthday present for Aline. Claude Ricci was a *santonnier* by trade. He made clay figurines for which *Provence* is famous. Originally these small clay statues —called "santons" in Provencial French, short for "saint homme" or holy man—were made to adorn the nativity "crèches." They included, of course the Christ-child, Mary, the Magi, shepherds, etc. Over the years, *santonniers* have branched out and now make figurines of local folk including bakers, fishermen, fishmongers, farmers—all dressed in traditional costumes. This craft, which originated in southern France, has become popular with Frenchmen from other parts of the country, not to mention the hordes of tourists who regularly visit *Provence*.

I first met Claude in the spring of 1988. I was as usual at a loss for ideas for Aline's birthday, when I happened to cycle past his *atelier's* boutique. It was 10 o'clock on a Saturday morning when I got to the door. Much to my surprise, it was locked. I found it strange that a shop like that would be closed during peak business hours. As I was about to leave, I spotted a heavy-set, bushy-bearded fellow of about forty, cautiously approaching the door. He was clutching a lit cigarette and wearing a white, paint-stained, artist's smock.

"Que voulez-vous?" (What do you want), he asked suspiciously from behind the closed door.

I explained that I was interested in seeing his wares, with a probable purchase in mind. That I would even have to explain that was amazing for I assumed that most merchants, and even artisans, are in business to sell and don't normally ask prospective customers what they want. As least that's what I thought.

Claude was not a typical shopkeeper in any sense of the word. In fact, he wasn't a shopkeeper at all. He was a temperamental artist. As we came to know him, Aline and learned to appreciate his extreme sensitivity and an uncanny gift for noticing small physical details that would make Sherlock Holmes and Colombo blush.

Cautiously, he unlocked the door, scrutinized me carefully, and let me into his shop, locking the door behind me. On the shelves were dozens of *santons* including the usual array of shepherds and Magi for the Nativity scenes to which they were destined, but some which were excellent replicas of the French actors Yves Montand, Emmanuelle Beart, and Daniel Auteuil, who had starred in the remake of Marcel Pagnol's famous story "Jean de Florette" and its sequel "Manon des Sources" (Manon of the Springs). As I looked around the shop, wondering about the strange behavior of the artist, and not knowing what might please my wife, a well-dressed, middle-aged woman came to the door. Nothing exceptional about that, you would think; it was a commercial boutique made to be visited by customers, right? Once again, Claude unlocked the door cautiously.

I continued looking around, admiring the numerous *santons* displayed on the shelves. I had seen many *santons* in different marketplaces and shops throughout the South of France, but few that could equal this craftsmanship. The faces were expressive and finely detailed. What a delicate stroke of the paintbrush it must take to create such artwork, I though.

As I was admiring his work, the woman customer said something to Claude about the comparatively high price of his *santons*. She had seen others in the nearby village which were considerably less expensive. Claude didn't take kindly to that remark.

The woman continued. Stopping before a *santon* on the shelf immediately in front of her, she inquired of the *santonnier:*

"Il fait combien celui-là?" (How much is this one?).

Claude got up from his work and walked to where the woman was standing and snapped at her gruffly.

"Madame, celui-là n'a pas de prix pour vous, car je ne vous le vend pas. Quittez mon atelier!" (Madame, this one has no price for you for I will not sell it to you. Get out of my shop!)

Observing the scene from just a couple of feet away, I was flabbergasted. What kind of merchant was this who would literally refuse to sell his wares to a customer, and even throw her out?

After the lady left indignantly, I started talking to Claude, who told me he was an artist and considered his *santon* creations his children, and refused to let his children be taken to a home by someone who would not appreciate them for their true value. This woman was not fit to own one of his "children," as she did not appreciate the difference between an artistically crafted *santon* and one of the cheaper, mass-produced imitations that are sold in department stores at half the price.

All *santons* are not created alike, he insisted. Claude's work was made with love and dedication to detail, and anyone who couldn't see that didn't deserve to own one. It was that simple.

I was blown away by this initial encounter with a man who eventually became a good friend. The nature of his work—sitting quietly behind his table in his atelier all day—afforded me opportunities to visit him fairly regularly, and I got to know him well.

I learned that a large part of his fear and suspicion at the approach of potential clients was due to the fact that he had been robbed at gunpoint on two occasions by Marseille riff-raff who had held a sawed-off shotgun under his chin. So he was understandably fearful when any stranger arrived at his door. A single man and "non-practicing homosexual," he had been victimized often enough in life to have grown cynical about the human race. There was even one young man whom he had helped considerably, both emotionally and financially, who had later betrayed him. All of this made Claude suspicious of anyone, even those of us with apparent good intentions. There would be no difficulty, I thought, in convincing Claude about man's inherently sinful nature.

Still, after I got to know and appreciate this highly strung artist, he began to accept my invitations to various church activities. He became a rather proficient *pétanque* player. That didn't surprise me as his hands, sensitive enough to paint the tiniest details on his exquisite *santons* would understandably be well coordinated for the less precise art of directing the trajectory of a *pétanque boule*.

Aline and I were amazed at Claude's most unusual perspicacious insights into the most subtle interactions between married couples; nothing escaped him. Ironically, I thought Claude should have made an excellent marriage counselor.

Total depravity notwithstanding, Claude seemed to be a well-meaning individual in a world of aggressive scoundrels. His disillusionment with the general selfishness of the human race should have made him more receptive to the biblical doctrine of original sin. That other people were sinful, Claude would not argue. Recognizing his own sin and need for a Savior, that was another thing altogether.

The little old lady from La Ciotat

I was working at my desk early one afternoon, preparing my Sunday sermon, when the phone rang. It was Claude, telling me that an elderly woman had just wandered into his shop. He wasn't able to communicate with her as she was obviously not in full possession of her faculties. He didn't know what to do so he asked if I wouldn't come over right away and help him figure out what to do with this poor lost soul.

I jumped on my bicycle and pedaled up the road to his atelier. When I got there, I found Claude attempting to communicate with a feeble looking octogenarian dressed in a plain robe and slippers. In spite of our best efforts, we weren't able to get through to her. According to Claude, she apparently had just stepped off the bus, which stopped a few meters in front of his shop. When we asked her where she was from, all we could understand was that she'd come from "La Ciotat," which was the name of a town about 20 miles east of Marseille.

After a half hour of fruitless attempt to communicate with her, the only useful information gleaned was the repeated name of La Ciotat. Was it a street name, or the name of her neighborhood? I decided that, rather than call the police, who would probably subject her to innumerable administrative formalities, I would simply drive her to La Ciotat, and get her home myself.

I cycled back home, got the car, parked in front of Claude's atelier, and escorted the confused old lady to my car. After buckling her in the front seat, I drove off towards the *Autoroute* which runs along the Mediterranean coast to Toulon, Nice and Cannes. I prayed as I drove, all the while wondering what I'd do with her once I got her to the part of La Ciotat she seemed to be referring to.

Meanwhile, my befuddled passenger just sat there with a slight smile on her wrinkled face, seemingly content to be going for a ride—or at least that's what is seemed to me.

Twenty miles down the highway, we reached La Ciotat, which had once been a major French ship-building town but had fallen on hard times,

I stopped at a local grocery store and a filling station or two before I got directions to the street the old lady mentioned several times. Her eyes lit up as her memory suddenly kicked when we approached what was apparently familiar territory for her. As we rounded a corner, she pointed to an old, dilapidated villa that sat back from the street about fifty meters or so. Judging by the length of the grass in the yard and the generally unkempt nature of the property, I assumed that no one lived there. Even the shutters were closed.

I decided to be prudent and check out the place a so I wouldn't leave my sweet, senile traveling friend in any danger. My suspicions were confirmed when I got out of the car and noticed that the rusted iron gate had a chain and lock to prevent anyone from trespassing. It was obvious that no one had entered that gate in years. It was now equally clear that the old lady had been simply reliving some memories from her youth as she spoke incoherently about her home in La Ciotat! I was trying to find the home of a woman who was clearly living in her own fantasy world.

What could I do now? This was a time for a quick prayer, à la Nehemiah (Nehemiah 2:4). The answer was on the ground in front of me. In the mailbox that was attached to the gate, there were some yellowed advertising flyers and assorted junk mail, some of which had probably been there for years. Some of the flyers still bore the name of the "Lavini" resident to whom they had been addressed. I decided to do a bit of detective work and found a telephone directory where I looked up the name Lavini. There were only a half-dozen or so in the Marseille area, so I made a few phone calls. Sure enough, by the third call, I reached a woman on the south side of Marseille who identified the address in La Ciotat and was puzzled to learn that her elderly mother was in the car with me in La Ciotat.

The story ends with me driving back towards Marseille to the south side of the city where I dropped my Alzheimer patient at the home of her forty-year-old daughter and son-in-law, who were both delighted and relieved to see her mother. As it turned out, she was a patient in a health care centre in Plan de Bottes just a five minute walk from Claude's atelier. She had apparently escaped from the center, slipped out the front gate, and walked up the road aimlessly, eventually wandering into Claude's shop. Although she had been with me for over three hours, she had not yet been missed by the folks at the care center, or at least not yet reported as missing.

The daughter was grateful for my efforts on behalf of her mother and for the providential confluence of factors that had led her to someone who took care of her. Of course I tried to use the opportunity for the gospel reminding the daughter of the identity of the Hand of Providence who had mercy on her mother. They seemed only mildly interested but listened politely out of gratitude.

Move to south Marseille

After seven years (1987-1995) in Plan de Botte, we decided, in collaboration with our church-planting teammates, that it was time for us to be moving on. Our tiny assembly of believers in Plan de Botte was more or less on its feet, so we needed to start another pioneering effort in a section of the Marseille area where there was no evangelical church. After a brief demographical study of the city with a colleague, we settled on the south side of Marseille in a neighborhood called "Roy d'Espagne" (King of Spain), whose largely white, well-educated population (200,000) was without a permanent evangelical assembly.

We got our things together and moved in September 1995, taking an apartment on the 10th floor of one of the sixteen-story residential "Tours" (towers) that had been built to accommodate some of the thousands of French expatriates returning from Algeria after the bloody revolution there in 1962, which expelled the French colonizers.

In spite of the beautiful surroundings, this turned out to be one of the most difficult periods in our family's short history. The tower we moved into was inhabited by a number of grumpy old people— including the dreadful Mme. Ravella, who lived on the 13th floor, and whose whole goal in life was to spread misery. She succeeded admirably.

The first week we were in the building, Mme. Ravella began to hassle us with phone calls ordering us not to flush our toilet after 9PM, as it disturbed the peace. She even scolded us for the noise of firecrackers, sure that it was our boys who were throwing them off the balcony, when our children were hundreds of miles away in the Alps at summer camp.

Mme. Ravella did not approve of our children practicing their instruments (harp and piano) at any hour of the day or night, something they needed to do to maintain their proficiency lest they be expelled from the Marseille conservatory.

A word about musical studies is in order here. Unlike the United States where there are many musicians and students of music, musical studies in France are prohibitively expensive unless one is admitted into one of the state-funded conservatories. In that case the studies are free i.e., paid by French taxes. Of course not everyone is admitted into the conservatory. Prospective students have to pass a *concours* (competition exam) and only a small number are chosen. Consequently, musical studies are somewhat elitist affair in France. All three of our children are blessed with musical talent. Still, regular practice is indispensable, as any musician will tell you.

So as not to offend our neighbors with practice at inconvenient hours, we asked them when it would bother them least. The answer of our immediate upstairs neighbor (Mme. Verrier) was categorical: "There is no hour for you to play. Get rid of your piano!" She was dead serious. One Saturday afternoon, while one of the children was playing a Chopin piece, Mr. Verrier (from the 11th floor) came down the stairs to the hallway in front of our door, banging on a casserole with a wooden spoon and screaming. I went to the door and followed him up the staircase to his apartment directly above ours. When we reached his apartment, I tried to reason with him, even as he tried to drag me in through the open door. At first I didn't understand, but later I realized that had he succeeded in dragging me into his apartment, he could have beaten me and called it self-defense as I would have been legally considered the intruder.

Our relationship with this couple ended only a few weeks later when M. Verrier, a distraught individual and a statistic of France's large unemployment problem, apparently fell off the balcony to his death some eleven floors below. His wife said he'd been up on a stepladder washing windows when he'd slipped. Perhaps. Still, the possibility of it being a suicide was in everyone's mind.

More obvious was the suicide of our 12th floor neighbor only a couple of months before. A quiet, sullen man of about 65 who never acknowledged my greeting in the elevator, M. Duboeuf always wore a fisherman's cap and seemed to stare down at the floor whenever our paths crossed. He was the physical incarnation of the dwarf "Grumpy" from the "Snow White" tale. His wife was a bit more civil. It seems that Mr. Duboeuf learned one day, after a doctor's visit, that he had pancreatic cancer, which would kill him in a matter of months. He got himself a pistol and, after writing a farewell letter to his wife, went out in the hills overlooking our building and put a bullet in his head.

I waited a couple of weeks before knocking on Mme. Duboeuf's door, introduced myself as a pastor, and asked to speak to her. She coolly allowed me a few minutes of her time, but made it abundantly clear that she had no faith whatsoever and wasn't at all interested in hearing anything about the gospel. Such is the hardness of many of the "Dupond" and "Durands" (Smiths and Jones) of France, alas.

Not only did our piano bother our neighbors, but even our daughter Anaïs' harp was considered an unacceptable noise by these nattering nabobs of negativism who were our upstairs neighbors. In fact, their aversion to "noise" was almost pathological as we learned one day through the building's *concierge.*

When the apartment building was built, a number of these future tenants had determined to have a shallow decorative water basin—too shallow for swimming—built over the underground garage for fear that this flat space adjacent to the building might be used for a play area by small children. Heaven forbid! The irony of this misanthropic maneuver was that the basin perpetually leaked and caused water damage in the parking garage underneath. Better still, bullfrogs began to take up residence in the basin and could be heard croaking into the night. That too was unacceptable. So the residents committee—influenced by misanthropes like the Verriers and Mme. Ravella—contracted to have the basin water poisoned regularly to kill the frogs!

I learned this from Mme. Durand, the building's compassionate *concierge,* whose impossible job involved listening to the constant

209

gripes of the likes of Mrs. Verrier and Ravella and trying to maintain peace.

Shocked by the sight of the exterminator company fishing a host of dead bullfrogs from the basin, I asked her what the neighbors would do in the summer months when the numerous *cigales* (katydids) in the hills around our building began their summer chirping sound. Would they hire a helicopter to spray the hillsides to kill these noisy insects?

What about the gale-like *mistral* wind raging through the trees? Would they have the trees chopped down or file a law suit against God? Mme. Durand shrugged.

This pathological obsession with noise created major difficulties for us. Apparently, Mme. Ravella was well-connected with someone at the police station. So I was summoned to appear before the men in blue, where I was informed that we could be fined for "*tapage diurne*" (daytime aggression) if our children persisted in playing the piano. The policemen were more understanding than Mme. Ravella and made it clear that they were only doing their job in warning me.

Mme. Ravella was persistent and managed to solicit police intervention one Saturday afternoon as I was about to leave the building. They camped at the bottom of the building (we could see them from the balcony) awaiting the first notes from the piano keyboard. I made it a point to leave before they got there, knowing they would be more compassionate in dealing with a woman than if the man of the house were home. I'm afraid Aline didn't understand my reasoning. Things got tense between us for a while.

Of *Pastis* and Pastoral visits

Part of any missionary's job is to visit the believers to encourage them in the faith, and to share the faith with non-believers. The tricky part of doing visitation in France is that most people's lives are busy, their weekly schedules so full—even more than in the States—that they don't have time to receive visitors. More and more women now work during the day, as two incomes are often necessary to assure even a modest standard of living. Unlike most Americans who live in single-family houses, the vast majority (ca. 80%) of French live in apartment buildings. Typically, they leave for work or school, like most Americans, at about 7:30-8:00 AM.

Unlike Americans, however, most French take a two-hour lunch break and don't get home from work until much later in the evening than most Americans. A school child would normally come home at around 5PM, have a snack called a *goûter*, do homework until 8 PM when he would eat with the family. Then it's to bed. He is off from school on Wednesday afternoons, but goes to class on Saturday mornings.

The more dedicated parents would be busy helping their children with their homework in the evenings. That means about the only people who would be home during the day would be some of the elderly folks—mostly women—who, like elderly folks the world over, are often lonely and enjoy company.

Consequently, by the time we left France, we had more than a few elderly friends we would call on regularly. Typically, during a late afternoon pastoral visit, one would often be given an *"apéritif"*—a small glass of alcohol offered guests before the evening meal. That was usually a local *liqueur* of some sort, occasionally the homemade pride of the host. The French are not only the largest producers, but also the greatest importers, of alcoholic beverages in the world. Consequently, if one can make a liqueur with something (one can make a *liqueur* out of anything), then the French do. For instance, we've lived in Florida and have never seen an orange-based liqueur. Though France grows no oranges, they produce several varieties of orange-based liqueur. In fact, there are probably as many *"liqueurs"* in France as there are cheeses—hundreds! It seems that each Frenchman has his favorite. In the Marseille area, the favorite *apéritif* is called *pastis*, an anise-based liqueur served with a carafe of water to dilute it to one's own taste. A visiting American guest told me that he thought it tasted like paregoric diarrhea medicine.

Other hosts will offer you a drink of their homemade "eau-de-vie" à la *cerise, aux abricots, aux amandes,* etc. (cherry flavored, apricot flavored, almond flavored fire-water). One of our neighbors, Robert M, whose wife was Polish, was always eager to have me sample some of his finest aromatic Polish vodka. Until I met Robert, I never realized that there was such a thing as fine vodka.

One had to be careful about this part of French culture as you couldn't refuse a drink of the host's favorite liqueur without offending him. But you didn't want to accept a second one for fear that, on an empty stomach, it could make you tipsy and make the presentation of the gospel less-than-coherent. That's why one always had to be careful to space out his afternoon visits prudently lest he drink an *apéritif* too many and defeat the purpose of his visit.

Ecole Lamenais

Aline and I were preoccupied with both the academic and spiritual plight of our children. By the grace of God, we'd managed to have all three of them enrolled at a Catholic school in Marseille (Ecole Lamenais), an institution with an excellent academic reputation. The spiritual was another matter. Unlike some Catholic schools in the States—especially in the South, where the gospel influence is pervasive—there is very little "evangelical" about a French Catholic school. For instance, the school's annual Christmas "talent show," which we were obliged to attend, was an interminably long affair where hundreds of parents sat patiently to listen to the often abominable "musical" presentations of the students. At the end of the show, the school's Dominican chaplain would normally give a word of closing. If ever there was an ideal opportunity to say something about the reason for the season, this was it. Alas, there was never even a remote mention of the birth or identity of the Christ child. On one occasion the priest concluded the evening by saying simply: "je n'ai qu'un seul mot pour vous ce soir: L'Esperance. Bonne nuit" (I have only one word for you tonight: Hope. Good night).

That lack of vision for the gospel was bad enough. We were more taken aback when we volunteered to host a series of home meetings organized by the chaplain for the senior students to discuss family concerns—marriage, raising children—from a Christian viewpoint. The only "qualification" required was that the hosting couple not be divorced. Divorce is the one unforgivable sin in most Catholic circles. We had one fellow, a retired colonel of the French army from a Catholic background, who used to attend our worship services. When I asked Colonel Lazare why he worshipped with us instead of at the Catholic church he told me: "I divorced my first wife years ago, so the Catholic church does not allow me to take the Eucharist. Had I killed her, and repented, that would be another story."

There were few parents who had volunteered to host the "family discussion group," so the school had put an announcement in a flyer that was distributed to all the parents. We were notified a short time later by a telephone call from the Dominican organizing the program that our offer to host was withdrawn from consideration as we were "Protestants" and some parents feared we might corrupt their children with our "unorthodox" viewpoint.

These students had the same preoccupations as any other adolescents with all the acute sensitivity of that age group to the great metaphysical questions of life. Failure to provide real answers to these questions, and the attraction of hedonism, had pushed some into experimentation with cannabis. Several had been caught and expelled for smoking hashish. That incident caused significant consternation amongst the parents and school director, M. de Varga, an admirably dedicated individual. In typical French fashion, the headmaster organized a symposium, bringing specialists down from Paris to address the parents.

It was Saturday morning and I was sitting in the packed chapel with 350 other parents, the vast majority of whom were well-educated members of the Marseille bourgeoisie. Mr. José Bartholet, the school's concerned and devoted headmaster, had brought in three specialists from Paris to enlighten the parents on the particulars of their adolescents' fascination with mind-altering drugs.

Their three-part presentation covered a number of legal and technical issues, of which most in the audience were ignorant. It included a brief explanation of the different types of drugs circulating and their physiological effects, as well as practical advice to help the concerned parents detect the presence of such drugs in their ostensibly well-bred progeny.

One of the panel experts, a Parisian writer and specialist on youth problems, rightly suggested that most young people who take drugs do so because of peer pressure but also in search of a "paradise." Some want to escape a hellish home environment often characterized by a lack of love.

A little more than halfway into the two-hour meeting, the floor was opened up to the parents for questions or comments. I prayed silently, asking the Lord, if it were His will, that I could speak a word on behalf of his gospel. For rarely would one have an opportunity to address such a large, concerned crowd. I was nervous, for any audience of well-educated Frenchmen is overwhelmingly humanist; there is, alas, little remaining of even the vague Roman Catholic tradition on which the school was founded. I confess that I wasn't particularly eager to share anything evangelical, much less to "preach" in such an atmosphere and invite ridicule. So I "threw out a fleece," deciding before the Lord that I would only speak if a specifically worded question arose concerning the motivations for taking drugs. Not five minutes later, I had my providential cue in the form of one woman's precisely stated inquiry. It was uncanny.

Nervous but convicted, I signaled for the microphone which was circulating, stood up and shared a brief testimony about my middle-class Roman Catholic background — similar to theirs — and the spiritual emptiness and metaphysical anguish that I had once tried to stifle with hallucinogenic drugs. I was delivered, I explained, by Him who offers real peace to His followers: "Peace I leave with you; my peace I give you. I do not give as the world gives" (John 14:27). I concluded quoting the Lord's promise and suggesting that much of the problem might be due to the absence of spiritual peace in the hearts of these sensitive youths.

To my amazement, the chapel erupted in applause! Surely the Lord's words can be powerful and effective in any environment, and even the most basic biblical truths can seem revolutionary to some who have never considered them.

The meeting ended a half hour later. As we shuffled out the door, a thirty-five year old man in a black *soutane* (cassock) — the school's chaplain — thanked me for my intervention. But his approval, like that of the applauding parents, is to be taken circumspectly. There's a great deal of ignorance and suspicion of our reformed evangelical perspective on the part of most French.

Two days after the drug symposium, I got a phone call from Headmaster Bartholet asking if I would be available to address the four classes of high school seniors! It seemed that the Lord had opened a door after all. I returned to Lamenais on January 5, 1995 (I remember the day as it coincided with the death of the late French President François Mitterand whose demise I learned of while having lunch with my hosts). On that day, I shared my testimony with five separate classes of high school seniors—about 150 students in all, including my own son. Once again, the Seed was sown.

EPILOGUE

AU REVOIR MARSEILLE/ BONJOUR USA

Open doors or not, after five consecutive years in the field, it was time for us to return to the States for our next "home ministry assignment" in the summer of 1997. We decided at that time to settle in Birmingham, Alabama, as our son Calix would be attending—or so we thought—Sanford University located in that southern city. We negotiated for lodgings with the help of a dear sister from a supporting church near Birmingham and got our two younger children enrolled at one of the better high schools in the area. Not only was Hoover High a public school financially accessible to us, but it also was in a magnificent new building in a beautiful section of Birmingham. In a public school, our children even had Christian science teachers who taught them that evolution is a theory—and a bad one at that. Not only that, but there were terrific Christians in the school who organized prayer meetings, and there were generally wholesome activities. This was most unlike France where high school sports teams don't exist, and where no one attends worship, and all athletic competitions are held on Sunday mornings. We were now in a country where our son Justin was able to play soccer on a terrific high school team. That may seem like a small thing to most people, but it wasn't to our athletic teenager.

Our daughter was blossoming amongst her Christian friends. Though our lodging was modest, it was adequate and conveniently located. We had friendly neighbors and no Mme. Ravella! Aline thought we'd gone to heaven.

When she could see how well our children were doing in such an atmosphere, Aline pleaded with me to allow them to finish their education in the United States. I was resistant to this idea, but the French proverb says: "Ce que la femme veut, Dieu veut" (What the wife wants, God wants). Or, as they say in the American South: "When momma ain't happy, ain't nobody happy."

I didn't accept the idea of having to stay in the States when I was sure the Lord was calling me to work with French-speaking folks. There wasn't much of a French-speaking contingent in Birmingham, Alabama. So I sought the counsel of the wise and godly pastor Frank Barker, at whose house we had a regular Saturday morning prayer meeting. When I explained my wife's strong preference to remain in the U.S., pastor Baker simply quipped: "You got a problem all right". I explained to him how even before I got married, I had planned to get a French wife. I saw my vocation as sort of a package deal with the wife and full-time language professor thrown in. Hence the irony of the situation in which my French wife, seeking what was best for her children, didn't want to return to her homeland. She vividly recalled a lengthy afternoon conversation with the American wife of a longtime missionary to France who expressed her bitter regret at having sacrificed the welfare of her children for the sake of her husband's ministry. "Don't make the same mistake I did," the woman had tearfully exhorted.

But what could I do in the States? How could I be useful to the Kingdom in the U.S.? What did the Lord of the Harvest have in mind for me? These questions I mulled over while on a visit to one of our supporting churches in Ft. Lauderdale, Florida, in April of 1998. I was praying for an answer and for direction for our lives.

As I arrived in Ft. Lauderdale, one of the first people I spoke to was a Frenchmen in a coffee shop. He was a south Florida resident. As we sipped our espresso together, I learned from him that there were about 30,000 Frenchmen living in south Florida, including 15,000 officially registered with the French Consulate in Miami and another

15,000 "parties à la nature" (unofficially here), as he colloquially put it. I hadn't realized that any more than most Americans do.

Then, at the church's missionary conference luncheon, I was seated next to a Haitian pastor with whom I spoke French the whole time. I learned from him that there are officially 380,000 Haitians (50% of whom speak French) in S. Florida. Once again, that's only the official figure. One of my Haitian students laughed when he heard that figure, explaining that he probably had that many cousins in S. Florida. In truth there are surely more than ½ million French-speakers in S. Florida. "Curiouser and "curiouser," as Alice of Wonderland fame would say.

That evening, at the mission banquet, I was again *coincidentally* seated next to a French-speaking *Quebecoise* from whom I learned that 250,000 of her compatriots are permanent residents in south Florida, a number that swells to ½ million when the "snowbirds" come down in the winter months. That's when it all clicked. If I needed to stay in the US while my children finished their education, S. Florida was the logical place. After making contact with our sister PCA churches, we joined the staff of Ministries in Action. Its vocation is to bring Bible training to some of he thousands of spiritually hungry but relatively uninstructed folk of the Caribbean, including the seven French-speaking Antillean islands.

That's where the story ends—for now at least. The hand of Providence has led us to a place where we can both contribute to the advancement of his French-speaking Kingdom and take into account the welfare of our children.

Shortly after our arrival in south Florida, I made a trip with a colleague to Guadeloupe in the French West Indies. I found a church numerically large but with little access to seminary like Bible training. Progressively and providentially, things have fallen into place for us and we now have three vibrant teaching programs going with spiritually hungry and eager believers in St. Maarten, Martinique, and Guadeloupe, which we access from S. Florida. We still work with the French, but it's the Antillean French. And Aline never complains of the cold anymore. What more could one ask for? Conclusion: The Lord works all things together to the good of those who love Him and are called according to His purpose.

Printed in the United States
59859LVS00007B/152

9 781600 342844